# MILLENNIALS
## and the
## WORKPLACE

# MILLENNIALS and the WORKPLACE

Challenges for Architecting the Organizations of Tomorrow

**PRITAM SINGH
ASHA BHANDARKER
SUMITA RAI**

Based on a research study by
All India Management Association

www.sagepublications.com
Los Angeles • London • New Delhi • Singapore • Washington DC

Copyright © All India Management Association, 2012
Pritam Singh, Asha Bhandarker, and Sumita Rai have asserted their rights under the Copyright Act to be identified as the authors of this work.

All rights reserved. No part of this book may be reproduced or utilized in any form or by any means, electronic or mechanical, including photocopying, recording or by any information storage or retrieval system, without permission in writing from the publisher.

First published in 2012 by

**SAGE Response**
B1/I-1 Mohan Cooperative Industrial Area
Mathura Road, New Delhi 110 044, India

**SAGE Publications Inc**
2455 Teller Road
Thousand Oaks, California 91320, USA

**SAGE Publications Ltd**
1 Oliver's Yard, 55 City Road
London EC1Y 1SP, United Kingdom

**SAGE Publications Asia-Pacific Pte Ltd**
33 Pekin Street
#02-01 Far East Square
Singapore 048763

**All India Management Association**
Management House
14, Institutional Area
Lodhi Road, New Delhi 110 003
India

Published by Vivek Mehra for SAGE Publications India Pvt Ltd, typeset in 11/15 pt Berkeley by Star Compugraphics Private Limited, Delhi and printed at Chaman Enterprises, New Delhi.

**Library of Congress Cataloging-in-Publication Data Available**

**ISBN:** 978-81-321-0898-6 (PB)

**The SAGE Team:** Sachin Sharma, Anupam Choudhury, and Vijay Sah

# Praise for the Book

This fascinating book builds upon empirical research and consulting to convincingly argue in what ways India's Millennials are unlikely to fit comfortably in today's corporations and points out how these will have to change to attract and retain the best Millennials in order to sustain the corporations' competitive advantage in a changing world.
—Alfredo Behrens, Professor, FIA, Sao Paulo, Brazil.

[The book] is a well-researched treatise. It makes a lucid, exhaustive, all-encompassing reading on the subject. [It is] an ultimate one-point reference book for the guidance of Millennials, and also for those who will pass on the baton to them. Surely, it is a treasure trove on the subject. My compliments to the learned authors, who have made untiring efforts to research this topic and publish this book.
—T. M. Bhasin, Chairman and Managing Director, Indian Bank, India

This book comes at a time when most organizations—private, public, and societal—are struggling with the paradigm shift involved in managing both the challenges as well as leveraging the potential of generational cohesion. In the context of the increasing significance and impact of the "Millenial Generation," the authors use their vast experience and knowledge to combine academic rigor with practical insights to break boundaries on both counts.

A comprehensive review of the literature, empirical research, and case studies are used to construct a new framework which explores both the art and science of architecting the "Organization of Tomorrow," which will unleash the potential of human and other resources.

A must read for leaders, managers and academics.

—Rajeev Dubey, President (Group HR and Aftermarket) and Member of the Group Executive Board, Mahindra & Mahindra Ltd, India

The book is of great interest in the current global context. The work is based on high-quality scientific research and findings. It highlights what the Millennials expect from the workplace and what they actually get in the workplace, and brings out how this gap can be bridged to make an organization more effective. This book is a must for all managers, and is highly recommended for all MBA programs. I would like to congratulate the authors on their achievement.

—Jyoti Gupta, Professor of Finance, ESCP Europe, Paris, and London

[This book] is a significant contribution to management literature and would be found useful by scholars and practitioners alike. The subject is important for a country like India which has a large young population with global aspirations. I hope corporate leaders can make use of the abundant insights featured in this book.

—Arun Kumar Jain, Professor of Strategy and Corporate Governance, Indian Institute of Management, Lucknow, India

I have found it extremely useful for many Indian as well as global companies who aspire to transform their organizations as well as leadership to future-proof themselves. I especially enjoyed going through the descriptions of Millennium Generation—who they are and what they expect—plus the profiles of future leaders who will get acceptance from young and upcoming managers. On the leadership role—in architecting the organizations of future—the book provides insightful guidance on the new paradigm of innovation, fairness, self-development, and free will so that the future direction for the organization can be accurately crafted. The HR leaders will also gain from this book on both organization evolution as well as building a new leadership DNA for future.

—Manoj Kohli, CEO (International) and Joint Managing Director, Bharti Airtel Ltd, India

A refreshing book devoted to the Millennials, the younger generation coming of age. The result of thorough research, the authors present the expectations and aspirations of the new generation, their demographic and psychographic background, and how organizations and institutions should adapt in view of them coming to the workplace. An important book that should be read by everybody involved in designing and running organizations of tomorrow.

—Dr Gregory Prastacos, Rector and Professor of Management Science, Athens University of Economics and Business, Greece

I believe that the human race with over 5,000 years of civilized living has not changed dramatically. However, humans are conditioned and socialized subtly by the dominant context and compulsions of their times. For a person without a discerning eye, these behavioral subtleties would either appear as absolute or he may totally miss it. The authors have through their "Millennial" lens amplified these subtleties without making absolute assertions. This sets up a thoughtful frame for comprehending the subtleties in behavior and attitude and understanding the larger social forces which are shaping it. The magnified rendition also sets up a very interesting theme for debate, without the tyranny of agreeing or disagreeing with the authors' presentation of the world we live in.

—K. Ramkumar, Executive Director—HR, Customer Service, and Operations, ICICI Bank Ltd, India

[This book] is a refreshing, insightful, and very [well] articulated research work. From start to end, the reader is provided with a frame of reference to understand the context and the key issues, as well as with insights on how to navigate through the issues of the changing workplace in the fast-changing world of organizations. Both the style and the content of the narrative are world class and make this work an outstanding reading for HR practitioners, corporate executives, scholars, and the public at large.

—Davide Sola, Associate Professor of Strategy and Management, ESCP Europe, London

[This book] gives a clarion call to the corporate world to re-think organizations of the future. The fundamental message that the authors give out is that 3G employees cannot be managed by 2G managers using 1G systems. The expectations of the 3G employees have been captured by the authors by a comprehensive survey. Basically, 3G employees expect to be liberated (intrapreneurial opportunities, self-development, and free will). The Millennials also expect equity, justice, and fairness in their organizations. The challenge is to architect a 3G organization that liberates the employees while not losing the focus on the goals and objectives of the organization. Consequently, new organizational structures and metrics to measure performance will have to be evolved for the 3G organization. This book is a must-read for the students of management, consultants, and practicing managers.

—M. J. Xavier, Director, Indian Institute of Management, Ranchi, India

*Dedicated to the Millennials,
the future leaders and builders of this nation.*

Thank you for choosing a SAGE product! If you have any comment, observation or feedback, I would like to personally hear from you. Please write to me at contactceo@sagepub.in

—Vivek Mehra, Managing Director and CEO,
SAGE Publications India Pvt Ltd, New Delhi

**Bulk Sales**

SAGE India offers special discounts for purchase of books in bulk. We also make available special imprints and excerpts from our books on demand.

For orders and enquiries, write to us at

*Marketing Department*
*SAGE Publications India Pvt Ltd*
*B1/I-1, Mohan Cooperative Industrial Area*
*Mathura Road, Post Bag 7*
*New Delhi 110044, India*
E-mail us at marketing@sagepub.in

Get to know more about SAGE, be invited to SAGE events, get on our mailing list. Write today to marketing@sagepub.in

*This book is also available as an e-book.*

# Contents

| | |
|---|---|
| List of Tables | xiii |
| List of Figures | xvii |
| List of Appendices | xix |
| Acknowledgments | xxi |
| Blueprint | xxiii |

| | | |
|---|---|---|
| 1. | Meaning of Work and Workplace: A Panoramic View | 1 |
| 2. | Who Are Millennials? | 45 |
| 3. | Meaning of Workplace: Millennials' Valence | 97 |
| 4. | Meaning of Workplace: Expectations vs Reality of Workplace Attributes | 152 |
| 5. | Architecting the Organization of Tomorrow | 201 |

| | |
|---|---|
| Index | 225 |
| About the Authors | 231 |

# List of Tables

| | | |
|---|---|---|
| 1A.1 | MOWP sample details | 33 |
| 1A.2 | Regional representation of students' data for BTech and MBA | 33 |
| 2.1 | Frequency and percentage: Demographic variables | 54 |
| 2.2 | Means and SDs: Psychosocial background variables | 57 |
| 2.3 | Means and SDs: Values and personality | 59 |
| 2.4 | Background variables and personality: A comparative picture | 71 |
| 2B.1a | Achievement orientation by background variables ($t$ test) | 75 |
| 2B.1b | Achievement orientation by background variables ($F$ test) | 76 |
| 2B.1c | Achievement orientation by background variables (Tukey Table) | 77 |
| 2B.2a | Locus of control by background variables ($t$ test) | 77 |
| 2B.2b | Locus of control by background variables ($F$ test) | 78 |
| 2B.2c | Locus of control by background variables (Tukey Table) | 79 |
| 2B.3a | Personal growth by background variables ($t$ test) | 80 |
| 2B.3b | Personal growth by background variables ($F$ test) | 81 |
| 2B.3c | Personal growth by background variables (Tukey Table) | 82 |
| 2B.4a | Self-fulfillment by background variables ($t$ test) | 83 |
| 2B.4b | Self-fulfillment by background variables ($F$ test) | 84 |
| 2B.4c | Self-fulfillment by background variables (Tukey Table) | 85 |
| 2B.5a | Community development by background variables ($t$ test) | 86 |
| 2B.5b | Community development by background variables ($F$ test) | 87 |
| 2B.5c | Community development by background variables (Tukey Table) | 88 |

| | | |
|---|---|---|
| 2B.6a | Progressive orientation by background variables ($t$ test) | 89 |
| 2B.6b | Progressive orientation by background variables ($F$ test) | 90 |
| 2B.6c | Progressive orientation by background variables (Tukey Table) | 91 |
| 3.1 | Meaning of workplace—mean values | 99 |
| 3.2 | Influence of demographic variables on meaning of workplace | 113 |
| 3A.1 | Meaning of workplace: Rotated component matrix | 122 |
| 3B.2a | Cronbach alpha values of the psychometric scales | 124 |
| 3B.2b | Inter-scale correlations | 124 |
| 3C.3a | Overall MOWP by selected demographic variables ($t$ test) | 125 |
| 3C.3b | Overall MOWP by selected demographic variables ($F$ test) | 125 |
| 3C.3c | Overall MOWP by selected demographic variables (Tukey test) | 126 |
| 3C.4a | Entrepreneurial innovation factor by selected demographic variables ($t$ test) | 126 |
| 3C.4b | Entrepreneurial innovation factor by selected demographic variables ($F$ test) | 127 |
| 3C.4c | Entrepreneurial innovation factor by selected demographic variables (Tukey test) | 128 |
| 3C.5a | Process centricity with shared vision factor by selected demographic variables ($t$ test) | 129 |
| 3C.5b | Process centricity with shared vision factor by selected demographic variables ($F$ test) | 129 |
| 3C.5c | Process centricity with shared vision factor by selected demographic variables (Tukey test) | 130 |
| 3C.6a | Sense of community factor by selected demographic variables ($t$ test) | 130 |
| 3C.6b | Sense of community factor by selected demographic variables ($F$ test) | 131 |
| 3C.6c | Sense of community factor by selected demographic variables (Tukey test) | 132 |
| 3C.7a | Sense of security factor by selected demographic variables ($t$ test) | 132 |

| | | |
|---|---|---|
| 3C.7b | Sense of security factor by selected demographic variables (F test) | 133 |
| 3C.7c | Sense of security factor by selected demographic variables (Tukey test) | 134 |
| 3C.8a | Conducive physical ambience factor by selected demographic variables (t test) | 134 |
| 3C.8b | Conducive physical ambience factor by selected demographic variables (F test) | 135 |
| 3C.8c | Conducive physical ambience factor by selected demographic variables (Tukey test) | 136 |
| 3C.9a | Sharing and celebrating culture factor by selected demographic variables (t test) | 136 |
| 3C.9b | Sharing and celebrating culture factor by selected demographic variables (F test) | 137 |
| 3C.9c | Sharing and celebrating culture factor by selected demographic variables (Tukey test) | 138 |
| 3C.10a | Technology savvy workplace factor by selected demographic variables (t test) | 138 |
| 3C.10b | Technology savvy workplace factor by selected demographic variables (F test) | 139 |
| 3C.10c | Technology savvy workplace factor by selected demographic variables (Tukey test) | 140 |
| 3C.11a | Company's brand image factor by selected demographic variables (t test) | 140 |
| 3C.11b | Company's brand image factor by selected demographic variables (F test) | 141 |
| 3C.11c | Company's brand image factor by selected demographic variables (Tukey test) | 142 |
| 3C.12a | Fair and ethical factor by selected demographic variables (t test) | 142 |
| 3C.12b | Fair and ethical factor by selected demographic variables (F test) | 143 |
| 3C.12c | Fair and ethical factor by selected demographic variables (F test) | 144 |

| | | |
|---|---|---|
| 4.1 | Means and standard deviations of MOWP items (expectations) | 155 |
| 4.2 | Means and standard deviations of MOWP items (availability) | 156 |
| 4.3 | Means and standard deviations of MOWP items (expectations and availability) | 158 |
| 4.4 | Millennials' workplace expectations | 161 |
| 4.5 | Experienced organizational reality | 171 |
| 4.6 | Expectations from a good leader | 181 |
| 4.7 | Intent to leave | 187 |
| 4.8 | Millennials through the lens of HR professionals | 191 |

# List of Figures

| | | |
|---|---|---|
| 1.1 | Impact of personality and demographics on the MOWP | 28 |
| 2.1 | Sample profile—age | 55 |
| 2.2 | Sample profile—nature of education | 55 |
| 2.3 | Sample profile—gender | 55 |
| 2.4 | Sample profile—prior work experience | 56 |
| 2.5 | Sample profile—place of upbringing | 56 |
| 2.6 | Sample profile—family type | 58 |
| 2.7 | Sample profile—parents' occupation | 58 |
| 2.8 | Sample profile—employment status of parents | 58 |
| 3.1 | MOWP total score and six predictor variables | 116 |
| 3.2 | Entrepreneurial innovation and five predictor variables | 117 |
| 4.1 | Graphical representation of Millennials' expectations from workplace | 162 |
| 4.2 | Graphical representation of "experienced organizational reality" | 172 |
| 4.3 | Graphical representation of the "expectations from a good leader" | 182 |
| 4.4 | Graphical representation of "intent to leave" | 188 |
| 4.5 | Graphical representation of "Millennials through the lens of HR professionals" | 192 |

# List of Appendices

| | | |
|---|---|---:|
| 1A | Background Information Questionnaire | 32 |
| 1B | MOWP Data Details | 33 |
| 1C | MOWP Questionnaire | 33 |
| 2A | Instruments Details | 73 |
| 2B | Differences in Personality by Background Factors | 75 |
| 3A | Rotated Component Matrix | 122 |
| 3B | Psychometric Properties of the Scales | 124 |
| 3C | Differences in MOWP by Background Factors | 125 |
| 3D | Stepwise Multiple Regression Analysis | 145 |

# Acknowledgments

In the odyssey of any research work, there are plenty of enablers, supporters, and advisors. It is extremely difficult to cite and acknowledge the contribution of each one of them. However, in this small space, we would like to try to acknowledge them all. First, we are grateful to Rekha Sethi, Director General, All India Management Association, for generously supporting this project financially. She has been very patient and graceful in handling delays in the completion of this project. Special thanks to Dr Kamal Singh, Dr Raj Agarwal, and Aseem Kumar for their support. We would like to express a deep sense of gratitude for Professor Mukul Gupta, Director, Management Development Institute (MDI, Gurgaon, India) and V. K. Nangia, Registrar, MDI, for providing all-out support in the execution of this project. We would like to appreciate our dear colleague, Dr Subir Verma, who was always available as a sounding board for intellectual sparring and, above all, helping us at critical stages in the project. Colleagues such as Professors B. A. Metri, S. K. Rai, Ashok Kapoor, A. K. Rath, V. K. Gupta, and many others deserve special thanks for extending tremendous moral support to us.

Dr A. Jose, Librarian, MDI, and his team have provided immense support by providing all the published material that we have used.

Kshipra Rustogi, Nidhi Yadav, Meeta Mishra, and Nidhi Mann—all worked tirelessly on data gathering, transcription, and content analyses of interview material.

We would like to express deep appreciation and gratitude to the thousands of Millennials who participated in this research very patiently and to all the HR professionals who shared their thoughts and perceptions about Millennials. We would also like to place on record the help we received from the Indian Institutes of Management, MDI, the Indian Institutes of Technology, and other lead institutions of India.

Most importantly, our respective families deserve our gratitude and appreciation for their patience and unstinting support through the entire journey of the work.

# Blueprint

Human history bears ample testimony to the fact that only those species, institutions, and organizations that had capability to appropriately adapt to and proact in the changing environment could survive, grow, and excel. The extinction of the dinosaurs took place because of their incapability to adapt to changing environmental conditions. World over, the downfall of kings, emperors, and monarchs has been the result of their insensitivity to the changing needs of their subjects. The famous French Revolution erupted in retaliation to Marie Antoinette's notorious statement to the agitated and hungry French people: "Let them eat cake [if they don't have bread]." The queen's statement reflects her utter ignorance, indifference, and insensitivity to the issues and problems of the common citizen. No wonder the reaction of the French public led to the downfall of the monarchy and the beheading of the queen.

Sensitivity to the contextual challenges therefore becomes an essential requirement for even mere survival of individuals and institutions. It goes without saying that when growth is the objective, the need for such sensitivity becomes even more critical not only for individuals but also for institutions. Thousands of years ago, Buddha made the profound statement that "nothing is permanent." Needless to say, this wisdom highlights the importance of understanding the unfolding and shifting patterns in the phenomena around us in order to cope with and adapt to the same. Therefore, it becomes important for organizations and individuals to develop an alert antenna/radar-like capability to gauge the emerging phenomena and prepare for them.

The perpetual quest of human beings has been to establish one's unique identity. In pre-modern societies, one's individual identity emanated primarily from the community, groups, clans, and family that one belonged to. In contemporary societies, however, the locus of identity has shifted from these sources to the individual level, emphasizing the role of achievement, power, freedom, contribution, and individuation in establishing one's identity. The organization becomes the primary domain where individual-level needs get expression. In contemporary societies, therefore, the march is toward individualism, and there is a search for routes that provide opportunities for individual achievement and expression. Our observation of contemporary individuals also reveals a dialectic process operating within the individual's psyche—one force struggling for independence and individuation and the other force seeking security, status, and self-identity. This is a paradoxical phenomenon that creates conflict and confusion at the individual level. It throws up complex management challenges for the organization—to evolve structure and processes that can satisfy these dialectic demands at the individual level.

In today's business world, people spend majority of their waking time immersed in the organization. People are increasingly relying on the organization for the fulfillment of their need for individuation as well as the need for security, power, belongingness, and status. This is because the other institutions—family, community, and religion—are gradually withering away in terms of their importance. Therefore, in a departure from the past, today the workplace has emerged as the dominant platform for fulfillment of individuation as well as security and belongingness needs. Scrutiny of these two needs indicates that they are diametrically opposite to each other and, therefore, at the individual level there is a constant struggle for establishing a fine blend of both. Achievement of such a blend of both is possible if the organization is sensitive to the needs of human beings and their struggle for both freedom/individuation and security/belongingness. This will help them create the appropriate structure and processes enabling individuals to reach the fine balance of both types of needs. In the absence of organizations making such efforts, individuals at the workplace will become disconnected and disenchanted, and not give their best. Consequently, organizations will be in no position to harness individual talent for performance excellence and growth.

The following two anecdotes narrated by two Indian CEOs have been presented here to illustrate and capture changing individual expectations and mindsets in the last 60 years.

## CEO 1

"When I was a small child, I believed that my father (who was a social leader) was the epitome of wisdom. I was a dabbling child, curious, exploring, and questioning. Whenever my father responded to some of my questions saying, 'I don't know,' I concluded that it was not worth knowing, because my father—the epitome of wisdom—did not think it is important enough to know and understand.

"I got married and my children started growing up. It was the electronic era and we started buying electronic gadgets—cameras, VCRs, music players, TV sets, cassette recorders, and so on. Owing to my dabbling nature, I continued experimenting with these gadgets and, frankly speaking, must have spoilt 5–6 of them. Things went to a level where my wife used to gently tell me, 'Don't touch it dear, I know you will break it!' However, I continued experimenting with these gadgets and could muster some ability to handle them. One day I was taken aback to hear my younger son tell my wife, 'Mum, you will be glad to know that even Daddy knows how to operate these gadgets!' I realized that I was witnessing an inflexion point: the mindset had changed from my generation to my son's generation—while I thought that my father was the epitome of wisdom, my son felt it important to remark that 'even Dad knew' something.

"Years passed and I went to the US to see my 11-year-old grandson. One day he was chatting nonstop with me on various topics while I was trying to concentrate on my yoga practice. In an effort to get some peace I tried to divert him by saying, 'Son, why don't you ask your Dad?' He quickly retorted, 'Oh grandpa, daddy doesn't know such things.' I was jolted into realizing that I was witnessing another inflexion point: the new generation had shifted the mindset to a different level (from the previous generation) in their attitude toward parents and authority figures. So, I have seen the shift from 'Daddy knows everything' to 'even Daddy knows' to 'Daddy doesn't know at all!' Looking back, I am overwhelmed by the enormity of the shifts taking place in our society."

# CEO 2

While talking about his family, CEO 2 narrated a very interesting story about his grandchild, who was about nine years old:

"As a doting grandfather, I used to frequently buy toys and gifts for Dhruv whenever I made business trips abroad. On a recent visit to Paris, I bought plenty of gifts for my grandson and sent the package to Pune, where he lives with his parents. My daughter-in-law, Smita, told little Dhruv, 'You lucky boy, just see how many gifts your grandpa has sent you!' In his excitement the young boy told Smita, 'Mum, I want to open all the gifts right now!' After checking them all, he said in a low voice, 'Mum, grandpa is not a good man.' Taken aback, Smita chided him, 'Do you know how much your grandpa loves you and how much we respect him?' Dhruv repeated, 'Grandpa is not a good man. He didn't even ask me what I wanted from Paris. I don't like any of his gifts!' When she responded, 'But how could he have consulted you when he was in Europe?' Dhruv quickly replied, 'I heard you and Dad talk to him many times. He could have also called and asked me what I wanted!'

"After three months when I visited Pune, this story was shared with me in detail. Smita said, 'Papa, your grandson said this about you and I was quite surprised!' I responded, 'OK, if that's what he feels, let's go to the mall and he can buy whatever he wants.' We entered a toy shop and I told Dhruv, 'Go ahead and choose all that you want!' On seeing the expensive electronic toy he had selected, Smita tried to dissuade him saying, 'No dear, it's too costly. Let's buy something else.' She finally persuaded him to buy a reasonably priced toy murmuring humorously to me, 'I don't want to spoil my son the way you have spoilt yours!'

"On the way back home, while Smita was driving the car, Dhruv asked her, 'Mum don't you think I am a good boy?' His mother responded enthusiastically and appreciated him saying, 'We all think you are a very good kid.' After a few minutes he asked Smita, 'Mum, don't you think I am obedient?' And once more Smita replied very positively saying, 'You are such a good boy, so obedient and sweet!'

"By this time the car had reached the main gates of the house and once more my grandson queried his mother, 'Mum, what do you think about yourself? Are you obedient or not?' To which she replied, 'What do you mean?' Then Dhruv said, 'Mum I am asking you because when Grandpa was persuading you to let me buy the toy of my choice you refused!' Very clearly, little Dhruv was actually challenging his mother and alleging that she was disobedient!"

These two stories powerfully illustrate the changing mindsets of young Indians. Incidentally, we have heard stories galore from our young MBA students about their bosses' capability to keep up with cutting-edge knowledge. They say things like, "Oh boss doesn't know"; or "surprise surprise, even boss knows!" We have also heard some of them say, "the boss is an old fogey; he doesn't know what's happening and to top it all, he is bossy!"

The young generation—Millennials—has moved from obedience to questioning; from acceptance to evaluation; from blind faith in the wisdom of authority figures to challenging, questioning, and judging. They have tremendous self-confidence and self-assurance; they are highly self-aware and well informed about the globe.

Contemporary organizations have to be well equipped and prepared to handle the complex challenge which is being thrown by the Millennials. This will be possible when organizations develop greater understanding, sensitivity, and appreciation about this generation and their aspirations, expectations, and mindsets. It is in this perspective that we undertook this project—*Millennials and the Workplace: Challenges for Architecting the Organizations of Tomorrow*—to map out the expectations and profiles of the Millennials. Findings of this study, it is assumed, will immensely help organizations to orchestrate their processes, structure, and systems and aligning these with emerging realities.

The role and importance of meaning of workplace has been emphasized by many scholars and thinkers. A plethora of studies also give pointers to the importance of creating meaning and matching expectations with reality. The experience of meaning at the workplace has been found to be linked to positive outcomes for both the individual and the organization including improvements in organizational performance, retention of key employees, effective management of change, and greater organizational commitment and employee engagement.

Lower harmony and mismatch between individual expectations and experience will undoubtedly result in disconnect with work and a redirection of energy and attention to other areas of life. Lack of meaning in the workplace has been found to be linked to negative outcomes, in particular, employee cynicism and turnover. On the other hand, greater match between expectations and workplace reality contribute to job satisfaction, which is closely associated with high productivity, low absenteeism, low turnover, and innovation at the workplace. This further highlights the criticality and importance of continuously understanding employees' workplace expectations and aspirations so that organizations align and realign workplace processes and practices to create the needed fit. Needless to say, such efforts by the organization will enable them to create a meaningful workplace.

## Architecture of the Book

This book has been organized in six chapters:

Chapter 1: "Meaning of Work and Workplace: A Panoramic View" deals with the literature on the significance of work in human life and human nature, and the meaning of workplace, all of which are closely intertwined with each other. It also deals with the factors leading to greater meaning of work and workplace in the existing literature. This chapter further highlights the salient findings of the expectations and aspirations of the Millennials from the workplace. Thus, Chapter 1 paints the background of the study and establishes the relevance and importance of this study for organizations and society.

Chapter 2: "Who Are the Millennials?" characterizes the Millennials in terms of their demographic and psychographic background profiles as well as selected personality factors such as achievement motivation, work locus of control, and personal values. The findings on personality have been examined across various demographic and psychographic variables.

Chapter 3: "Meaning of Workplace: Millennials' Valence" delves into the phenomenon of expectations of Millennials and examines this across (*a*) various demographic factors like age, gender, nature of education, prior work experience, family type, parents' occupations and employment status, place of upbringing and parental styles; and (*b*) selected personality factors—achievement motivation, work locus of control, and personal values. The chapter studies the impact of the demographic and personality variables on the meaning of workplace.

Chapter 4: "Meaning of Workplace: Expectations vs Reality of Workplace Attributes" brings out the gap between what Millennials expect from the workplace and what they get. This chapter also examines the Millennials' expectations from their immediate superior as well as factors triggering the intention to leave the organization.

Chapter 5: "Architecting the Organization of Tomorrow" attempts to sketch the contours of the new workplace that would create alignment between the individual's expectations and the organizational offerings.

**Pritam Singh**
**Asha Bhandarker**
**Sumita Rai**

**Ugadi**
**March 23, 2012**

# Meaning of Work and Workplace

## A Panoramic View

Through centuries, there has been a perennial quest for evolving institutions which can meet the needs and expectations of respective constituencies and stakeholders. This paradigm has been unequivocally emphasized by thinkers and scholars like Socrates, Aristotle, Plato, Chanakya, Confucius, Machiavelli, Goethe, Kant, Dewey, Sartre, Seneca, Drucker, McGregor, Eric Fromm, Herzberg, Jim Collins, Singh, and Bhandarker, etc. All of them stress the need to bring convergence between aspirations of the masses and various social–economic–political institutions, the assumption being that the aspirations and desires are the core requirement and must be met by appropriately designing and building institutions. Lincoln's famous statement that democratic institutions ought to be built on the tenets "of the people, by the people, for the people" (Basler, 1953) illustrates the core principle of good governance of institutions.

A cursory reflection on the collapse of monarchies and the rise of democracy, as well as the rise and fall of communism, hold lessons for building institutions adequately equipped to meet the requirements of the stakeholders. Across various streams of public life—political, religious, social, corporate, etc.—it has been observed that those leaders and institutions which were insensitive to the needs of their stakeholders were rejected by the latter. The corporate world also has many instances of insensitive leaders and institutions who demonstrated apathy and lack of concern for the stakeholders resulting in ruination of organizations. The above instances powerfully bring out the relevance and importance of aligning institutional governance processes, systems, and thrust, and leadership styles with the demands and challenges thrown up by stakeholders at different points in time.

Jim Collins brings out that many of the companies he studied and presented as models of excellence in his previous work *Built to last* (Collins and Porras 1997) disappeared by the time he wrote his next book, *Good to great* (2001). Similar experience has been reported by De Gues (1997) in his book, *The living company*. Among several factors which contributed to the collapse of many corporations, perhaps the most critical one has been their lack of response to stakeholders' needs, aspirations, and demands, and emerging business imperatives. They did not continuously align and realign their organizational strategies, systems, processes, and skills with stakeholders' demands and aspirations.

On the other hand, our recent work, *In search of change maestros* (2011) brings out that great institutions like L&T, ABG, Biocon, Airtel, ICICI, UTI, and JSW, became great because they ceaselessly aligned themselves to stakeholders' requirements as well as responded to contextual challenges in order to continuously grow and deliver excellent performance. They have demonstrated enormous capacity to enfold the future into the present; passion to move to the next orbit; entrepreneurial innovation and game-changing style; and above all, looking within, looking around, and looking beyond. All these companies have achieved exceptional growth and performance through the power of alert antenna and radar-like sensing of the environmental issues and stakeholders' expectations. Thus aligning institutions with stakeholders' aspirations, expectations, and needs has been the key mantra for their robust growth and continued excellence.

The biggest raison d'être compelling institutions to change are the techno-economic-psycho-social shifts being experienced by contemporary society. Today, globally, companies are grappling with the issues thrown up by unprecedented changes in these areas. They are seeking appropriate solutions to overcome the above challenges. Our decades of experience in the corporate world brings out that worldwide industries have managed smooth absorption and adoption of technology. Companies are however still struggling with complex issues of evolving a suitable culture and designing a workplace, which could meet the changing expectations of the stakeholders.

Today the greatest challenge facing organizations worldwide is that of acquiring, retaining, and grooming the right kind of talent. In a study conducted by DDI (Krishnan and Wellins, 2010), it was found that 77 percent of Indian leaders identified improving and leveraging talent as the most important business priority, second only to growth, which was identified by 79 percent of the sample. Similar trends were seen in the global sample in their study where leadership talent was rated number 1 (75 percent); while growth was rated number 2 (69 percent). Today's workplaces thus face the critical challenge of keeping people motivated, creating meaning in work on a continuous basis in order to retain them, and harness their full potential. Although this phenomenon has been deliberated at length, over the years, it has assumed greater importance in the light of generational changes in priorities. The popular literature dealing with Millennials (Chatman and Flynn 2001; McGuire, By, and Hutchings 2007; Stauffer 1997; Ott, Blacksmith, and Royal 2008; "Cara" 2009, cited in Myers and Sadaghiani 2010; Raines 2002); as well as the serious research (Twenge and Campbell 2001; Twenge and Nolen-Hoeksema 2002; Twenge 2000; Greenfield (cited in Neisser, 1998); George 2009; Kowske, Rasch, and Wiley 2010; and Smola and Sutton 2002) conclude that they are different in their value systems, life priorities, goals, aspirations, and styles. Therefore the greatest challenge for organizations and other sociopolitical institutions is to understand this new generation and their mindsets and evolve compatible systems and processes which can help in unleashing their energies to the fullest possible extent. Failure to do this will result in the flight of talent, de-motivation, and lack of commitment, which would be catastrophic for organizations.

Organizations the world over lay great emphasis on carefully doing their growth and resource planning; rigorous efforts are made at scenario mapping and matching resources to realize growth plans. Companies also engage in detailed study for technology planning as well as product planning. There are detailed reviews of what the external customer wants and needs and efforts are made by most companies to meet these requirements. In contrast organizations pay scant attention to people planning. Surprisingly people planning boils down to mere enumeration of head count and the needed skills without seeking to identify, understand, and assess their needs, aspirations, and value systems.

Our experience in conducting strategy workshops for many organizations shows us that barring exceptions, little attempt is made by companies to identify and understand why people join organizations and what they expect and aspire to. This has assumed a much more critical role with the rise of the contemporary knowledge society and the emergence of Millennials. When people join companies all-out efforts are made to socialize and induct them to fall in line with organizational systems, processes, and culture. This approach worked quite well in traditional monopolistic organizations where people stayed on more out of compulsion than out of choice. Today, as talent becomes scarce and people have global opportunities, such an approach fails to attract people to join such organizations and give their best for a reasonable time period. Even more importantly, those coming into workplaces with certain expectations only to find them belied, will experience dissonance and look for other and better companies to move to. It is therefore hardly surprising that most companies globally are faced with high degree of turnover and are grappling with retention and motivational strategies. From the above analysis it is clear that organizations invariably seek to mold people to existing organizational realities rather than molding, designing, and aligning organizations to face various emerging people-related new realities. Thus organizations continue to perpetuate the past rather than evolve newer ways of organizing for the future, in tune with new requirements and demands of people entering organizations.

We commenced this research so as to help organizations prepare today for tomorrow by enfolding the future into the present. The old adage goes, those who think of tomorrow today, make their today as well as their tomorrow. However, those who do not think of tomorrow, spoil their tomorrow as well as today. Even in ancient times, there existed the quest to know the future primarily to help people adequately prepare for the same. Emperors and kings in early times in fact used the power of oracles, mystics, and soothsayers to divine the future and prepare institutions and organizations for the same. Although we make no claims to be either oracles, or mystics, an attempt is made in this work to map out the likely scenarios on the people front which can enable organizations to reorient themselves for the same. It is in this perspective that we decided to embark on the present research work to map the likely people-related challenges in the emerging scenario.

## Contours of the Study

This chapter has been organized to:

1. present a gestalt view of the literature regarding meaning of work and human nature;
2. highlight the selected variables affecting Meaning of Workplace (MOWP); and
3. discuss the research design and framework utilized in this work.

## Panoramic View of the Literature: A Gestalt View

This part purports to examine (a) the significance of work in human life; (b) human nature; and (c) meaning of work and workplace. All of them are closely interwoven with each other and understanding significance of work in human life and human nature are very important in order to understand meaning of work and workplace in a holistic sense.

### Meaning of Work in Human Life

Work has been an important element of human societies as well as people's lives since time immemorial. In fact human beings seem to be innately wired to engage in work in some form or the other. Thinkers (Hillman, 1989) have gone to the extent of calling the orientation to work an instinctual phenomenon and by implication something which human beings feel compelled to do. "Work instinct is the innate and powerful tendency to exert one's physical and mental powers, one's skills and talents, in order to reach a goal, to create, to express one's self etc" (Morin, 2004).

According to Viktor Frankl (1984), "Man's search for meaning is the primary motivation in his life." John Burroughs, the poet, said:

> The secret of happiness is—something to do; some congenial work. Take away the occupation of all men and what a wretched world it would be! ... Few persons realize how much happiness is dependent upon their work, upon the fact that they are kept busy and not left to feed upon themselves... Blessed is the man who has some congenial work, some occupation in which he can put his heart, and which affords a complete outlet to all the forces there are in him. (cited in Watson, 1951)

"Three grand essentials to happiness in this life are something to do, something to love and something to hope for" (Addison cited in Watson, 1951).

> Work and thou canst escape the reward; whether thy work be fine or coarse, planting corn or writing epics, so only it be honest work, done to thine own approbation, it shall earn a reward to the senses as well as to the thought... The reward of a thing well done is to have done it. (Emerson cited in Watson, 1951)

"The mintage of wisdom is to know that rest is rust, and that real life is in love, laughter and work" (Hubbard cited in Watson, 1951).

> Thank god every morning when you get up that you have something to do which must be done, whether you like it or not. Being forced to work and forced to do your best, will breed in you temperance, self control, diligence, strength of will, content and a hundred other virtues which the idle never know. (Kingsley cited in Watson, 1951)

Thomas Carlyle (2008) said in his highly acclaimed poem, "Past and Present," "Blessed is he who has found his work; let him ask for no other blessedness; he has work, a life purpose and will follow it ... labour is life." He further stated, "Get your happiness out of your work or you will never know what real happiness is." "It is only well with me when I have a chisel in my hand" (said Michelangelo [2010], the great sculptor). "Work is its own end and brings its own joy" (Hillman, 1989). In the broader belief system of the West, "work is worship," and the famous adage goes, "An idle mind is the devil's workshop," illustrating the importance given to work in Western societies. "Work is the grand cure of all the maladies and miseries that ever beset mankind" (Carlyle cited in Daintith, 1997); "The harder you work the luckier you get (Player cited in Daintith, 1997); "Work is much more than fun itself" (Coward cited in Daintith, 1997); "I wish to preach, not the doctrine of ignoble ease, but the doctrine of the strenuous life" (Roosevelt cited in Daintith, 1997); "The only place where success comes before work is in the dictionary" (Sassoon cited in Daintith, 1997).

"Whatever thy hands findeth do it, do it with thy might; for there is no work, nor device, nor knowledge, nor wisdom in the grave, whither thou goest" (Bible: Ecclesiastes 9:10, Eccles [1997]). "Work is as much a necessity to man as eating and sleeping..." (Humboldt cited in Edwards, 1999); "Not alone to know, but to act according to thy knowledge, is thy destination, proclaims the voice of thy inmost soul...for action was existence given to thee; thy actions and thy actions alone determine thy worth" (Fichte cited in Edwards, 1999).

In the words of Moore and Weiss (1955),

> To the typical man...working means having a purpose, gaining a sense of accomplishment, expressing himself. He feels that not working would leave him aimless and without opportunities to contribute... It is through the producing role that most men tie into society.

"There is no truer and more abiding happiness than the knowledge that one is free to go on doing day by day, the best work one can do..." (Collingwood cited in Edwards, 1999); "The greatest asset of any nation is the spirit of its people and the greatest danger that can menace any nation is the breakdown of that spirit- the will to win and the courage to work" (Cortelyou cited in Edwards, 1999). "I believe in work, hard work and long hours of work. Men do not break down from overwork, but from worry and dissipation" (Hughes, 1999). "The man who does not work for the love of work but only for money is not likely to make money nor to find much fun in life" (Schwab, 1999).

Gini (2001) viewed work as necessary for procuring the necessities of life, an essential component of personal identity, and a major form of shaping, and being shaped by the society. The economic rationale has been highlighted as one of the important reasons for working by many thinkers (Braude, 1975; Firth, 1948; Friedman and Havighurst, 1954; Miller, 1980). Anderson (1961) defines work as an "activity of some purpose" or in more direct terms as time given to a job for which one is paid. According to Donald and Havighurst (1959) one of the important functions of work is to serve society. The Work in America group (Special Task Force, 1973) defines work as an activity that produces something of value for other people. Salz (1955) defines work as an activity one does in the execution of a task or project. Morse and Weiss (1955) found that working gives people a feeling of being tied into the larger society. Work is also seen as a source of identity and peer-group relations (Friedman and Havighurst, 1954; Steers and Porter, 1975).

Work has been seen as a tonic for personal identity and self-esteem. When an individual does meaningful work he actually develops a sense of identity, worth, and dignity (Morin, 2004). According to Eric Fromm, work acts as an effective means to deal with the angst of death and void (Morin, 2004). He once wrote, "The principle can be formulated thus: I am because I effect" (cited in Morin, 2004). "Therefore working is a meaningful way to prove one's existence and hopefully, that it is worth to be lived" (Morin, 2004).

In the Western world, the Protestant Work Ethic (PWE), characterized by diligence, punctuality, deferment of gratification, and primacy of the work domain (Rose, 1985) has played a dominant role in transforming the way they view work and the workplace. Both work and workplace are viewed as vehicles for achievement (being productive), autonomy (being independent) and contribution (creating something useful/meaningful). The PWE significantly transformed the meaning of work and workplace. In the period post-religious reformation in Europe, hard work became a religious duty and hence was performed to ensure rewards. Career success and the accumulation of wealth accruing from hard work were considered to be highly desirable. According to Weber (1904), PWE contributed to the rise and success of modern capitalism.

The landmark study by England and colleagues (MOW International Research Team, 1987) brought out that working carries both instrumental and expressive meanings—work is necessary to procure the means to satisfy physical needs but is also directly linked to a person's self-concept, identity, and social standing. The central role of work in people's lives has also been brought out in many empirical studies (Brief and Nord, 1990; England and Misumi, 1986; Harpaz, 1990, 1999; Kaplan and Tausky, 1974;

Mannhein, 1993; Morse and Weiss, 1955; MOW International Research team, 1987; Parker, 1971, Warr, 1982). The importance attached to work has been studied across countries (England, 1991; Harding and Hikspoors, 1995; Harpaz, 1999; Kuchinke, Kang, and Oh, 2008; MOW International Research team, 1987; Ruiz-Quintanilla and Wilpert, 1991).

From the above presentation it is evident that work in the western world has been viewed as an important and an integral part of human life. Work and workplace provide opportunities to human beings to productively channelize energy and create something useful and meaningful and fulfill many of their needs. In this sense then both work and workplace are critical factors in creating purpose and focus in human life.

In the Indian context work has been considered to be one's dharma or duty. The first *shloka* of the Bhagavad-Gita, "*Dharma Kshetre Kuru Kshetre*" brings out the pivotal role of both dharma (duty) and karma (work) and emphasizes that life without these has no meaning. This tome of Indian wisdom stresses that work must be performed without I-centric, reward-centric, and ego-centric mindset. While discussing about karma, Lord Krishna counseled Arjuna, "Yogastha Kuru Karmani Mohatakta Dhananjaya" [Oh Arjuna, you must engage in your work in the mode of a Yogi—a detached mode—without lust for the rewards. It is only by performing action without attachment that one can attain perfection and excellence, because one is completely absorbed in work itself and finds that work is its own reward] (Chinmayananda, 1976). He further said, "Perform your bounded duty, for action is superior to inaction." He also said that even the maintenance of the human body is not possible without action. In the Bhagavad-Gita, the wise person is one who acts without attachment to the reward, unlike the ignorant person who acts only to gain rewards (Chinmayananda, 1976).

In "Anushasanparvam" of the Mahabharata, it is said, "Through good deeds one gets happiness and through bad deeds sorrow. Everywhere it is work that brings result and nothing which has not been earned can be got anywhere. Heaven, earthly enjoyment, habits, intelligence, all these are the result of the work done here in this world" (Advaita Ashrama, 2010). While highlighting the characteristics of the highly evolved person, the great Indian sage Sri Ramakrishna said that such a person is so completely absorbed in his work and action that he "foregoes all the ideas or results of the actions in life." He follows the principle, "Duty for duty's sake and work for work's sake" (Anusasanparvan cited in Advaita Ashrama, 2010). The other great Indian epic, the Ramayana extols the virtues of karma (work and action) in human life: In this world work is the most important component of human life and human beings get results only on the strength of their work and contributions.

Both the Mahabharata and the Ramayana—two of India's most renowned epics shaping and defining Indian civilization—convey that work is at the core of human existence. They convey that the person who is completely absorbed in his work would create perfection, excellence, and contribute to the larger goal of society. To such a person, the reward will automatically follow. Through his actions and work, such a person would continuously create his future.

According to Ali (1995), Quranic principles and the Prophet's prescriptions serve as a guide for Muslims in conducting their life, family, and business. The Quran instructs Muslims to pursue whatever work is available, whenever it is available. He further states that according to the Prophet, hard work causes sins to be absolved and also that no one eats better food than that which he earns through his own efforts. Imam Ali, the fourth successor of the Prophet, said, "Persist in your actions with a noble end in mind ... failure to perfect your work while you are sure of the reward is injustice to yourself" (Imam Ali cited in Ali, 1999). Strong adherence to Islamic work ethics is manifested in a number of ways: (a) Emphasis on hard work; (b) meeting deadlines and persistence. Work is viewed not as an end in itself but as a means to foster personal growth and social relations. Dedication to work and work creativity are seen as virtuous in Islam.

According to Confucius, the great Chinese philosopher who defined and codified the Chinese way of life, "If you choose a job you love, you will never have to work a day in your life" (Confucius, n.d.), highlighting that doing what you love is itself a deep source of joy and happiness. Hui (1992) has stated that Confucian ethics promote a desire to succeed, achieve, and be entrepreneurial. Along with strong work ethics, it also stresses high value for interpersonal harmony, hierarchy, family integrity, kinship affiliation, and individual responsibility.

The Buddha has been equally emphatic on the role of work in human life. According to the Buddha (n.d.), "Your work is to discover your world and then with all your heart give yourself to it." This statement of Buddha suggests that one must find one's work and then totally immerse oneself into it, thus emphasizing total involvement and commitment to work. The essence of Buddha's philosophy is succinctly captured by the following quote: "To be idle is a short road to death and to be diligent is a way of life; foolish people are idle, wise people are diligent."

Weaving together the wisdom across major philosophies of the world brings out the following salient commonalities:

- Work has been viewed as an integral and core aspect of human life
- Work provides the platform for self expression and transformation
- Work is the route to self actualization
- Work is the fountainhead of happiness and joy
- Work is the major source of meaning in life
- Work defines the identity of a human being
- Work leads to contribution to society and individual well being

## Kaleidoscope of Human Nature

Organizations and institutions are normally orchestrated around the postulated organizational goals and the assumptions and understanding of human nature. In other words, the correct understanding and assumptions of human nature and the setting of desired and relevant goals are the core for building great institutions and organizations. Inadequate understanding about human beings can therefore be catastrophic and result in creation of dysfunctional organizations. The mismatch between human aspirations and nature on the one hand and organizational processes and practices on the other leads to negative and dysfunctional consequences both at the individual as well as organizational levels. At the individual level, it leads to demoralization, alienation, and neuroticism; and at the organizational level, failure to achieve the intended goals. In a nutshell, it is therefore desirable that organizations be created around the true nature of human beings, their motivation, aspirations, and goals.

In our observation across 400–500 organizations as trainers and consultants in the last three decades, we have found that many CEOs create organizational processes, systems, and practices around their basic beliefs and assumptions about human nature, which are many times inadequate and incomplete and not conducive to fulfilling human aspirations. Those who hold the Taylorian view of man as selfish, lazy, and indolent would tend to incorporate practices and processes designed to control and even coerce human beings. CEOs, who overwhelmingly subscribe to the hedonistic and economic view of the human being, evolve organizational processes and systems geared to satisfying the material and economic needs of human beings. On the other hand, leaders subscribing to the humanistic worldview develop processes and practices which seek to uphold human dignity, justice, fairness, freedom, and empowerment. Leaders with such beliefs also create a community culture in their organizations thus satisfying the human need for social connect. Top-level role holders of organizations who carry an integrated view of human beings orchestrate organizational practices and processes to fulfill holistic human needs at the level of body, mind, and soul. It is in this perspective that the present section traces the dominant idea of human nature dealt by philosophers, thinkers, poets, artists, and management scientists in order to create the complete canvas of human nature.

There has been a continued quest through millennia to understand the human being and map various aspects of the self. In fact, some writers and thinkers despair of human nature while others extol human virtues. While writing about man, Shakespeare said, "What a piece of work is a man! How noble in reason! How infinite in faculties! In form and moving how express and admirable! In action how like an Angel!" (cited in Daintith, 1997). Other writers have expressed similar views: "On earth there is nothing great but man…" (Hamilton cited in Daintith, 1997); "Man himself is the crowning wonder of creation…" (Gladstone cited in Edwards, 1999). The Chinese philosopher Mencius considered the original nature of man to be essentially good. Likewise Lao Tzu also expressed a similar view of human nature. Confucianism emphasizes that the essential nature of man is characterized by compassion, sympathy, righteousness, and Zen (Radhakrishnan and Raju, 1995). In the Islamic worldview, man is the highest creation and has a free will to make his own decisions. Hindu philosophy views the human soul as immortal and an inseparable part of divinity.

Rogers (1961), one of the foremost proponents of humanistic psychology indicated in his writings that man is innately positive with potential for self-realization. This view has also been propounded by psychologists like Fromm (2003) and Maslow (1968) and has been the basic assumption of scholars on leadership like Bennis (1994), Burns (1978), and Singh and Bhandarker (1997). Branden (1984) emphasized the role of self-esteem and positive self-evaluation for self-actualization the crowning achievement of a human being in Western psychology.

According to McGregor (1960) man is self-directed and self-controlled; he is a learning human being and accepts responsibility; he has a high degree of imagination and creativity which he uses for problem solving; man likes work and finds work to be a source of satisfaction. Mayo's (n.d.) writing conveyed two assumptions about human nature: (a) human beings are gregarious and (b) prefer living in social relationships with other people. According to Locke (cited in Scott and Hart, 1948), majority of the people is good barring a few who are corrupted. Rousseau believed that in the state of nature man was born with an innate predisposition toward self-preservation, mitigated by a compassion for all other men. Men were simple, good, naive, and trusting (Rousseau, 1950, cited in Scott and Hart, 1971). Marx (1887) viewed the human being as a social animal who is also driven by economic gains. He emphasized the need for human beings to stay in touch with nature and other human beings in order to stay whole and healthy.

Just as some writers have highlighted the best qualities of a human being, others have brought out the darker side. "I love mankind; it's people I can't stand," said Schulz (n.d). Hsun Tzu, the Chinese philosopher, said that human nature is essentially and originally selfish and evil (n.d.). Augustine saw mankind as a "massa peccati," a mess of sin, incapable of raising itself from spiritual death (Fitzgerald and Cavadini, 1999). According to Frederick Taylor (1971), human beings have a tendency to be self-destructive and need to be controlled. Commenting on the assumptions about man implicit in the works, classical organizational theorist, Haire, said that man is viewed as "lazy," "shortsighted," "selfish," "liable to make mistakes," has "poor judgment," and "may even be a little dishonest" (1962).

Anthony Downs (1965) is of the opinion that the "Organization Man" of today is suspicious, distrustful, jealous, deceitful, self-centered, apathetic, immature, intolerant of differences, poor communicator, as well as myopic in his vision. The mechanistic model of organization assumes that man is like a machine—predictable, repairable, and replaceable (Gibson, 1966). According to Gibson's (1966) interpretation, classical scientific management theorists like Gulick, Taylor, Fayol, Mooney, and Urwick are of the view that man is motivated solely and predictably by economic considerations and is an isolated factor of production, independent of social and group pressures.

A third view of human nature as a blend of the beastly as well as godly attributes, has been expressed by some writers: "Our humanity were a poor thing but for the divinity that stirs within us" (Bacon cited in Edwards, 1999); "As there is much beast and some devil in man, so is there some angel and some God in him..." (Coleridge cited in Edwards, 1999); "He is of the Earth, but his thoughts are with the stars. Mean and petty his wants and his desires; yet they serve a soul exalted with grand, and glorious aims, with immortal longings, with thoughts which sweep the heavens and 'wander through eternity'. A pigmy standing on the outward crest of this small planet, his far-reaching spirit stretches outward to the infinite and there alone finds rest" (Carlyle cited in Edwards, 1999); "There are depths in man that go to the lowest hell, and heights that reach the highest heaven..." (Carlyle cited in Edwards, 1999); "A man's nature, runs either to herbs or weeds; therefore let him seasonably water the one, and destroy the other" (Bacon cited in Edwards, 1999); "Man is, 'either a beast or a God'..." (Aristotle cited in Daintith, 1997). In Jewish thought Image and Dust express the polarity of the nature of Man. Man is not only the image of God, but also a product of physical nature (Radhakrishnan and Raju, 1995). Ancient Indian scriptures stated that human beings possess three attributes or *gunas*—*Satoguna* (intellectual, wise, and virtuous), *Rajoguna* (active, spirited, and aggressive), and *Tamoguna* (dull, unthinking, ignorance, inactive, id-like, and hedonistic).

Maslow (1968), Herzberg, Mausner, and Snyderman (1959), Alderfer (1969), and McClelland (1961) postulated that human beings are the amalgam of multiple needs. Maslow emphasized five levels of needs in ascending order, with Self Actualization being at the highest level. Human beings are a mix of intrinsic and extrinsic needs. Herzberg (1959) emphasized on Hygiene factors and Motivators.[1] According to McClelland, human beings operate on three basic needs—achievement, affiliation, and power; and in Alderfer's view human beings have existence, relatedness, and growth needs. Humanistic psychologists (Ryff, 1989) identified six needs—autonomy, personal growth, positive relations with others, purpose in life, environmental mastery and self acceptance. Locke (1948) also reasoned that all men had natural rights among which were liberty and right to personal property. The above views regarding the multiple levels of human nature indicate the human potential to attain both the zenith of all virtues as well as reach the nadir of animalistic and selfish depths.

In the course of our extensive work in training, counseling, and mentoring people across various kinds of institutions right from schools, colleges to the corporate world, we have experienced that every human being has the seed to become a full-fledged banyan tree. We have seen that human beings have vast potential which unfortunately does not get fully actualized. Generally speaking we have seen people striving, struggling, and demonstrating the intense urge to evolve themselves into becoming better human beings. In the Freudian sense human personality is like an iceberg with most of the potential lying hidden and untapped. Similar view has been expressed by Joseph Luft and Harry Ingham (1955), the creators of the Johari Window model. In fact, the greatest challenge for human societies and institutions is to facilitate greater self-actualization of human potential. Our experience has led us to conclude that in essence human beings are characterized by deep curiosity, need to create, need to innovate, and need to self-actualize. They have intense desire for freedom and autonomy; and along with this, they are also social beings with need for social connect, need to be part of communities, need to be compassionate, caring and loving. In many ways the Statue of Liberty in New York symbolizes the intense desire of human beings for Liberty, Equality and Fraternity. All these three needs are so high among human beings that wars, uprisings, revolutions, through centuries have taken place in a bid

---

[1] Hygiene factors—Working conditions, policies and administrative practices, salary and benefits, supervision, status, job security, fellow workers, personal life. Motivators—Recognition, achievement, advancement, growth, responsibility and job challenge.

by human beings to get liberty, equality, and fraternity and break free from the shackles of control and despotic rule.

From the above discussion the following salient features about the nature of man emerge:

- Philosophers and thinkers overwhelmingly see human beings as essentially good, virtuous, compassionate, social, helpful, etc.
- Many thinkers and philosophers have held the view that human beings have the potential to be both good and bad. In other words they possess the capability to be virtuous as well as non-virtuous.
- The human beings have also been seen as a bundle of needs. Their needs, motivations, and *gunas* are moderated and magnified depending upon society, community, and the organization they are engaged in. In other words, social and economic institutions through their processes, systems, and culture, and community and society through social norms and expectations, powerfully shape the individual's needs, motivations, and aspirations.

## Meaning of Work and Meaning of Workplace (MOWP)

After going through the section elucidating the centrality of work and its role in creating happiness, meaning, and motivation in human life, readers may be curious to identify the work components which create greater or lesser motivation and contribution focus. The reader may be equally curious to understand which work parameters have stronger linkage with human nature, work motivation, and contribution as delineated in 'Meaning of Work—Survey of Literature'.

It is in this perspective that the present section has been organized. It deals with some of the prominent constructs related to meaning of work and workplace and their impact on human happiness, need fulfillment, motivation, and contribution.

Ideally, the goal of a nation, society as well as work institution is to create prosperity, growth, and happiness for individuals and society. This is possible only when individuals are passionate for achieving performance, growth, and excellence. Study of the growth of nations across the world has brought out clearly that it is human resources rather than natural resources which are critical for growth and prosperity of the nation. It would be worthwhile to mention that prosperity of a society depends on myriad factors like natural resources, technological prowess, socioeconomic and political structures as well as human skills and capabilities. However in harnessing the above-mentioned resources for development it is the human passion and human capability which play an overriding role. The growth differential in any society therefore can mainly be explained in terms of differential human capabilities, their passion, and motivation (Drucker, 1988; Maslow, 1954; McClelland, 1961; Singh and Bhandarker, 1990). The rise of nations like Singapore, Japan, and Germany, despite being disadvantaged on many natural resources, is a testimony to the human spirit, determination, and ingenuity. The core challenge facing nations and organizations is to excite, inspire, and motivate the human force for excellent contribution and growth. This phenomenon can be examined at multiple levels—individual, family and society, institutions, and the nation.

Thinkers and scholars (Argyris, 1962; Bennis, 1966; Maslow, 1970; McClelland, 1961; Rousseau, 1950) have highlighted the need for the development of national policies, programs, educational systems, institutional arrangements and various socio-political-economic organizations. They have also emphasized the need to evolve appropriate strategies, processes, and systems, significantly focusing on creating passion to work and motivation to create excellence in contribution. Rousseau talked about the need for institutional arrangements for liberating human beings from the bonds of societal chains. Maslow (1970) advocated the creation of the Eupsychian man and self-actualizing human beings by fulfilling their basic needs. McClelland stresses the influence of achievement, power, and affiliation motives for realizing holistic human potential and creating the achieving society (McClelland, 1961). Argyris (1962) and Bennis (1966) wrote on the need for new organizational forms, since bureaucracy stifles human development and creativity. Fromm (1973), Maslow (1954), Bennis (1966), Argyris (1962), Blauner (64), and Kanungo (1992, 1982) reflect upon and suggested ways and means to reduce alienation and anomie, and create healthy human beings.

All religions—Hinduism, Buddhism, Islam, Christianity, Judaism, and Zoroastrianism—unequivocally emphasize the need to inspire human beings to fully actualize themselves and make significant contribution to the uplifting of institutions and society.

However the exclusive focus of the present work is to explore the expectations and aspirations of people from the workplace with a view to creating organizations which can match these expectations and aspirations of individuals so that they can contribute their best to institution and nation building and becoming self-actualizing human beings.

## Meaning of Work—Survey of Literature

Before examining the research literature on meaning of work and workplace, it would be appropriate to highlight the way meaning of work has been conceptualized. Morin (2004) suggested, "the concept of 'meaning of work' can be defined as the significance the subject attributes to work, his representations of work, and the importance it has in his life." Wrzesniewski and Dutton (2001) provided initial empirical validation for taxonomy of work meanings, consisting of work as a job, a career, and a calling. Quintanilla and Wilpert (1988) described five dimensions of working—subjective work definition, work motivation, work centrality, social work norms, and dominant work roles. These include not only meanings attributed by individuals to their current work but also the importance and value of work in general.

People experience meaning at work when there is harmony or balance between their needs and aspirations and the nature of the work they are engaged in (Csikszetmihalyi, 1990; Morin, 2004). In other words there is higher meaning of work when there is convergence between the internal world of the individual—needs, aspirations, and expectations—and the external context of the workplace—job, work, and workplace characteristics. Meaning of work is an outcome of the alignment between individuals' competencies, values and purpose, and workplace attributes which gratify higher level needs. The alignment between sense of self and work itself produces an integrated and holistic meaning of work (Chalofsky, 2003).

There is a plethora of literature studying the valence of workplace attributes (Campbell and Pritchard, 1976; Chen, and Pritchard, 2008; Kanfer, 1987; Kanfer, Parker and Wall, 1998; Latham and Pinder, 2005; Morgeson and Humphrey, 2006; Parker, Wall, and Cordery, 2001; Roberts and Glick, 1981; Wall and Martin, 1987). The prominent and classic work has been that by scholars and researchers like Herzberg et al. (1959), Hackman and Oldham (1976), Vroom (1964), Adams (1963a), and Porter and Lawler (1968).

Based on his extensive research, Herzberg (1976) concluded that both extrinsic and intrinsic factors are critical for creating meaning in work and work motivation. Fulfillment of extrinsic factors can create satisfaction; it, however, does not necessarily create a motivated employee if fulfillment on intrinsic factors is low. In case he is dissatisfied on both types of work parameters—Hygiene factors and Motivators—he would be unhappy and see no meaning in work.

Vroom (1964) postulated the importance of expectancy, valence, and instrumentality for creating motivation and meaning of work and workplace. According to him work motivation and meaning of work depend on the strength of desire one has for a particular job factor and the probability one sees of achieving that. In other words, motivation and the meaning one derives from the workplace depend on perceived valence × instrumentality of workplace attributes. In his model, Vroom also introduced the concept of levels of outcomes for work motivation, emphasizing that the level of motivation and meaning of work individuals derive is not necessarily governed by the first level of outcome; rather it is governed by a series of subsequent outcomes. Porter and Lawler (1968) proposed a model of intrinsic and extrinsic work motivation—intrinsic being where people do an activity out of interest and in doing this they experience satisfaction; and extrinsic, when satisfaction comes not from the activity per se but from instrumental factors linking reward to performance of that activity. Path Goal Theory propounded by House (1971) is a powerful extension of Vroom's model. It has roots in the expectancy theory of motivation which postulates that leaders motivate their followers by providing greater personal payoffs from the workplace. The basic assumption here is that increase in personal payoffs from work would meet the employees' expectations and thereby lead to higher motivation. Locke and Latham (1990) viewed levels of motivation and meaning of work which individuals perceive as an outcome of interactive effects between one's personal goals and workplace factors. They suggest that people will be highly motivated and see meaning when they set specific and difficult goals and feel competent to display those needed behaviors. Using Action Regulation Theory, scholars like Hacker (1994) have emphasized that freedom in making decisions promotes greater motivation and meaning.

Adams (1963) extensively discussed the need for equity, fairness, and distributive justice for enhancing work motivation. In his postulation an individual's motivation and the meaning he derives from work depends not only on what he gets but relative to what others get for similar nature of work and performance. In other words meaning of work is not a pure outcome of the absolute value of the reward; it is an outcome of the comparative value, relative to what others get for the same level of performance.

Findings of a recent global survey on 15,000 corporate executives (*Economic Times*, 2010) indicated that people separate from their organizations when they see that their promotion is not linked to performance. In other words, meaning of work is enhanced when there is equity, justice, and fairness in organizational processes; participation in goal setting; and clear connection established between performance and reward. Porter and Lawler's (1968) model synthesized elements of Vroom's postulates (power of valence, instrumentality, and expectancy); Locke's goal setting model and Adam's equity theory and presented a comprehensive conceptual paradigm for heightening work motivation and meaning in work.

Maslow (1968) conceptualized the legendary hierarchy of needs—physiological, safety, belongingness, self-esteem and self-actualization—in human beings, which get sequentially activated. Thus unless lower order needs are satisfied, higher order needs are not activated. According to the Maslovian conceptualization the workplace should provide the opportunity for fulfillment of individuals' self-esteem and self-actualization needs. When the workplace gratifies these needs, human beings can self-actualize and become Eupsychian. Subsequent research (Haslam, Powell, and Turner, 2000; Rauschenberger, Schmitt, and Hunter, 1980; Ronen, 2001; Wicker et al., 1993; Wahba and Bridwell, 1976) using Maslow's model has shown that multiple needs operate simultaneously with different degrees of intensity. Further it has been found that when satisfaction of higher order needs is blocked, the individual tends to focus on satisfaction of lower order needs (Alderfer, 1969; Singh and Das, 1976). Need for competence and autonomy underlie Intrinsic Motivation, according to the SDT theory (Gagné and Deci, 2005). In fact, SDT defines needs as universal necessities for optimal human development (Ryan et al., 96). Gagné and Deci (2005) further state that satisfaction of these needs will lead to intrinsic motivation, which in turn contributes to effective performance, job satisfaction, positive work-related attitudes, organizational citizenship behaviors, psychological adjustment, and well-being. Clearly, the needs–supplies fit influence workplace attitudes.

Researchers (Bandura, 2001; Bottger and Chew, 1986; Parker, 2003) have brought out the role of personality factors like self-efficacy and growth need strength on workplace behavior and motivation to work. Parker (2003) and Bandura (2001) suggested that when people are characterized by poor self-efficacy, they are likely to exert little or no effort even when the environment provides opportunities for growth. As against this, when people have high self-efficacy, they exert themselves even in difficult situations and this in turn enhances their likelihood of success. Bottger and Chew (1986) concluded from their research that those with high growth need strength (that is, the extent to which individuals value complex and challenging work), would respond very well to job enrichment as compared to those with low growth need strength.

Morin (2004) identified six factors creating higher meaning of work—social purpose, moral correctness and workplace ethics, achievement-related pleasure, autonomy, recognition, and positive relationships. The famous Meaning of Work study (MOW International Team, 1987) examined five major domains of work and assessed their relative importance. These are work centrality, societal norms regarding work, valued work outcomes, importance of work goals and work-role identification. More recent studies (Chalofsky, 2003; Mitroff and Denton, 1999a) have consistently demonstrated that people rate purpose, fulfillment, autonomy, satisfaction, close working relationships, and learning as more important than money for deriving meaning at work.

Hackman and Oldham (1980) have done seminal work highlighting the importance of job characteristics in creating meaning at the workplace. They (Hackman and Oldham, 1976) concluded that work becomes more meaningful when it is characterized by skill variety, task identity, task significance, autonomy, and feedback from work. According to their conceptualization, the individual must perceive that his job is meaningful, valuable, and worthwhile; provides freedom and accountability at work and regular feedback on job performance. In order to enhance meaning at the workplace, Hackman and Oldham proposed the introduction of both job enlargement and job enrichment, also known as horizontal and vertical job loading. Porter and Lawler (1968) suggested that organizations should restructure work in such a way that effective performance would result in intrinsic and extrinsic rewards and subsequently lead to job satisfaction.

In studies of a Dutch bank and school, Houkes et al. (2001) found that there is a positive relationship between work content (skill variety) and work motivation, and between erosion of work content and emotional exhaustion. Warr's Vitamin Model (Warr, 1987) outlines the key features of the work environment associated with employee well-being and meaning of work. According to Warr (1987) employees need to have opportunities to exercise personal control and use skills, job variety, get money, goal fulfillment, supportive supervision, physical security, environmental clarity, opportunity for interpersonal clarity, and a valued social position for creating meaning of work and work motivation.

Chalofsky (2003) emphasizes the centrality of the job itself as a source of meaning in the workplace and so reinforces the continuing importance of traditional content theories of work motivation (e.g. Herzberg, 1966), job design (e.g., Hackman and Oldham, 1976, 1980) and the work environment (e.g. Warr, 1987). Turner, Barling, and Zarcharatios (2002) have similarly stressed the relevance of designing jobs which encourage employees to actively engage in their tasks and work environments in order to gain meaningfulness from their work. Cables and De Rue (2002) found from their research that employees differentiate among three varieties of fit of a person with organizational values, rewards, and job demands. Person–organization fit perceptions have been found to predict job satisfaction and organizational commitment much better than demands and abilities fit (Cables and Judge, 1996).

## Millennials' Preferences and Expectations from Work

People of a generation are bound to be more similar to each other owing to the influence of various social, political, economic events occurring during pre-adult years. This can result in individuals developing distinctive sets of values, beliefs, expectations, and behaviors different from previous generation/s resulting in a distinct generational identity (Inglehart, 1997).

Given the characteristics of the youth entering organizations and the events that have defined their lives (notably globalization, rapid technological advancement, increasing demographic diversity) various authors have labeled the new generation as Generation Y, Millennials, Nexters, and the Nexus Generation (Barnard, Cosgrove, and Welsh, 1998; Burke and Ng, 2006; Zemke, Raines, and Filipczak, 2000).

According to Wong et al. (2008), Gen Y is used to technology. People of this generation are comfortable with change, value development, and enjoy the challenges of new opportunities that come their way. Similar to Baby Boomers, they are also viewed as driven and demanding of the work environment and are also likely to be optimistic. They enjoy collective action and are highly socialized. They value having responsibilities and having input into decisions and actions.

Many studies (Bibby, 2001; Dewhurst, Guthridge, and Mohr, 2009; Harpaz, Honig, and Coetsier, 2002; Corporate Leadership Council, 2004; Erikson, 2009; Lancaster and Stillman, 2002; Yang and Guy, 2006; Price Waterhouse Coopers, 2008; Lyons, 2003; Ng, Schweitzer, and Lyons, 2010; SHRM, 2009; Gursoy, Maier, and Chi, 2008; Martin, 2005; Remo, 2006; Alsop, 2008) have been conducted on Millennials to identify employee preferences and expectations from the workplace. In a research conducted on 10,000 young people, Bibby (2001) sought to ascertain the characteristics which were considered to be critical to a "good job." It was found that respondents considered interesting work (86%), a feeling of accomplishment (76%), friendly and helpful colleagues (63%) were more important than pay (66%), and job security (57%).

A recent *McKinsey Quarterly* survey (Dewhurst et al., 2009) underscores the changes in expectations from the workplace. Findings indicated that the respondents view praise from immediate managers, leadership attention, and a chance to lead projects or task forces—as equally if not more effective motivators than money and stock options. Findings indicate that the top three motivators are important (a) in making employees feel valued by their companies; (b) indicating that the companies are concerned about their well-being; and (c) that they strive to create opportunities for career growth (Dewhurst et al., 2009).

Millennials look for work that is meaningful and fulfilling (Lancaster and Stillman, 2002; Yang and Guy, 2006). A recent study by Price Waterhouse Coopers (2008) found that corporate responsibility is critical to Millennials and 88% indicated that they will seek an employer whose work values match their own. They have low tolerance for less than challenging work and often perform poorly in high volume and non-stimulating work (Corporate Leadership Council, 2005). In addition, Millennials appear to be seeking the opportunity to broaden their horizons through job mobility and international assignments (Price Waterhouse Coopers, 2008).

"Manager Quality" (one's immediate boss) has been rated as a top motivational factor (after pay) for Millennials (Corporate Leadership Council, 2005). High rating has also been assigned to collaborating closely with and learning from colleagues and managers and forming friendships with their coworkers (Corporate Leadership Council, 2005). Another study echoed the above finding where it was found that Millennials emphasize the social aspects of work (friendly coworkers, fun environment) (Lyons, 2003).

Ng et al. (2010) studied the career expectations and priorities of the Millennials and found that the Millennials rated the opportunities for advancement as the most desirable work-related attribute. They also rated good people to report to among the leading factors when making career decisions. Good training and developing new skills were next, indicating a strong desire for professional growth to take on high impact positions. Items related to pay, benefits, and security ranked in the middle behind career advancement.

The SHRM study (2009) brought out that Millennials rate close relationships and frequent feedback from supervisors as the most important expectation from the workplace. This is followed by the expectation of open communication from their supervisors and managers, even about matters normally reserved for more senior employees (Gursoy et al., 2008; Martin, 2005; Remo, 2006; SHRM, 2009). Third, Millennials prefer to work in teams, in part because they perceive group-based work to be more fun, but also because they like to avoid risk (Alsop, 2008; Gursoy et al., 2008). A seven-country study by Harpaz et al. (2002) on youth brought out that the two most valued work goals are interesting work and good pay.

It has been argued that the growing emphasis on the intrinsic aspect of work marks a shift from materialistic expectations to a need for a greater sense of meaning and purpose in their working lives (Guevara and Ord, 1996; Hutton, 2003).

The foregoing analysis brings out the following noteworthy features:

- Scholars, thinkers, and researchers dealing with meaning of work and work motivation unequivocally emphasize the importance of fit of individual's needs, values, personality, expectations, and aspirations with workplace and job characteristics. It is this fit which provides the chance for an individual to experience holistic meaning of work.
- When there is a mismatch between the two—that is, individual needs and workplace characteristics—there is disconnect of the individual from the organization, experience of demotivation, and lack of meaning.
- Another important feature is the focus which individuals lay on equity, justice, and fairness. This is especially true in terms of the reward one gets for performance where people focus more on peer comparisons rather than on the absolute value of the reward which they receive.
- While the importance of intrinsic motivators has been emphasized for decades, it has now assumed heightened intensity with the emergence of the new generation, the Millennials.
- Extensive work has been done in this area in the West. However in the Indian context there is scant research on this topic to enable building the theoretical constructs necessary to design a better workplace for Millennials.

## Meaning of Work and Workplace: Definitions

Workplace meanings have been defined differently by different people: some intrinsic, some extrinsic. Sverko and Vizek-Vidovic (1995) concluded that meaning of work is the set of general beliefs about work held by an individual, who acquires them through interaction with the social environment. It is generally assumed that these beliefs are related to the person's career orientation and behavior in the work situation, including job performance, turnover, absenteeism, and job satisfaction (p. 3). According to Morin (2004), "the concept of 'meaning of work' can be defined as the significance the subject attributes to work, his representations of work, and the importance it has in his life" (p. 4).

Meaning of workplace is a broader concept in that it incorporates the expectations regarding the physical environment at work as well. For the purpose of the present research, MOWP is the type of work and workplace attributes which an individual prefers, values, and desires. It is a preference for working in an organization characterized by a set of physical, social, and psychological factors which are derived from work practices and work culture. It is assumed that when a person is able to get a preferred workplace it would result in higher meaning and therefore lead to greater motivation.

## Other Variables Used in This Research

### Demographic and personality[2] attributes

Demographic and personality attributes have also been used in the present work as factors which are antecedent to MOWP and which can help in predicting preferred workplace factors. These are now discussed below:

- Demographic factors related to family have been used in this research since they reflect the family socialization styles, nature of exposure to the world, and familial values which are crucial to the formation of the worldview of the millennials. Previous research (Feij, 1998; Maccoby, 1992; Sanders et al., 1998) has established that the socialization process is one of the main sources of work attitudes. This includes factors such as family structure and process, parental

---

[2] Definitions presented in Chapter 2.

employment history, parental roles and cultural and religious upbringing, as well as educational institutions, the mass media, and types of jobs, whether full-time or part-time. It has also been found that parental employment has a significant impact on the attitude formation process of children (Barling and Kelloway, 1999).
- After family, the other major socialization realms are educational institutions and the workplace (Ibarra, 1999; van Maanen, 1975; van Maanen and Schein, 1979), and all these have a powerful influence on the individual's value formation and reinforcement. Therefore, it is expected that the demographic variables have a significant impact on personality, values, and MOWP.
- Age and work experience reflect the individual's level of experience, exposure to work as well as stages in life. Education reflects the type of professional-level value shaping which an individual would be exposed to in the major socialization process. Personality factors have been found to influence job attitudes (Judge and Bono, 2001, Judge et al., 1999), goal setting, goal commitment, and effort to achieve the goals (Barrick, Mount, and Strauss, 1993; Gellatly, 1996). The impact of specific personality attributes on workplace attitudes and behavior has been well researched and have been presented in detail in Chapter 2.
- Demographic factors, as well as personality play an important role in creating, mindsets, attitudes, and expectations at the individual level. Hence in order to get greater insights into the expectations from the workplace, demographic factors—both psychographic and sociographic; and personality factors like values, locus of control, and achievement motivation, are assessed in this research.
- The preference for certain work and workplace characteristics, it is assumed, will thus be influenced strongly by the selected personality and demographic factors.

The importance of this work cannot be underestimated. Understanding the meaning of workplace will enable organizations to build a preferred workplace which in turn can help in managing Millennials' turnover, commitment, and stress. This will also enable organizations to tap into the creativity and energies of the Millennials.

The authors have developed Figure 1.1 on the basis of the foregoing discussion of the research literature.

Figure 1.1  Impact of personality and demographics on the MOWP

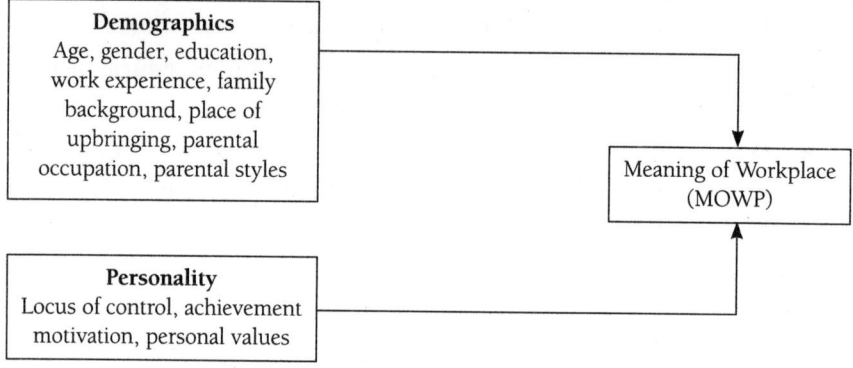

## *Demographic factors*

Demographic variables like age, education, gender, family type, place of upbringing, prior work experience, educational stream, parental occupation, parental styles, etc., have been assessed (see Appendix 1A for the details).

## *Personality*[3]

Personality is defined as an individual's preferred or typical way of behaving, thinking and feeling (Saville et al., 1984). Three personality constructs—personal values, achievement motivation and locus of control[4]—have been assessed in this research, the details of which are given subsequently:

1. **Personal Values:** Values are defined as beliefs and personal standards that guide individuals to function in a society and thus, values have both the cognitive and affective dimensions (Rokeach, 1973). Work attitude and work behavior are governed by work values to a large extent (Chew and Putti, 1995). Researchers have argued that different cultural and social experiences play an important role in

---

[3] The term includes personality and values for ease of presentation.
[4] A detailed presentation on the personality variables and values is provided in Chapter 2.

creating different value premises (Bass et al., 1979; England, 1986; Hofstede, 1980). According to England (1978), knowing the value system will allow organizations to design effective motivational systems. A number of social, economic and technological changes have resulted in the formation of new work values (Chew and Putti, 1995) and hence understanding the value preference of Millennials would be very important for organizations.

2. **Achievement Motivation:** The American Psychological Association (APA) Concise Dictionary of Psychology defines motivation as "the impetus that gives purpose or direction to human or animal behavior and operates at a conscious or unconscious level" (2008: 29). According to McClelland (1961) the need for achievement (n-Ach) is characterized by the desire to take responsibility for solving problems, to master complex tasks, as well as set goals and get feedback on level of success. Achievement motivation has an effect on workplace preferences and expectations. Research has shown that individuals with high achievement motive are attracted to work environments in which they have opportunities for self development, personal growth, skill upgradation (to develop their full potential), to do something important, and to make a contribution. They need to be in control of their work (work autonomy), have sufficient influence to determine the nature of tasks, to act without consultation and permission, and to affect decisions made by the managers (Atkinson 1957, 1978; Bandura, 1986; McClelland, 1985a; McClelland, Koestner R, Weinberger, 1989; Spence and Helmreich, 1983; Turban and Keon, 1993; Weiner, 1991, 1990, 1979). Achievement motivation has been found to correlate with other desirable work outcomes like Organizational Commitment and Organizational Citizenship Behavior (Salami, 2008).

3. **Locus of Control:** Locus of control is a personality orientation characterized either by the belief that one can control events in one's life by one's own efforts (internal locus of control) or that what happens in one's life is determined by forces outside one's control like fate, luck, or chance (external locus of control). Julian Rotter (1954) first conceptualized this orientation and the construct has been very widely used in a large number of researches.

Studies have found significant relationships of work locus of control to numerous outcomes including work-related stress and strain (Spector and Fox, 2003), counterproductive behaviors (Fox & Spector, 1999), job satisfaction (Leung, Siu, and Spector, 2000) and job performance (Blau, 1993). Volansky and Habinski (1998) found that internal-external locus of control is an important personal attribute related to an individual's organizational commitment. Research has also shown a relationship between work ethics and locus of control (Cherry, 2005; Deflumeri, 1982; Forte, 2005; Jones, 1993). Hence, a person's locus of control has a significant effect on his/her work attitude, organizational behavior, satisfaction, performance, and commitment.

Personal values, achievement motivation, and locus of control have been the three personality attributes used in this research to understand Millennials' profile.

# Research Design and Framework

## Objectives of the Research

The key thrust of this research is on the Millennial generation which comprises people born after 1977 (Chen and Choi, 2008; Tapscott, 1998) since they are emerging as future leaders of the organizations. Youth are often at the cusp of the cultural shifts and value preferences. According to Harpaz et al. (2002), they adapt to new technologies, styles, and modes of behavior thus hastening change in both society and organization. Hence understanding their expectations and MOWP will be immensely useful to create the desired organization of the future. This in turn can help both individuals and organizations to reach their potential.

The following are the objectives of this research:

- To map the psychological profile of Millennials.
- To identify the workplace expectations of Millennials.

- To understand how to create a workplace which that not only attract Millennials to join but which is aligned to the expectations of Millennials.

This book is an outcome of extensive research carried out by the team from 2007–10. It is the product of both rigorous quantitative and qualitative research. The data for this work was gathered from 2,170 respondents from leading engineering and management schools representing the four regions—north, south, east, and west—of the country through structured questionnaire. Final usable responses were 2,158 (see Appendix 1B for the sample details). Qualitative data has been gathered from much smaller numbers the details of which are presented in the relevant sections that follow.

## Instrument Design

The MOWP questionnaire was developed in three phases. In Phase 1, focused group interviews were conducted with 115 corporate executives and 130 engineering and management students. Students and executives responded to a single open-ended question, "What does work mean to you? Kindly mention five characteristics of the workplace where you would like to work." Their responses were content analyzed resulting in 71 themes. These were then converted into statements and incorporated into the questionnaire for Phase 2. In Phase 2, data were gathered from a sample of 312 students. Based on the mean analysis of the data, the number of items was reduced from 71 to 49 by selecting the top 49 items. This was done in order to make the data more manageable.

In Phase 3, the final MOWP questionnaire consisting of 49 items (for details see Appendix 1C of this chapter) was administered on 2170 students (covering top-ranked management and engineering colleges across North, South, East, and West). Other tests (personal values, achievement motivation and work locus of control) were also included in the test battery (for details see Appendix 2A in Chapter 2).

In addition to the above data, the team was curious to understand the perspective of those MBAs with work experience regarding the extent to which they actually found the workplace characteristics which the larger group had filled up as expectations. The MOWP questionnaire was administered to a sample of 600 students from across B Schools with at least two years of work experience and asked the question, "To what extent have you found the following characteristics at your workplace?" Out of the lot, 567 usable responses were received.

In addition 100 students were interviewed to get an in-depth understanding of the expectations from the workplace. Open-ended interviews were also conducted with 50 HR heads in order to understand observations and insights regarding Millennials' attitude, and profile which would help in devising a better future workplace.

# Appendix 1A: Background Information Questionnaire

## Individual Background

1. Age:
2. Name of the Institute:
3. Prior Work Experience:
4. Education:
   (1) Graduate (2) Post Graduate
5. Nature of Education:
   (1) MBA (2) Non MBA (please mention)
6. Gender:
   (1) Male (2) Female
7. Family Background (Parents' occupation):
   (1) Service (2) Agriculture (3) Business
8. Kindly indicate the employment status of your parents:
   (1) Mother employed (2) Father employed (3) Both employed
9. Family Type:
   (1) Nuclear (2) Joint
10. Kindly indicate the decision making process in your family:
    (1) Highly autocratic (2) Autocratic (controlling) (3) Mixed (4) Democratic (5) Highly democratic (open)
11. Think about your father and kindly rate his typical style on five-point rating scale:
    (1) Highly critical (2) Critical (3) Nurturing (4) Highly nurturing

12. Think about your father and kindly rate your father's typical style on a five-point rating scale:
    (1) Highly rational (2) Rational (3) Emotional (4) Highly emotional
13. Kindly rate your parents' style on a five-point scale in terms of "Risk Taking Ability:"
    (1) Very low (2) Low (3) Medium (4) High (5) Very high
14. Place of your upbringing:
    (1) North India (2) South India (3) Eastern India (4) Western India (5) Central India
15. Parental expectations from you in terms of your career—please mention below:
    (1)
    (2)
    (3)

## Appendix 1B: MOWP Data Details

Table 1A.1 MOWP sample details

| Type of Sample | Students | | Executives | Total |
| --- | --- | --- | --- | --- |
| | BTech | MBA | Working Executives | |
| IITs, IIMs, MDI and other leading institutions | 792 | 864 | 502 | **2158** |

Table 1A.2 Regional representation of students' data for BTech and MBA

| | BTech | MBA | Total |
| --- | --- | --- | --- |
| North | 231 | 500 | 731 |
| South | 166 | 185 | 351 |
| East | 118 | 127 | 245 |
| West | 277 | 52 | 329 |
| Total | 792 | 864 | 1656 |

## Appendix 1C: MOWP Questionnaire

### Questionnaire A

This questionnaire is designed to measure one's expectations from the *work place*. Please rate the importance of each attribute according to you—1 being the least important and 5 being the most important.

## I would like to work at a place which:

| (1) Least important | (2) Somewhat important | (3) Moderately important | (4) Highly important | (5) Most important |
|---|---|---|---|---|

| No. | | 1 | 2 | 3 | 4 | 5 |
|---|---|---|---|---|---|---|
| 1 | Helps me to earn respect from society | | | | | |
| 2 | Has modern equipments to facilitate work | | | | | |
| 3 | Contributes to the economy of the country | | | | | |
| 4 | Is ethical in dealings | | | | | |
| 5 | Gives freedom for many coffee breaks | | | | | |
| 6 | Has a strong brand value | | | | | |
| 7 | Encourages innovation and idea generation | | | | | |
| 8 | Brings discipline among its employees | | | | | |
| 9 | Has high prestige | | | | | |
| 10 | Provides opportunities to influence others | | | | | |
| 11 | Provides opportunities for personality development | | | | | |
| 12 | Believes in fairness and justice | | | | | |
| 13 | Provides opportunity for social networking | | | | | |
| 14 | Encourages learning | | | | | |
| 15 | Encourages team work | | | | | |
| 16 | Follows rules and regulations | | | | | |
| 17 | Provides opportunity to exercise power | | | | | |
| 18 | Is well lit | | | | | |
| 19 | Is flexible with work timings | | | | | |
| 20 | Provides constructive feedback for my development | | | | | |
| 21 | Requires working in a planned manner | | | | | |
| 22 | Has a well defined "shared vision" | | | | | |
| 23 | Gives autonomy and freedom to express my views | | | | | |
| 24 | Provides opportunities to take initiatives | | | | | |
| 25 | Has wide open spaces | | | | | |
| 26 | Takes initiatives for planned change | | | | | |
| 27 | Encourages experimentation | | | | | |
| 28 | Has latest technology | | | | | |
| 29 | Has a green environment (trees, etc.) | | | | | |
| 30 | Brings people closer | | | | | |
| 31 | Is conveniently located from my residence | | | | | |
| 32 | Provides job security | | | | | |
| 33 | Encourages people to voice their concerns | | | | | |
| 34 | Is open to suggestions for improvement | | | | | |

| No. | 1 | 2 | 3 | 4 | 5 |
|---|---|---|---|---|---|
| 35 Recognizes contribution | | | | | |
| 36 Encourages leadership development | | | | | |
| 37 Values work–life balance | | | | | |
| 38 Has a crèche | | | | | |
| 39 Celebrates success | | | | | |
| 40 Encourages trust and transparency | | | | | |
| 41 Empowers people | | | | | |
| 42 Has role clarity | | | | | |
| 43 Takes care of financial needs | | | | | |
| 44 Reduces fear of losing job | | | | | |
| 45 Cares about physical and mental health of its employees | | | | | |
| 46 Provides a platform for forming life-long relationships | | | | | |
| 47 Provides opportunities for decision making | | | | | |
| 48 Recognizes performance | | | | | |
| 49 Provides a sense of community | | | | | |

# References

Adams, J. S. (1963a). Toward an understanding of inequity. *Journal of Abnormal and Social Psychology*, 67 (5), 422–436.

Advaita Ashrama. (2000). "Vivekananda: The Great Spiritual Teacher". Kolkata: Advaita Ashrama.

Alderfer, C. (1969). An empirical test of a new theory of human needs. *Organizational Behavior and Human Performance*, 4 (2), 142–175.

Ali, A. J. (1995). The evolution of work ethics and management thought: An Islamic view. In H. S. R. Kao, D. Sinha & B. Wilpert (Eds.), *Management and cultural values: The indigenization of organizations in Asia* (p. 140). New Delhi/Thousand Oaks, London: Sage Publications.

Alsop, R. (2008). *The trophy kids group up: How the Millennial generation is shaping up the workplace*. San Francisco: Jossey-Bass.

Anderson, N. (1961). *Work and leisure*. London: Routledge & Kegan.

Argyris, C. (1962). *Interpersonal competence and organizational effectiveness*. Homewood, Ill: Irwin Press.

Atkinson, J. W. (1957). Motivation determinants of risk-taking behavior. *Psychological Review*, 64 (6/1), 359–372.

Atkinson, J. W., & Birch, D. (1978). *An introduction to motivation* (2nd Ed.). New York: Van Nostrand.

Edwards, T. (1999). *The world's greatest quotations*. New Delhi: Crest Publishing House.

Bandura, A. (1986). *Social foundations of thought and action: A social cognitive theory*. Englewood Cliffs, New Jersey.: Prentice Hall.

———. (2001). Social cognitive theory: An agentic perspective. *Annual Review of Psychology*, 52 (1), 1–26.

Barling, J. & Kelloway, E. K. (1999), Introduction. In J. Barling & and E. K. Kelloway (Eds.), *Young workers: Varieties of experiences*. Washington, DC: American Psychological Association.

Barnard, R., Cosgrove, D., & Welsh, J. (1998). *Chip & pop: Decoding the nexus generation*. Toronto: Malcolm Lester Books.

Barrick, M. R., Mount, M. K., & Strauss, J. P. (1993). Conscientiousness and performance of sales representatives: Test of the mediating effects of goal setting. *Journal of Applied Psychology, 78* (5), 715–722.

Basler, Roy P. (Ed.) (1953). *The collected works of Abraham Lincoln*. New Brunswick, New Jersey: Rutgers University Press.

Bass, B. M, Burger, P. C, Doktor, R., & Barrett, G. V. (1979). *Assessment of managers: An international comparison*. New York: Free Press.

Bennis, W. G. (1994). *On becoming a leader*. New York: Perseus Books.

———. (1966). *Changing Organizations*. New York: McGraw-Hill Book Company.

Bibby, R. W. (2001). *Canada's teens: Today, yesterday and tomorrow*. Toronto: Stoddart Publishing Co. Limited.

Blau, G. (1993). Testing the relationship of locus of control to different performance dimensions, *Journal of Occupational and Organizational Psychology, 66* (2), 125–138.

Blauner, R. (1964). *Alienation and freedom: The factory worker and his industry*. Chicago: University of Chicago Press.

Bottger, P. C., & Chew, I. K. H. (1986). Job characteristics model and growth satisfaction: Main effects of assimilation of work experience and context satisfaction, *Human Relations, 39* (6), 575–594.

Branden, N. (1984). The benefits and hazards of the philosophy of Ayn Rand: A personal statement. *Journal of Humanistic Psychology, 24* (4), 39–64.

Braude, L. (1975). *Work and wonders: A sociological analysis*. Praeger Publishers: New York.

Brief, A. P., & Nord, W. R. (Eds.) (1990). *Meanings of occupational work: A collection of essays*. Lexington, Massachusetts: Lexington Books.

Buddha. (n.d.). *Buddhist Quotes*. Retrieved September 5, 2010, from About.com: http://quotations.about.com/od/spiritualquotes/a/buddhistquotes.htm.

Burke, R. J., & Ng, E. (2006). The changing nature of work organizations: Implications for human resource management. *Human Resource Management Review, 16* (1), 86–94.

Burn, J. M. (1978). *Leadership*. New York: Harper & Row.

Cable, D. M., & De Rue, D. S. (2002). The convergent and discriminant validity of subjective fit perceptions. *Journal of Applied Psychology, 87* (5), 875–884.

Cable, D. M., & Judge, T. A. (1996). Person–organization fit, job choice decisions, and organizational entry. *Organizational Behavior and Human Decision Processes, 67* (3), 294–311.

Campbell, D. J., & Pritchard, R. (1976). Motivation theory in industrial and organizational psychology. In M. D. Dunnette (Ed.), *Handbook of Industrial and Organizational Psychology* (pp. 63–130). Chicago: Rand McNally.

Carlyle, T. (2008). *Past and present*. Charleston, Seychelles: BiblioBazaar.

Chalofsky, N. (2003). An emerging construct of meaningful work. *Human Resource Development International, 6* (1), 69–83.

Chatman, J. A., & Flynn, F. (2001). The influence of demographic heterogeneity on the emergence and consequences of cooperative norms in work teams. *Academy of Management Journal, 44*, 956–974.

Chen, Po-Ju, & Choi, Y. (2008). Generational differences in work values: A study of hospitality management. *International Journal of Contemporary Hospitality*, 20 (6), 595–615.

Cherry, J. (2005). The impact of normative influence and locus of control on ethical judgments and intentions: A cross-cultural comparison. *Journal of Business Ethics*, 68 (2), 113–132.

Chew, I., & Putti, L. (1995). Relationship on work-related values of Singaporean and Japanese managers in Singapore. *Human Relations*, 1149–1170.

Collins, J. (2001). *Good to great*. New York: HarperCollins.

Collins, J., & Porras, J. I. (1997). *Built to last: Successful habits of visionary companies*. New York: HarperCollins.

Confucius. (n.d.). BrainyQuote.com. Retrieved September 5, 2010, from http://www.brainyquote.com/quotes/quotes/c/confucius134717.html.

Corporate Leadership Council. (2004). *Generation X and Y employees*. Washington, DC: Corporate Executive Board.

———. (2005). *HR considerations for engaging Generation Y employees*. Washington, DC: Corporate Executive Board.

Csikzentmihalyi, M. (1990). *Flow: The psychology of optimal experience*. New York: Harper & Row.

Daintith, J. (Ed.). (1997). *Thematic Dictionary of Quotations*. London: Bloomsbury Publishing Plc.

De Geus, A. (1997). *The living company: Habits for survival in a turbulent business environment*. Boston, Massachusetts: Harvard Business School Press.

Deflumeri, J. (1982). *Teachers' moral reasoning*. Unpublished manuscript, Doctoral School of Education Doctoral Dissertation.

Dewhurst, M., Guthridge, M., & Mohr, E. (2009). Motivating people getting beyond money. *McKinsey Quarterly*, 1, 12–15.

Donald, M. N., & Havinghurst, R. J. (1959). The meaning of leisure. *Social Forces*, 37, 357–360.

Downs, A. (1965). A theory of bureaucracy. *Academy of Management Journal*, 9 (3), 233–245.

Drucker, P. (1988). *The coming of the new organization. Harvard Business Review*, 66 (1), 45–53.

*Economic Times*. (2010). Promotion denial prime cause of attrition: Study. *Economic Times*, September 4, 2010, New Delhi Edition, Page 5, Column no. 6.

Edwards, T. (1999). *The world's greatest quotations*. New Delhi: Crest Publishing House.

England, G. W. (1978). Managers and their value systems: A five-country comparative study. *Columbia Journal of World Business*, 13, 33–44.

———. (1986). National work meanings and patterns—constraints on management action. *European Management Journal*, 4 (3), 176–184.

———. (1991). The meaning of work in the USA: Recent changes. *European Work and Organizational Psychology Journal*, 1, 111–124.

England, G. W., & Misumi, J. (1986). Work centrality in Japan and the United States. *Journal of Cross Cultural Psychology*, 17, 399–416.

Morin, E. M. (2004). The meaning of work in modern times, 10th World Congress on Human Resources Management, Rio de Janeiro, Brazil, August, speech.

Erikson, T. J. (2009). Gen Y in the workforce: How I learned to love Millenials and stop worrying about what they are doing with their iPhones. *Harvard Business Review*, February 2009.

Feij, J. A. (1998). Work socialization of young people. In P. Drenth & C. de Wolff (Eds.), *Handbook of work and organizational psychology* (2nd ed.) (Vol. 3, Chapter 10). Hove: Psychology Press.

Firth, R. (1948). Anthropological background to work. *Occupational Psychology, 22,* 94–102.

Fitzgerald, A., & Cavadini, J. C. (1999). *Augustine through the ages: An encyclopedia.* Grand Rapids, Michigan: Wm. B. Eerdmans Publishing.

Forte, A. (2005). Locus of control and the moral reasoning of managers. *Journal of Business Ethics, 58* (1), 65–77.

Fox, S. & P. E. Spector. (1999). A model of work frustration-aggression. *Journal of Organizational Behavior, 20,* 915–931.

Frankl, V. E. (1984). *Man's search for meaning.* Boston: Beacon.

Friedmann, E. A., & Havighurst, R. J. (1954). Chicago: University of Chicago Press.

Fromm, E. (1973). *The anatomy of human destructiveness.* New York: Holt: Rinehart and Winston.

———. (2003). *On being human.* New York: The Continuum International Publishing Group Ltd, The Tower Building.

Gagné, M., & Deci, E. (2005). Self-determination theory and work motivation. *Journal of Organizational Behavior, 26,* 331–362.

Gellatly, I. R. (1996). Conscientiousness and task performance: Test of a cognitive process model. *Journal of Applied Psychology, 81,* 474–482.

George, L. (2009). Dude, where's my job? Retrieved May 5, 2010, from http://www2.macleans.ca/2009/01/14/dude-where%E2%80%99s-my-job/

Gibson, J. L. (1966). Organization theory and the nature of man. *The Academy of Management Journal, 9* (3): 233–245.

Gini, A. R. (2001). *My job, myself: Work and the creation of the modern individual.* New York: Routledge.

Greenfield, P. M. (1998). The cultural evolution of IQ. In U. Neisser (Ed.), *The rising curve: Long-term gains in IQ and other measures* (pp. 81–123). Washington, DC: American Psychological Association.

Guevara, K., & Ord, J. (1996). The search for meaning in a changing work context. *Futures, 28* (8), 709–722.

Gursoy D., Maier, T. A., & Chi, C. G. (2008). Generational differences: An examination of work values and generational gaps in the hospitality workforce. *International Journal of Hospitality Management, 27,* 458–488.

Hacker, W. (1994). Action regulation theory and occupational psychology: Review of German empirical research since 1987. *German Journal of Psychology, 18,* 91–120.

Hackman, R. J., & Oldham, G. R. (1976). Motivating through the design of work: Test of a theory. *Organizational Behaviour and Human Performance, 16,* 250–279.

———. (1980). *Work redesign.* Reading, Massachusetts: Addison-Wesley.

Harding, S. H., & Hickspoors, E. J. (1995). New work values: In theory and in practice. *International Social Science Journal, 47,* 441–455.

Harpaz, I. (1990). The importance of work goals: An international perspective. *Journal of International Business Studies, 21* (1), 75–93.

———. (1999). Work values in Israel: Stability and change over time. *Monthly Labor Review, 122,* 46–50.

Harpaz, I., Honig, B., & Coetsier, P. (2002). A cross-cultural longitudinal analysis of the meaning of work and the socialization process of career starters. *Journal of World Business, 37,* 230–244.

Haslam S. A., Powell, C., & Turner, J. C. (2000). Social identity, self-categorization, and work motivation: Rethinking the contribution of the group to positive and sustainable organizational outcomes. *Applied Psychology: International Review, 49*, 319–339.

Herzberg, F. (1966). *Work and the nature of man.* Cleveland, Ohio. Holland.

———. (1976). *The managerial choice: To be efficient and to be human.* Homewood, Illinois: Dow-Jones-Irwin.

Herzberg, F., Mausner, B., & Snyderman, B. B. (1959). *The motivation to work* (2nd ed.). New York: John Wiley & Sons.

Hillman, J. (1989). *A blue fire. Selected writings.* New York: Harper & Row.

Hofstede, G. (1980). *Cultures consequences: International differences in work related values.* Beverly Hills, California.

Houkes, I., Janssen, P. P., de Jonge, J., & Nijhuis, F. J. (2001). Specific relationship between work characteristic and intrinsic work motivation, burnout and turnover intention: A multi- sample analysis. *European Journal of Work and Organizational Psychology, 10* (1), 1–23.

House, Robert J. (1971). A path-goal theory of leader effectiveness. *Leadership Quarterly, 7* (3), 323–352.

Hui, C. H. (1992). Values and attitudes. In R. I. Westwood (Ed.), *Organisational behaviour: Southeast Asian perspectives* (pp. 63–90). Hong Kong: Longman.

Hutton, W. (2003). Wear kid gloves when tackling Generation Y, *Personnel Today, 17.*

Ibarra, H. (1999), Provisional selves: Experimenting with image and identity in professional adaptation, *Administrative Science Quarterly, 44* (4), 764–791.

Inglehart, R. 1997. *Modernization and postmodernization: Cultural, economic, and political change in 43 societies.* Princeton, New Jersey: Princeton University Press.

Rousseau, J. J. (1950). A discourse on the origin of inequality. In J. J. Rousseau (Ed.), *The social contract and discourses* (G. D. H. Cole, Trans.) (p. 222, 223, & 226). New York: Everyman's Library, E. P. Dutton.

Jones, G. E. (1993). Unethical behavioral intentions in organizations: Empirical exploration of an integrative model (Ethics). Unpublished doctoral dissertation, State University of New York at Albany.

Judge, T. A., & Bono, J. E. (2001). Relationship of the core self-evaluation traits—self esteem, generalized self efficacy, locus of control and emotional stability—with job satisfaction and job performance: A meta analysis. *Journal of Applied Psychology, 86*, 80–92.

Judge, T. A., Higgins, C. A., Thoresen, C. J., & Barrick, M. R. (1999). The big five personality traits, general mental ability and career success across the life span. *Personnel Psychology, 52*, 621–652.

Kanfer, R. (1987). Task-specific motivation: An integrative approach to issues of measurement, mechanisms, processes, and determinants. *Journal of Social & Clinical Psychology, 5*, 237–264.

Kanfer, R., Chen, G., & Pritchard, R. D. (2008). *Work motivation: Past, present, and future.* New York: Routledge.

———. (1992). Alienation and empowerment: Some ethical imperatives in business. *Journal of Business Ethics, 11*, 413–422.

Kanungo, R. N. (1982). *Work alienation: An integrative approach.* New York: Praeger Publisher.

Kaplan, H. R, & Tausky, C. (1974). The meaning of work among the hard-core unemployed. *Pacific Sociological Review, 17*, 185–198.

Kowske, B., Rasch, R., & Wiley, J. (2010). Millennials' (lack of) attitude problem: An empirical examination of generational effects on work attitudes. *Journal of Business and Psychology, 25*, 265–279.

Krishnan, R. D., & Wellins, R. S. (2010). *Global leadership forecast: India highlights*. Pittsburgh, Pennsylvania: Development Dimensions International, Inc., MMX, p. 5.

Kuchinke, P. K., Kang, H. S., & Oh, S. Y. (2008). The influence of work values on job and career satisfaction, and organizational commitment among Korean professional level employees. *Asia Pacific Education Review*, 9 (4), 552–564.

Lancaster, L. C., & Stillman, D. (2002). *When generations collide: Who they are. Why they clash. How to solve the generational puzzle at work*. New York: Harper Collins.

Latham, G. P., & Pinder, C. C. (2005). Work motivation theory and research at the dawn of the twenty-first century. *Annual Review of Psychology*, 56, 485–516.

Leung, T. W., Siu, O. L., & Spector, P. E. (2000). Faculty stressors, job satisfaction, and psychological distress among university teachers in Hong Kong: The role of locus of control. *International Journal of Stress Management*, 7, 121–138.

Locke, E. A., & Latham, G. P. (1990). *A theory of goal setting and task performance*. Englewood Cliffs, New Jersey: Prentice Hall.

Luft, J., & Ingham H. (1955). The Johari window a graphic model of interpersonal awareness. Proceeding of western training laboratory in group development. Los Angeles: UCLA.

Lyons, S. (2003). *An exploration of generational values in life and at work*. Unpublished doctoral dissertation, Carleton University, Ottawa, Canada.

Maccoby, E. E. (1992). The role of parents in the socialization of children: An historical overview, *Developmental Psychology*, 2 (6), 1006–1017.

Mannheim, B. (1993). Gender and the effects of demographics status and work values on work centrality. *Work and Occupation*, 20, 3–22.

Martin C. A. (2005). From high maintenance to high productivity: What managers need to know about Generation Y. *Industrial and Commercial Training*, 37: 39–44.

Marx, K. (1887). *Das Kapital*. Moscow, USSR: Progress Publishers.

Maslow, A. (1954). *Motivation and personality*. New York: Harper.

———. (1970). *Motivation and personality* (2nd ed.). New York: Harper.

———. (1968). *Toward a psychology of being*. New York: D. Van Nostrand Company.

Maslow, A. H. (1968). Toward a psychology of being (2nd ed.). New York: Van Nostrand Reinhold.

Haire, Mason (Ed.). 1962. *Organization theory in industrial practice*. New York: John Wiley and Sons, p. 86.

McClelland, D. (1961). *The achieving society*. Princeton, Jersey: D. Van Nostrand.

McClelland, D. C. (1985a). How motives, skills, and values determine what people do. *American Psychologist*, 41, 812–825.

McClelland, D. C., Koestner R., & Weinberger J. (1989). How do self-attributed and implicit motives differ? *Psychological Review*, 96: 690–702.

McGregor, D. (1960). *The human side of enterprise*. New York: McGraw-Hill, p. 47.

McGuire, D., By, R. T., & Hutchings, K. (2007). Towards a model of human resource solutions for achieving intergenerational interaction in organizations. *Journal of European Industrial Training*, 31, 592–608.

Michelangelo. (n.d.). Think Exist.com. Retrieved September 5, 2010, from Thinkexist.com Web site: http://thinkexist.com/quotes/Michelangelo/2.html

Miller, G. (1980). The interpretation of nonoccupational work in modern society: A preliminary discussion of typology, *Social Problems*, 27, 381–391.

Mitroff, I. I., & Denton, E. A. (1999a). *A spiritual audit of corporate America: A hard look at spirituality, religion and values in the workplace*. Jossey-Bass: San Francisco, California.

Morgeson, F. P., & Humphrey, S. E. (2006). The work design questionnaire (WDQ): Developing and validating a comprehensive measure for assessing job design and the nature of work. *Journal of Applied Psychology*, 91, 1321–1339.

Morin, E. (2004, August). *Meaning of work in modern times*. Paper presented at the 10th World Congress on Human Resources Management, Rio de Janeiro, Brazil, p. 4.

Morse, N. L. & Weiss, R. S. (1955). The function and meaning of work and job. *American Sociological Review*, 20, 191–198.

MOW International Research Team. (1987). *The meaning of working*. London: Academic Press.

Myers, Karen K., & Sadaghiani, K. (2010). Millennials in the workplace: A communication perspective on Millennials' organizational relationships and performance. *Journal of Business Psychology*, 25 (2), pp. 225–238.

Ng, Eddy, Schweitzer, L., & Lyons, S. T. (2010). New generation, great expectations: A field study of the Millennial generation. *Journal of Business and Psychology*, 25 (2), 281–292.

Ott, B., Blacksmith, N., & Royal, N. (2008, March 13). What generation gap? Job seekers for different generations often look for the same things from prospective employers, according to recent Gallup research. Retrieved from, http://gmp.gallup.com.

Parker, R. S. (1971). *The Future of work and leisure*. London: MacGibbon & Kee.

Parker, S. K. (2003). Longitudinal effects of lean production on employee outcomes and mediating role of work characteristics. *Journal of applied Psychology*. 88, 620–634.

Parker, S. K., & Wall, T. D. (1998). *Job and Work Design*. London: Sage.

Parker, S. K., Wall, T. D., & Cordery, J. L. (2001). Future work design and research and practice: Towards an elaborated model of work design. *Journal of Occupational and Organizational Psychology*, 74, 413–440.

Porter, L. W., & Lawler, E. E. (1968). *Managerial Attitudes and Performance*. Homewood, Illinois: Irwin.

Price Waterhouse Coopers. (2008). *Millenials at work: Perspectives from a new generation*. Retrieved May 20, 2010 from http://www.pwc.com/gx/en/managing-tomorrows-people/future-of-work/pdf/mtp-millennials-at-work.pdf

Radhakrishnan, S., & Raju, P. T. (Eds.). (1995). *The Concept of Man—A Study in Comparative Philosophy*. Harper Collins Publishers India, p. 350.

Raines, C. (2002). *Connecting generations: The sourcebook for a new workplace*. Berkeley, California: Crisp Publications.

Rauschenberger, J., Schmitt, N., & Hunter, J. E. (1980). A test of the need hierarchy concept by Markov model of change in need strength. *Administrative Science Quarterly*, 25 (4), 654–670.

Remo, N. (2006). *The effects of the reciprocity norm and culture on normative commitment for Generation Y*. Unpublished Master's thesis, University of Windsor, Windsor, ON, Canada.

Roberts, K. H., & Glick, W. (1981). The job characteristics approach to task design: A critical review. *Journal of Applied Psychology*, 66, 193–217.

Rogers, C. (1961). *On becoming a person: A therapist's view of psychotherapy*. London: Constable.

Rokeach, M. (1973). *The nature of human values*. New York: The Free Press.

Ronen, S. (2001). Self-actualization versus collectualization: Implications for motivation theories. In Erez, M., Klenbeck, U. & Thierry, H. K. (Eds.). Work motivation in the context of a globalizing economy, pp. 341–68. Hillsdale, NJ: Lawrence Erlbaum.

Rose, M. (1985). *Reworking the work ethic: Economic values and socio-cultural politics*. London: Schocken.

Rotter, J. B. (1954). Social learning and clinical psychology. New York: Prentice-Hall.

Ruiz Quintanilla, S. A., & Wilpert, B. (1988). The meaning of working—scientific status of a concept. In V. de Keyser, T. Qvale, B. Wilpert, and S. Ruiz Quintanilla (Eds), *The Meaning of Work and Technological Options* (pp. 3–14). New York: John Wiley.

Ruiz Quintanilla, S. A., & Wilpert, B. (1991). Are work meaning changing? *European Work and Organizational Psychology*, 1, 91–109.

Ryan, R. M., Sheldon, K. M., Kasser, T., & Deci, E. L. (1996). All goals were not created equal: An organismic perspective on the nature of goals and their regulation. In P. M. Gollwitzer & J. A. Bargh (Eds.), *The psychology of action: Linking cognition and motivation to behavior* (pp. 7–26). New York: Guilford.

Ryff, C. (1989). Happiness is everything, or is it? Explorations on the meaning of psychological well-being. *Journal of Personality & Social Psychology*, 57 (6), 1069–1081.

Salami, S. O. (2008). Demographic and psychological factors predicting organizational commitment among industrial workers. The anthropologist. *International Journal of Contemporary and Applied Study of Man*, 10 (1), 31–38.

Salz, B. R. (1955). The human element in industrialization, *Economic Development and Cultural Change*, 4 (1/2), i–ix and 1–265.

Sanders, M. M., Lengnick-Hall, M. L., Lengnick-Hall, C., & Steele-Clapp, L. (1998). Love and work: Career-family attitudes of new entrants into the labor force, *Journal of Organizational Behavior*, 19 (6), 603–619.

Saville, P., Holdsworth, R., Nyfield, G., Cramp, L., & Mabey, W. (1984). *The Occupational Personality Questionnaire (OPQ)*. Thames Ditton: Saville-Holdsworth, Ltd.: London.

Scott, W. G., & Hart, D. K. (1971). The Moral Nature of Man in Organizations: A Comparative Analysis (p. 244). *The Academy of Management Journal*. 14 (4), 241–255.

SHRM (Society for Human Resource Management). (2009). Employee job satisfaction. Retrieved from http://www.shrm.org/Research/SurveyFindings/Articles/Documents/09-0282_Emp_Job_Sat_Survey_FINAL.pdf (on 6 February 2012).

Singh, P., & Bhandarkar, A. (1990). *Corporate success and transformational leadership*. New Delhi: Wiley, Eastern.

Singh, P. & Das, G. S. (1976). Organizational culture and its impact on commitment to work. *Indian Journal of Industrial Relations*, 13 (4, April), 511–524.

Singh, P., & Bhandarker, A. (1997). Five mantras to lead: Some pertinent reflections. *Vision Journal*, July–December issue, 1–10.

Singh, P., & Bhandarker, A. (2011). *In search of change maestros*. New Delhi: Sage International, New Delhi.

Smola, K. W., & Sutton, C. D. (2002). Generational differences: Revisiting generational work values for the new millennium. *Journal of Organizational Behavior*, 23 (4): 363–382.

Special Task Force. (1973). *Work in America*. Cambridge, Massachusetts: MIT Press.

Spector, P. E. (1988). Development of the work locus of control scale. *Journal of Occupational Psychology*, 61 (4), 335–340.

Spector, P. E., & Fox, S. (2003). Reducing subjectivity in the assessment of the job environment: Development of the factual autonomy scale, FAS. *Journal of Organizational Behavior*, 24, 417–432.

Spence, J. T., & Helmreich, R. L. (1983). Achievement-related motives and behavior. *Achievement and Achievement Motives: Psychological and Sociological approaches*. Freeman: San Francisco.

Stauffer, D. (1997). For generation Xers, what counts isn't work or all play. *Management Review*, 86 (11), 7–19.

Steers, R. M., & Porter, L. W. (1975). *Motivation and Work Behavior.* McGraw-Hill, New York.
Sverko, B., & Vizek-Vidovic, V. (1995). Studies of the meaning of work: Approaches, models, and some of the findings. In D. E. Super (Ed.), *Life roles, values, and careers: International findings of the work importance study* (pp. 3–21). San Francisco: Jossey-Bass.
Swami Chinmayananda. (1976). *The Holy Gita.* Bombay: Central Chinmaya Mission trust, p. 175, 187.
Tapscott, D. (1998). *Growing up digital: The rise of the net generation.* New York: McGraw-Hill.
Taylor, F. W. (1919). The principles of scientific management, *The Academy of Management Journal. 14* (4), 241–255.
Thinkexist.com. (2010) Buddha Quotes. Retrieved September 5, 2010, from http://thinkexist.com/quotation/your_work_is_to_discover_your_world_and_then_with/200312.html
Turban, D. B., & Keon, T. L. (1993). Organizational attractiveness: An interactionist perspective. *Journal of Applied Psychology, 78* (2), 184–193.
Turner, N., Barling, J., & Zarcharatios, A. (2002). Positive psychology at work. In C. R. Snyder & S. J. Lopez (Eds.), *The handbook of positive psychology* (pp. 715–728). New York: Oxford University Press.
Twenge, J. M. (2000). The age of anxiety? The birth cohort change in anxiety and neuroticism, 1952–1993. *Journal of Personality and Social Psychology, 79* (6): 1007–1021.
Twenge, J. M., & Campbell, W. K. (2001). Age and birth cohort differences in self-esteem: A cross-temporal meta-analysis. *Personality and Social Psychology Review, 5* (4): 321–344.
Twenge, J. M., & Nolen-Hoeksema, S. (2002). Age, gender, race, socioeconomic status, and birth cohort differences on the children's depression inventory: A meta-analysis. *Journal of Abnormal Psychology, 111* (4): 578–588.
Vandenbos, G. R. (2008). *APA Concise Dictionary of Psychology.* American Psychological Association.
Van Maanen, J. (1975), Police socialization: A longitudinal examination of job attitudes in an urban police department. *Administrative Science Quarterly, 20* (2), 207–228.
Van Maanen, J., & Schein, E. H. (1979). Toward a theory of organizational socialization. *Research in Organizational Behaviour, 1,* 209–264.
*Vivekananda: The great spiritual teacher.* (n.d.). Calcutta: Advaita Ashram Publication Department.
Volansky, A., & Habinski, A. (1998). The emerging role of school leadership in Israel: From external to internal locus of control. *New Directions in School Leadership, 9* (Fall), 87–105.
Vroom, V. H. (1964). *Work and motivation.* New York: Wiley.
Wahba, M. A., & Bridwell, L. G. (1976). Maslow reconsidered: A review of research on the need hierarchy theory. *Organizational Behavior and Human Performance, 15* (2), 212–240.
Wall, T. D., & Martin, R. (1987). Job and work design. In C. L. Cooper & I. T. Robertson (Eds.), *International Review of Industrial and Organizational Psychology* (pp. 61–91). Oxford: Wiley.
Warr, P. (1982). A national study of non-financial employment commitment. *Journal of Occupational Psychology, 55* (4), 297–312.

Warr, P. (1987). *Work, unemployment, and mental health.* Oxford: Clarendon Press.
Watson, L. E. (Ed.). (1951), *Light from many lamps.* New York: Simon & Schuster Inc.
Weber, M. (1904). *The protestant ethic and the spirit of capitalism. Archiv fur sozialwissenschaft*, pp. 20–21. (T. Parsons, Trans.). New York: Charles Scribner's Sons.
Weiner, B. (1990). History of motivational research in education. *Journal of Educational Psychology, 82* (4), 616–622.
Weiner, B. (1991). On perceiving the other as responsible. In R. Dienstbier (Ed.), *Nebraska symposium on motivation* (Vol. 38, pp. 165–198). Lincoln, Nebraska: University of Nebraska Press.
Wicker, F. W., Brown, G., Wiehe, J. A., Hagen, A. S., & Reed, J. L. (1993). On reconsidering Maslow: An examination of the deprivation/domination proposition. *Journal of Research in Personality, 27* (2), 118–133.
Wiener, B. (1979). A theory of motivation for some classroom experiences. *Journal of Educational Psychology, 71* (1), 3–25.
Wong, M., Gardiner, E., Lang, W., & Coulon, L. (2008). Generational differences in personality and motivation: Do they exist and what are the implications for the workplace? *Journal of Managerial Psychology, 23* (8), 818–890.
Wrzesniewski, A., & Dutton, J. E. (2001). Crafting a job: Revisioning employees as active crafters of their work. *Academy of Management Review, 26* (2), 179–201.
Yang, S., & Guy, M. E. (2006). GenXers versus boomers: Work motivators and management implications. *Public Performance and Management Review, 29* (3), 267–284.
Zemke, R., Raines, C., & Filipczak, B. (2000). *Generations at work: Managing the clash of veterans, boomers, Xers and Nexters in your work place.* American Management Association: New York.

# Who Are Millennials? 2

In the last three decades, in our consulting and training experience working on organizational design and architecting work processes on several occasions, we have found that many organizations neither have adequate understanding about the people working there, nor make serious efforts to map the demographic, personality, and value profiles of the employees. As a result it is not surprising that organizations fail to create the needed fit between employees' profiles (needs, attitudes, values, and personality) and organizational requirements. In the absence of such a strategy, people are invariably assigned tasks for which they have neither competencies, nor aptitude and psychological predisposition. It is like asking a bird to run and rabbit to fly, for which they neither have the needed disposition nor the competencies. Organizations continue to fit square pegs in round holes, creating problems both for individuals as well as the organization.

Organizations invariably expect individuals to fit into the existing job, role, and culture rather than developing a fit between individual expectations and aptitude and the organizational processes to meet people's needs and demands. Many scholars have described modern organizations as monolithic, rigid, mechanistic, hierarchical, and soulless (Argyris, 1973; Cox Jr. 93; Burns and Stalker 94; Handy, 1995; Singh, Bhandarker, and Bhatnagar, 2006; Bains and Bains, 2007) because of the poor fit between the employees' profile and organizational processes, systems, culture, and styles of functioning. Those organizations which have attempted to bring a fit and develop alignment between individual needs and demands with organizational processes have succeeded in significantly tapping into the capabilities and talents of the people.

Findings of our research (Singh and Bhandarker, 2011) on outstanding Indian organizations clearly bring out that they focused on creating a fit between individual profile, psychological predisposition, and organizational requirements. It is no surprise therefore that these organizations are admired, growing, and continuously creating excellence.

It is in this background that we have mapped the profile of Millennials in order to get insights into who they are in terms of their psycho-social background as well as their personality profile and values disposition. Such a work will immensely benefit Indian organizations enabling them to develop appropriate ways to build person–organization fit, by evolving an appropriate work culture which will help both the individuals and organizations and create an enabling, exciting, inspiring, and productive workplace. This will help promote performance excellence, entrepreneurial innovation, along with motivating, inspiring, enthusing the workforce, and unleashing their potential.

The chapter is divided into two parts: Part 1 portrays the research on personality and value dispositions of Millennials, while Part 2 brings out the empirical findings on background (demographic variables), personality and values of Millennials. Part 1 examines the literature on three key personality-related attributes—locus of control, achievement motivation, and personal values.

# Part 1: Personality Attributes in the Research Literature

There are few constructs in the field of psychology which continue to attract and fascinate people like personality does. The outpouring of research, the range of theories, and the large publication of self-help books all indicate its relevance and importance. The fact that all major religions have debated, discussed, and mapped the idea of the person is testimony to its importance through centuries.

All the work on personality in the last century by leading thinkers—Jung, Adler, Fromm, Horney, Sullivan, Erikson, Murray, Allport, Cattell, Kelly, Rogers, Bandura, Mischel—(see Hall, Lindazey, and Campbell, 2007) has primarily been used in understanding and developing human personality.

According to Bernstein et al. (2003), "Personality is the unique pattern of enduring thoughts, feelings, and actions that characterize an individual." According to Andre (2009), "personality is the expression of the total sum of who you are biologically, psychologically and behaviorally." Personality thus is a complex synthesis and amalgamation of an individual's biological characteristics, habits, emotional expression, and social skills, demonstrating an enduring pattern over a period of time. Understanding personality is relevant and important at the workplace because it contributes to predicting human behavior, attitudes, and styles.

While personality has been assessed using many different frameworks and instruments, in this work however, we have used three constructs—locus of control, achievement orientation, and personal values. These constructs have been selected because most of the research literature in organizational psychology and in the management world has found them to be useful in predicting workplace predispositions, human aspirations, and styles, the details of which are now presented in the following paragraphs.

## Locus of Control

According to Lao-Tse, "He who gains a victory over other men is strong; but he who gains a victory over himself is all powerful" (cited in Watson, 1988: 151). "We cannot walk through life on mountain peaks," eloquently pointed out the poet, John Burroughs (cited in Watson, 1988: 73). These sayings express the essence of human life and affirm that all human beings have to face the dualities of both peaks and valleys, ups and downs, successes and failures, happiness and sorrow, hope and despair, and excitement and boredom in their lives while talking about great people. Philosophers and thinkers have, through the ages, highlighted that great people always seek to convert adversities into opportunities, failure into success, despair into hope, by confronting reality and accepting and handling it proactively. In fact, facing and accepting failure is the first step for effectively dealing with it. It has been seen that great people continuously strive to face reality, reflect and own up mistakes and search for solutions. They believe in the philosophy, "whether you prevail or fail, endure or die… depends more on what you do to yourself than on what the world does to you" (Collins, 2009). This philosophy portrays the profile of great people as inner directed with the courage to accept and internalize failure, then go on to do something about it, rather than externalize and blame others for their problems and take no action to improve things. Such people believe in Henley's (cited in Watson, 1988: 85) famous line, "I am the master of my fate: I am the captain of my soul." Nelson Mandela was known to be continually inspired by this line while incarcerated on Robben Island and used to recite the poem to fellow prisoners (Eddie, 1998).

Julian Rotter (1966) conceptualized this philosophy as locus of control and extensively researched this construct. It has emerged as one of the most powerful constructs in explaining human behavior in various domains of life and work. It has been defined as the way individuals see their own actions affecting the events that surround their lives (Lefcourt, 1982). Paul E. Spector (1988) extended the locus of control concept within organizational settings through measurement of an individual's work locus of control. This construct reflects a person's specific belief and disposition about controlling work-related outcomes. Individuals with an internal work locus of control would tend to believe they can have influence over what happens to them at work, such as, opportunities relating to promotions, salary, and performance (Spector, 1988).

People with high internal locus of control accept responsibility for events (Davis and Davis, 1972) and external locus-of-control individuals blame their environment for failures (Phares, Wilson, and Klyver, 1971). Internal locus of control individuals ("internals") believe they control the events in their lives. Such individuals subscribe to the view that the probability of goal attainment is directly proportional to their efforts and their ability to learn from repeated experiences (Lefcourt, 1982). People with internal locus of control would also tend to set more difficult goals for themselves (Yukl and Latham, 1978), which reflect their perception of control (Murray, 1990). Internals may be more satisfied and perceived as having less emotional exhaustion because they have some control over their environment. Externals on the other hand do not see the relationship between their efforts and the ultimate results of these efforts (Lefcourt, 1982). Therefore, those persons with high external locus of control ("externals") generally attribute high probability to luck as the cause of significant happenings in their lives (Friedland, 1992).

Many studies have been conducted to assess locus of control and its association with workplace outcomes. Significant relationships have been found between work locus of control and workplace outcomes like job satisfaction (Dailey, 1980; Fuqua and Couture, 1986; Garson and Stanwyck, 1997; Leung, Siu, & Spector, 2000; Rees and Cooper., 1992; Schafer and McKenna, 1991; Whitebook et al., 1982), less emotional exhaustion (Fuqua and Couture, 1986; Whitebook et al., 1982), job performance (Blau, 1993), organizational commitment (Volansky & Habinski, 1998), work ethics (Forte, 2005), greater participation in jobs (Dailey, 1980), greater involvement (Knoop, 1981), task orientation, stress resistance, ability to take risks and intrinsic motivation (Boone, 1992; Boone and De Brabander, 1992), effectiveness at work and greater emotional intelligence (Singh, 2006), higher positive affect and greater life satisfaction (Kulshreshtha and Sen, 2006), and high entrepreneurial orientation (Kundu and Rani, 2004). A recent study (Jha and Nair, 2008) found that internally controlled people responded favorably to empowerment practices at the workplace.

In contrast, external locus of control, which is the belief that the events in one's life are occurring regardless of one's own efforts, has been found to be negatively correlated to feelings of personal accomplishment (Lunenburg and Cadavid, 1992) and job satisfaction (Blegen, 1993; Kasperson, 1982). Further, external locus of control (Kasperson, 1982) has been found to be positively correlated with negative work attitudes, engaging in unethical behavior at the workplace (Forte, 2005), and greater alienation from the work settings (Mitchell, Smyser, and Weed, 1975; Seeman, 1967; Wolfe, 1972).

Locus of control has been found to be related to work-related meaning and attitudes. Spector's (1982) review demonstrated that internals very often have higher levels of job motivation, job performance, job satisfaction, and leadership than do externals. Further, internals report more favorable job or role characteristics. Internals have been found to set more difficult goals and have stronger need for achievement (n-Ach) than do externals, reflecting internals' stronger intrinsic motivation to obtain desired outcomes (Yukl and Latham, 1978). Role efficacy has been found to be associated positively with emotional intelligence and internal locus of control, but negatively with external locus of control (Singh, 2006).

Cross-cultural research across 24 nations/territories—including an Indian sample (Spector et al., 02)—found that internal locus of control was positively associated with job satisfaction, absence of psychological strain, and absence of physical strain in all countries. Thus, it appears that regardless of cultural background and nationality, a person's belief system around locus of control would tend to have a significant effect on his/her work attitude, organizational behavior, satisfaction, performance, and commitment.

The above review shows that the impact of locus of control has been examined on work attitudes, job performance, commitment, work ethics, effective task and job performance, and psychological and physical strain. However there is paucity of empirical work studying the impact of locus of control on MOWP. It is in this background that we have chosen this personality construct (see Appendix 2A for scale details).

In this study the definition of locus of control by Spector (1988) has been used. Those with an internal locus of control (internals) believe that work outcomes are based on their own effort, will, initiative, and ability. Conversely, those with an external work locus of control (externals) believe that work outcomes depend on external factors, such as luck, fate, circumstance, or knowing the right people.

## Achievement Motivation

Human needs channel and direct energy towards desired goals. Needs, therefore, drive people's actions, behavior, expectations, and aspirations at the workplace. In other words there is likely to be a strong correlation between individual's needs, their aspirations, meaning of work, and workplace expectations. According to McClelland (1961), achievement motivation can be defined as an individual's need to meet realistic goals, receive feedback, and experience a sense of accomplishment. A person with high achievement motivation tends to have a different set of workplace expectations and seeks different kind of meaning at work as compared to those with lower n-Ach.

Need for achievement is the basic fulcrum for building performance excellence and growth of the organization. It is the engine driving the growth of individuals, organizations, as well as societies towards greater achievement, contribution, and prosperity. Great organizations therefore constantly seek processes, practices, modes for inculcating and heightening achievement motivation among their people for creating high-performing organizations.

Over the years a great deal of research has gone into the analysis of n-Ach originating in the work of Murray (1938), which was taken forward by McClelland and Atkinson in the 1950s and further continued in the recent work of Heckhausen and Spence (1995). The study of achievement motivation has focused on the intensity and persistence of the achievement-related strivings by an individual and prediction of performance outcomes.

At the individual level achievement motivation is a great power which drives the individual to ceaselessly strive, struggle, and achieve the desired goals. All behaviors motivated by the need for achievement include two primary components (a) confronting oneself with a challenge, and (b) matching solutions (means, strategies, and answers) to problematic situations. There has been growing interest in recent years in the analysis of achievement motivation as a basic personality trait leading to personal achievements as well as excellence (Elizur, 1986; Grote and James, 1991; Spence, Pred, and Helmreich, 1989; Yamauchi and Li, 93). Weaving together the findings of seminal work in this field (Atkinson, 1974, 1958, 1957; McClelland, 1965, 1961; McClelland et al., 1953; Cassidy and Lyon, 1989; Elizur, 1979; Jackson, Ahmed, and Heapy, 1976; Sagie, 1994; Spence et al., 1989; Cooper, 1983; Veroff, 1982; Yeo and Neal, 2004; Stewart et al., 2003; Feather., 1962; Weiner, 1992; Merritte, 2000; Heintz and Steele-Johnson., 2004) bring out the following salient features of the profile of those with high need for achievement:

- Need for achievement is a prominent human drive leading to striving for personal achievement as well as excellence.

- People with high need for achievement are found to be hard working, calculated risk takers, facing uncertainties rather than avoiding them, and seeking to solve problems.
- nAch has been found to be associated with workplace outcomes such as risk preference, performance, entrepreneurship, and social adjustment.
- Those with high need for achievement also demonstrate high persistence.
- They enjoy accepting challenging assignments, pursue their goals relentlessly, and with enormous tenacity. They are not satisfied with their achievement and tend to set higher goals, raise the bar of performance thus striving for higher and higher achievements.
- They confront challenges and demonstrate canny sense in matching solutions to problematic situations.
- They demonstrate entrepreneurial zest and follow the unbeaten track.

Personal achievement motivation has been defined for the purpose of this study as characterized by mastery, work orientation, competition, and personal unconcern (Helmreich and Spence, 1978).

## Personal Values

The genesis of the term values lies in the Latin word "Valere"—to be strong and to be of worth. The American heritage dictionary defines values as, "a principle, standard or quality considered worthwhile or desirable" (Harper, 2011). Values are therefore socially sanctioned and provide the normative standard in society regarding what is good and desirable.

According to Rokeach a value is "an enduring belief that a specific mode of conduct or end-state of existence is personally or socially preferable to an opposite or converse mode of conduct or end-state of existence" (see Rokeach, 1973 for details). Values have the following components (Bilsky and Schwartz, 1994): They (a) are about concepts and beliefs; (b) are about desirable end states or behaviors; (c) transcend specific situations; (d) guide election or evaluation of behavior and events; and (e) are ordered by relative importance.

Values have been a subject of study in the last four decades (see reviews by Bilsky and Schwartz, 1994; Clugston, Howell, and Dorfman, 2000; Connor and Becker, 2003; Fischer and Smith, 2006; Glazer, Daniel, and Short, 2004; Lenartowicz and Johnson, 2003; Murphy and Gordon, 2004; Roe and Ester, 1999; Rokeach, Miller, and Snyder, 1971; Zhao, He, and Lovrich, 1998, 1999). Distinction has been made between personal values a la Rokeach (1973) and broader culture bound values a la Hofstede (1980). Differentiation has also been made between general values and work values (Ros, Schwartz, and Surkiss, 1999). Values have been given importance because they are considered to be stable and core characteristics of human personality (see McGuire et al., 2006).

Numerous studies in the 70s had in fact shown the close relationship between values, attitudes and behavior (see Rokeach and Regan, 1980 for details). Values have been found to influence work-related outcomes like organizational commitment, job satisfaction, and work performance (Box, Dom, and Dunn, 1991; Finegan, 2000; Glazer et al., 2004, Kirkman and Shapiro, 2001; Pearson and Chong, 1997; Wasti, 2003). Values also have also been found to have a significant impact upon workplace decision making (McGuire et al., 2006; Keast, 1996), decision styles (Ali, Ahmed, and Krishnan, 1995), and leadership styles (Agrawal and Krishnan, 2000). When employee values and firm values match, it has been found to result in greater satisfaction (Meglino, Ravlin, and Adkins, 1989) and less turnover (Sheridan, 1992).

Thus, the values an individual holds indicate his preference for desired end states of existence and means towards attaining those ends. Values significantly influence an individual's attitude and behavior in a given situation and therefore values have tremendous power in predicting an individual's behavioral predispositions.

For the purpose of this study values are viewed as a set of specific modes of conduct or the end state of existences that are preferable to an opposite mode of conduct or end state of existence (Rokeach, 1973).

## Part 2: Millennials—Who Are They?

This study is the outcome of a research conducted on a sample of 2,158 respondents born in the period 1977–1984, based on the generally accepted and used age criterion by scholars (Chen and Choi, 2008; Tapscott, 1998) to define Millennials. This part highlights Millennials' profile in terms of (a) their background; (b) their personality and values; and (c) influence of background factors on Millennials' personality and their value systems.

## Section A

The background profile of Millennials has been studied across five demographic variables—age, educational background, gender, work experience, and place of upbringing (see Table 2.1 and Figures 2.1 to 2.5). Millennials in this study are found to be predominantly around 22.1–28 years of age (49.80 percent); followed by 17–22 years (40 percent), and 29–34 years of age (10 percent). Around 53.5 percent Millennials are with an MBA background and 46.5 percent are with an engineering background. Majority of the Millennials in the study are males (79.2 percent), while the balance (20.8 percent) constitutes females. Almost half of the sample (48%) is without work experience while the rest have work experience

Table 2.1 Frequency and percentage: Demographic variables

| S. No. | Background variable | Groups | N | Percentage |
|---|---|---|---|---|
| 1. | Age | 1) 17–22 years | 815 | 40.03 |
|  |  | 2) 23–28 years | 1,014 | 49.80 |
|  |  | 3) 29–34 years | 207 | 10.17 |
| 2. | Nature of education | 1) MBA | 920 | 53.49 |
|  |  | 2) Engineering | 800 | 46.51 |
| 3. | Gender | 1) Male | 1,702 | 79.20 |
|  |  | 2) Female | 447 | 20.80 |
| 4. | Prior work experience | 1) Nil | 893 | 47.96 |
|  |  | 2) 3 months–3 years | 284 | 15.25 |
|  |  | 3) 3–5 years | 470 | 25.24 |
|  |  | 4) 5–12 years | 215 | 11.55 |
| 5. | Place of upbringing | 1) North India | 808 | 42.19 |
|  |  | 2) South India | 436 | 22.77 |
|  |  | 3) Eastern India | 261 | 13.63 |
|  |  | 4) Western India | 318 | 16.61 |
|  |  | 5) Central India | 92 | 4.80 |

*Note:* There is variation in sample size owing to incomplete information on the demographic variables.

Who Are Millennials? 55

**Figure 2.1 Sample profile—age**

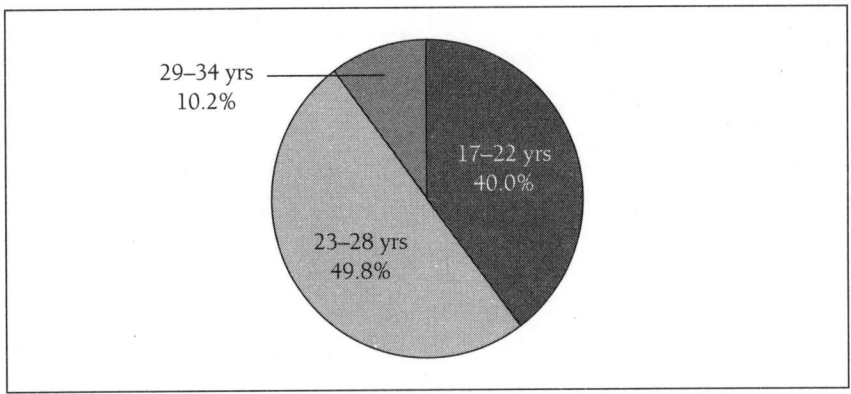

**Figure 2.2 Sample profile—nature of education**

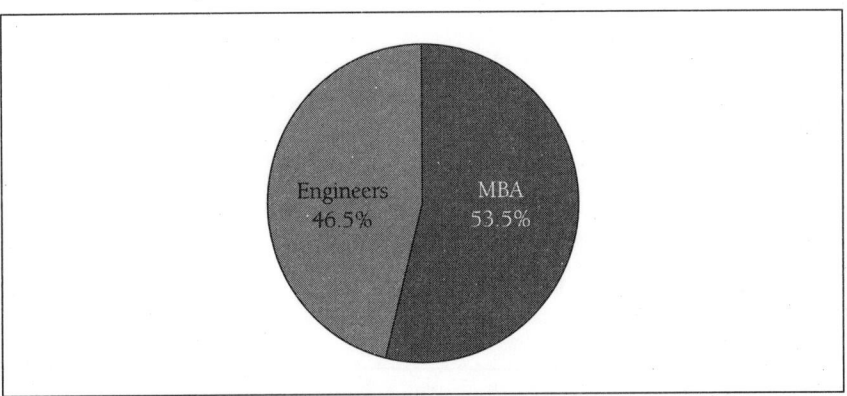

**Figure 2.3 Sample profile—gender**

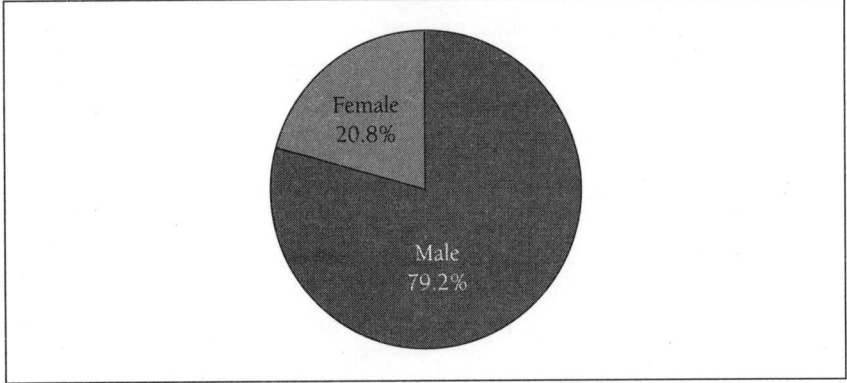

**56** Millennials and the Workplace

**Figure 2.4** Sample profile—prior work experience

**Figure 2.5** Sample profile—place of upbringing

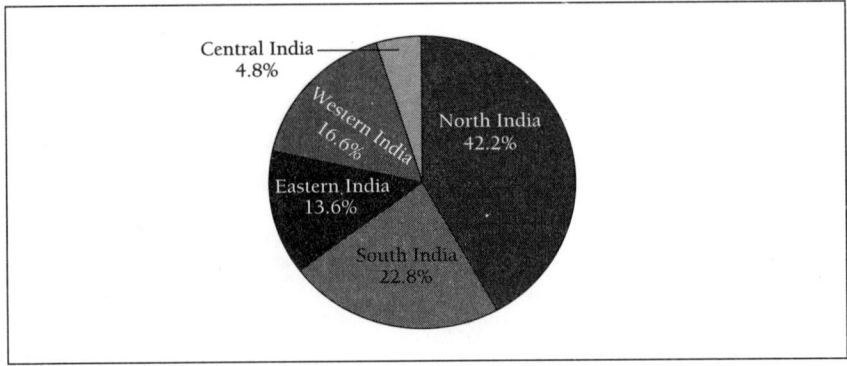

ranging from 3 months to 12 years. Figure 2.5 indicates that the sample has been drawn from top engineering and business schools from north, south, east, and west, with 42.2 percent from the north, 22.8 percent from the south, 16.6 percent from the west, 13.6 percent from the east, and 4.8 percent from central India.

## Who are the Millennials?: Psychosocial profile

Table 2.2 (and Figure 2.6, Figure 2.7, and Figure 2.8) present Millennials' psycho-social profile around family structure, parental occupation, and prental styles. Majority of the Millennials in the sample (69.70 percent) belong to nuclear families with only 1/3rd (30.30 percent) hailing from joint families. Out of the lot, 2/3rd of the sample of Millennials is from

Table 2.2 Means and SDs: Psychosocial background variables

| S. No. | Background variable | Groups | N | Mean | SD |
|---|---|---|---|---|---|
| 1. | Family type | 1) Nuclear | 1,496 | 1.30 | 0.46 |
|  |  | 2) Joint | 651 |  |  |
| 2. | Parental occupation | 1) Service | 1,445 | 1.52 | 0.84 |
|  |  | 2) Agriculture | 150 |  |  |
|  |  | 3) Business | 462 |  |  |
| 3. | Employment status of parents | 1) Mother employed | 188 | 2.16 | 0.57 |
|  |  | 2) Father employed | 1,254 |  |  |
|  |  | 3) Both employed | 496 |  |  |
| 4. | Father's style | 1) Highly critical | 49 | 3.08 | 0.77 |
|  |  | 2) Critical | 278 |  |  |
|  |  | 3) Nurturing | 805 |  |  |
|  |  | 4) Highly nurturing | 502 |  |  |
| 5. | Father's style | 1) Highly rational | 133 | 2.43 | 0.76 |
|  |  | 2) Rational | 838 |  |  |
|  |  | 3) Emotional | 552 |  |  |
|  |  | 4) Highly emotional | 151 |  |  |
| 6. | Family decision-making style | 1) Highly autocratic | 37 | 3.08 | 0.79 |
|  |  | 2) Autocratic | 299 |  |  |
|  |  | 3) Mixed | 929 |  |  |
|  |  | 4) Democratic | 392 |  |  |
|  |  | 5) Highly democratic | 58 |  |  |
| 7. | Family risk-taking ability | 1) Very low | 120 | 2.86 | 0.93 |
|  |  | 2) Low | 445 |  |  |
|  |  | 3) Medium | 783 |  |  |
|  |  | 4) High | 290 |  |  |
|  |  | 5) Very high | 76 |  |  |

*Note:* There is variation in sample size owing to incomplete information on the demographic variables. SD = Standard Deviation.

service family background, 22.5 percent from business background, and 7.3 percent hails from agriculture background. In other words, the bulk of the Millennials in the study belongs to urban and metro areas.

In terms of their family structure, around 64.7 percent Millennials come from households where the father has been the sole bread winner, while about 1/4th are from families where both parents are employed and a miniscule percentage (9.7 percent) comes from families where the mother is the sole bread winner.

Millennials perceive their father's style as moderate, being neither highly autocratic, nor highly democratic (3.08 mean value)—although tending

**Figure 2.6 Sample profile—family type**

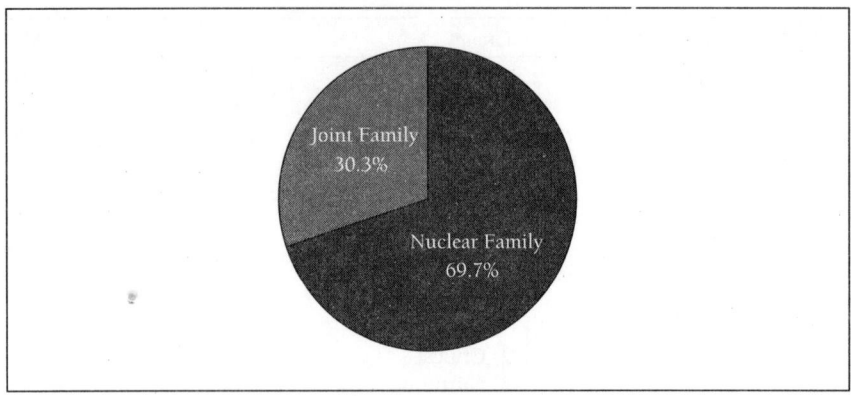

**Figure 2.7 Sample profile—parents' occupation**

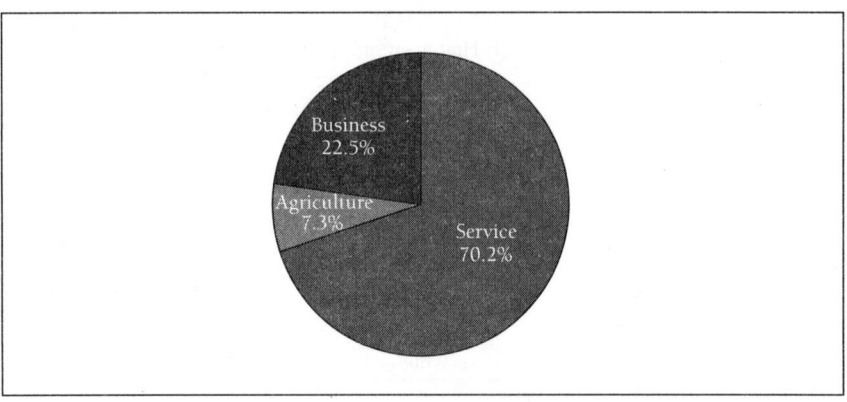

**Figure 2.8 Sample profile—employment status of parents**

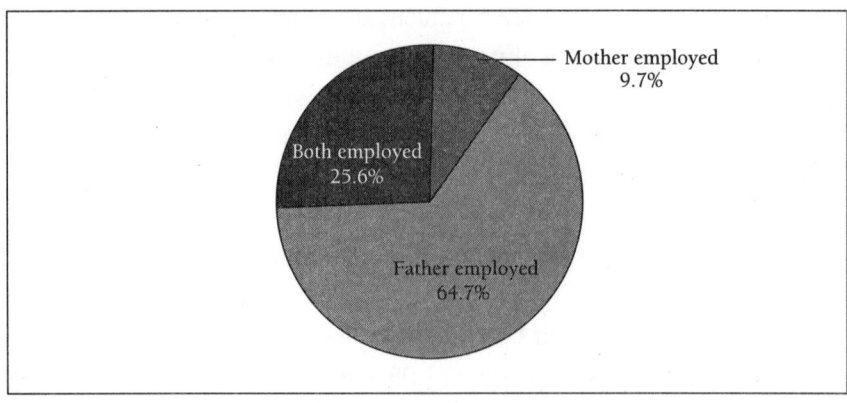

slightly towards democratic. The father has also been perceived as moderate on being critically nurturing (3.08 mean value) (although slightly tending towards being more nurturing). Father has been rated as tending towards being more rational (2.43 mean value) rather than emotional in style. Parental style has been seen to be moderately risk taking (2.86 mean value).

## Section B: Personality and Values of Millennials

This section examines the personality profile of the Millennials including results on values, locus of control and achievement orientation. Table 2.3 presents the means and SDs on personality attributes like locus of control, achievement orientation, and value dispositions (personal growth, self-fulfillment, progressive orientation, and community development[1]). Analysis of this table shows that Millennials are characterized by an above-average achievement orientation (3.65 mean value on a five-point scale); above-average internal locus of control (3.48 mean value on a five-point scale). Among the values highest importance has been given to personal growth (4.17 mean value on a five-point scale), followed by self-fulfillment (4.01 mean value on a five-point scale), progressive orientation (3.93 mean value on a five-point scale), and community development (3.80 mean value on a five-point scale).

Table 2.3  Means and SDs: Values and personality

| Variables | Mean | SD |
|---|---|---|
| *Personality*: | | |
| 1) Achievement orientation | 3.65 | 0.46 |
| 2) Locus of control** | 3.48 | 0.46 |
| *Values*: | | |
| 1) Personal growth | 4.17 | 0.54 |
| 2) Self-fulfillment | 4.01 | 0.59 |
| 3) Progressive orientation | 3.93 | 0.67 |
| 4) Community development | 3.80 | 0.79 |

*Notes*: N = 2158; ** Higher score indicates internal work locus of control (on a five-point scale) and lower score indicates external locus of control.

---

[1] See Appendix 2A for definitions in each category and questionnaire details.

Thus the overall sample comprises people who have an above average need to achieve, strive, and prove themselves.

Their above average internal locus of control suggests that they would tend to focus on making things happen rather than blaming the environment or fate. The value priorities seem to indicate that they focus most on self-fulfillment (which includes various domains of one's life including family, mature love, true friendship, happiness, freedom, inner harmony, pleasure, a world at peace, salvation, wisdom, and self-respect) after personal growth (characterized by items like opportunity to realize one's potential, opportunity for self-development, sense of accomplishment, and opportunity to be creative), which is rated number 1. They are progressive (social recognition, status, and work itself) and also think of community, society, and nation (contribution to society, to nation, and national security). Relatively speaking, this table brings out that the Millennials assign the highest weight to personal growth.

Analysis of Table 2.3 brings out the following salient features about the personality profile and values of Millennials:

- Achievement orientation is on the higher side, the mean value being 3.65 (on a five-point scale). In other words, Millennials are ambitious, have high achievement orientation, and would like to strive and persevere to achieve the goal.
- A similar picture is emerging about internal locus of control the mean value being 3.48. In other words Millennials in this sample accept responsibility for events, rather than attributing to others or to circumstances. They demonstrate above average capability to confront with failures, accept the same, and strive to convert failure into success.
- Although Millennials have above-average achievement orientation and internal locus of control, it is important to mention however that the score are not in the very high zone.
- Perusal of the value disposition of Millennials brings out that they attach highest priority to personal growth, followed by self-fulfillment, progressive orientation and community development in that order.

## Section C: Variables Influencing Personality and Personal Values Priorities of Millennials

Section C purports to examine the impact of demographic variables on Millennials' value systems and personality disposition. This has been done with a view to providing readers insights regarding the influence of background on the personality dispositions and values of the Millennials. Twelve demographic variables—educational background, gender, family type, family style decision-making process, father's style critical nurturing, father's rational and emotional style, parents' risk-taking ability; age, work experience, parental occupation, parental employment status, and place of upbringing have been utilized to examine their impact on two personality variables—achievement orientation and locus of control; and four personal value priorities—self-fulfillment, personal growth, community development, and progressive orientation.

### Achievement orientation

Tables 2B.1a and 2B.1b examine the impact of demographic variables on the Millennials' achievement orientation. Perusal of Table 2B.1a indicates that Millennials from the MBA stream have significantly[2] higher achievement orientation (mean value 3.66) as compared to those from the engineering stream (mean value 3.62). A study of the data on gender brings out that relatively speaking males have higher achievement orientation as compared to females, although the difference is not significant (see $t$ value insignificant at $p \geq .05$ level). Family type that one belongs to—whether nuclear or joint—does not make much difference to achievement orientation as indicated by the insignificant $t$ value at $p \geq .05$ level.

Achievement orientation is identical in subgroups by family decision-making process—whether autocratic or democratic (3.65); it is also similar regardless of whether father's style is more critical (3.65) or more nurturing (3.66) indicating that these two family variables do not significantly

---

[2] Significance has been tested using the $t$ test; only those values significant at $p \geq .05$ level and above are statistically significant and not due to chance and other measurement related factors.

impact achievement orientation. Further perusal of the table shows that achievement orientation is higher when the father's style is seen as more emotional (3.69) as compared to when the father's style is seen as more rational (3.64) and this difference is significant (see the $t$ value significant at $p \geq .05$ level). The table also shows that achievement orientation is significantly higher (3.68) in the group which rates family risk taking as high.

Perusal of Table 2B.1b indicates that Millennials in the age group of 23 to 28 years have the highest achievement orientation followed by those in the age groups of 29 to 34 years and 17 to 22 years. However age does not make a significant impact on achievement orientation (see the insignificant $F$ value).

Further study of the table brings out the impact of work experience on achievement orientation. Along with increasing age a trend of increasing achievement score is visible—3.61, 3.65, 3.66, 3.69—although the $F$ value is not significant at $p \geq .05$ level. Achievement mean values by parental occupation brings out that those from agriculture background have the highest mean value of 3.77 compared to those from service and business—3.64 each. The significant $F$ value and Tukey test show that the achievement orientation of those from agriculture background is significantly higher than that of the other groups. Parental employment status also makes a significant difference to achievement orientation (see the significant $F$ value $p \geq .05$ level). Those Millennials whose mother has been the sole bread winner, have the highest achievement orientation (3.72) while those who reported both parents employed have the least achievement orientation. Region of upbringing (north, south, east, west, or central India) also appears to significantly influence achievement orientation (see the significant $F$ value $p \geq .05$ level). Those from eastern India have the highest achievement orientation (3.73), followed by south (3.67), north (3.64), west (3.63) and central (3.61).

## Conclusions

Analysis of this section brings out the following striking conclusions:

- Six of the twelve demographic variables—parental occupation, parents' employment status, place of upbringing, educational stream,

father's style (rational and emotional), and parents' risk-taking ability—have a significant influence on achievement orientation.
- The other six demographic variables—gender, family type, family decision-making process (autocratic and democratic), father's style critical nurturing, age, prior work experience—do not significantly influence achievement orientation.
- An interesting trend in the data is that Millennials' achievement orientation seems to increase with increasing work experience.
- It is revealing that those hailing from agriculture background have significantly higher achievement orientation as compared to others.
- It is equally noteworthy that Millennials coming from families where the mother is the sole bread winner have the highest achievement orientation.
- Place of upbringing appears to have a significant influence as those Millennials from east India have the highest achievement orientation.
- Millennials from the MBA stream as compared to those from the engineering stream; Millennials hailing from families where the father displays more of an emotional style (rather than a rational style); and those from families with high risk-taking ability (rather than low-taking ability), have significantly greater achievement orientation.

## Locus of control

Tables 2B.2a and 2B.2b examine the impact of demographic variables on the Millennials' locus of control. Perusal of Table 2B.2a indicates that Millennials from the MBA stream have significantly[3] higher internal locus of control (mean value 3.52) as compared to those coming from engineering stream (mean value 3.42). A study of the data on gender brings out that relatively speaking females have slightly higher internal locus of control as compared to males, although the difference is not significant (see, $t$ value insignificant at $p \geq .05$ level). Family type that one belongs to–whether

---

[3] Significance has been tested using the $t$ test; only those values significant at $p \geq .05$ level and above are statistically significant and not due to chance and other measurement related factors.

nuclear or joint—does not make much difference to Millennials' locus of control as indicated by the insignificant t value at $p \geq .05$ level.

The locus of control score is the same when studied by the family decision making process—thus whether the family decision making style is rated as autocratic or democratic, the locus of control score is almost the same—3.47 and 3.50 respectively. The locus of control score also tends to be the same across father's style that is, whether the father's style is more emotional or more rational, the locus of control scores do not vary much the value being 3.49 in the case of the former group and 3.48 in the case of the latter group. The only family-level demographic factor which influences locus of control is father's style, whether critical or nurturing. Those who have experienced nurturing fathers appear to have significantly (see the significant t value) greater internal locus of control (3.51) as compared to those with critical styles (3.46).

A study of Table 2B.2b indicates that Millennials in the age group of 23 to 28 years have the highest internal locus of control (3.53), followed by those in the age groups of 29 to 34 (3.51) and 17 to 22 years (3.42). Age has a significant impact on locus of control (see the significant F value).

Further perusal of the table brings out that Millennials' work experience has a significant impact on locus of control (see the significant F value $p \geq .05$ level). A trend of increasing internal locus of control score is visible—3.44, 3.51, and 3.55—among those Millennials with nil experience, 3 months to 3 years, and 3.1 years to 5 years work experience, respectively. However, the score goes down among those Millennials with 5.1 years to 12 years of work experience. Parental occupation has a significant impact on locus of control scores of Millennials (see the significant F value $p \geq .05$ level). Perusal of the means indicates that those Millennials from service background have the highest internal locus of control (3.50) compared to those from agriculture (3.35) and business (3.48) background. The significant F value and Tukey test show that the internal locus of control score of those Millennials from service background is significantly higher than that of the other groups. Parental employment status makes no difference to locus of control (see the insignificant F value $p \geq .05$ level). Relatively speaking however, those Millennials whose mother has been the sole bread winner have the highest internal locus of control (3.51). Perusal of the table brings out that those Millennials hailing from western India have the highest internal locus of control (relatively speaking). However, insignificant F values indicate that region of upbringing (north, south, east, west, or central India) does not significantly influence locus of control of Millennials.

## Conclusions

The above analyses of the influence of Millennials' background on their locus of control brings out the following noteworthy conclusions:

- Only five out of twelve demographic variables—age, prior work experience, parental occupation, educational stream, and father's style (critical nurturing)—have a significant influence on Millennials' locus of control. The remaining seven do not significantly influence locus of control.
- Millennials in the age group 23 to 28 years and with 3.1 years to 5 years work experience, have significantly higher internal locus of control.
- Those Millennials coming from the MBA stream and hailing from families where the father has a nurturing style also have significantly higher locus of control.
- Parental background also reveals some interesting features—Millennials from service family background, where the mother is the sole bread winner and those hailing from Western India demonstrate higher Internal locus of control as compared to other categories within each of the variables.

## Personal growth value

Tables 2B.3a and 2B.3b present the impact of the demographic variables on personal growth value. Table 2B.3a shows that Millennials from the MBA stream attach significantly higher weight to personal growth (4.17) in comparison with engineering students (4.09); Millennials hailing from democratic family background (4.26); Millennials who have experienced nurturing father (4.22); Millennials who have experienced emotional style of father (4.27); and who hail from families with high risk-taking ability (4.23) attach significantly higher weight to personal growth (see the

$t$ values significant at $p \geq .05$ level, Table 2B.3a). Gender and family type also do not significantly influence personal growth value rating (see the insignificant $t$ values at $p \geq .05$ level).

Perusal of Table 2B.3b brings out that Millennials' preference for personal growth significantly (see the $F$ significant at $p \geq .05$ level) increases with increasing age as indicated by the mean values which increase from 4.09 (17–22 years) to 4.20 (23–28 years) and 4.36 (29–34 years). The table shows that there is a similar increase in personal growth score by prior work experience—the longer the experience, the higher the personal growth mean value. While those with no experience have 4.08 mean value, it increases to 4.16 with 3 months to 3 years work experience; then 4.24 for 3.1 years to 5 years work experience and 4.29 in the case of the highest work experience category—5.1 years to 12 years. Work experience has a significant impact on personal growth value preference (see the significant $F$ value $p \geq .05$ level).The means of personal growth analyzed by parental occupation show that Millennials from service families have the highest score (4.20) compared to those coming from agriculture (4.11) and business (4.11). The significant $F$ value shows that parental occupation has a significant impact on personal growth value priority with those from service background having the highest personal growth score. Similarly place of upbringing also has a significant influence on personal growth value preference (see the significant $F$ value). The highest preference to personal growth has been given by Millennials from western India, closely followed by those from north India, then south and east and lastly central India. Parental employment status does not have a significant influence on personal growth preference (see the insignificant $F$ value at $p \geq .05$ level).

## Conclusions

The above analyses of the influence of Millennials' background on their personal growth value brings out the following noteworthy conclusions:

- Nine of the twelve background variables have a significant impact on the Millennials' personal growth value preference.
- Older Millennials (29–34 years age) have significantly higher personal growth value score as compared to younger Millennials.

- The higher the work experience the greater the personal growth value score.
- Those coming from the MBA stream have significantly greater personal growth score as compared those from the engineering stream.
- Those hailing from families with a service background, those who hail from western India and north India have significantly higher personal growth orientation; and
- Those from families with democratic decision-making style, where father displays more emotional style, where parents have high risk-taking ability, have significantly greater personal growth scores.

## Self-fulfillment (SF) value

In this section Millennials' valence of self-fulfillment has been examined across the 12 demographic variables. Results reported in Table 2B.4a show that four of the seven demographic variables—family decision-making process, father's style critical nurturing, father's style (rational and emotional), and parents' risk-taking ability—have a significant influence on Millennials' SF preference (see the significant $t$ values at $p \geq .05$ level). Millennials whose family practices democratic decision making, where the father demonstrates a nurturing style; where the father demonstrates emotional style and where the family is high on risk taking ability have significantly higher SF (4.04, 4.04, 4.06, and 4.06) values as compared to those where the family is autocratic in decision making, critical and rational in style, and low on risk taking. Millennials' SF preference is however not significantly influenced by stream of education, gender, and family type (see the insignificant $t$ values at $p \geq .05$ level).

Analysis of Table 2B.4b brings out that Millennials have rated SF value 4.00 and above in all the three categories. Overall analysis of age-related data however suggests that age does not have a significant influence on Millennials' preference for SF value. Data regarding work experience and SF value presented in this table shows that work experience does not have a significant influence on SF value preference. Similar is the finding using parental occupation and parental employment status. Both these background variables do not significantly influence SF value preference (see the insignificant $t$ values at $p \geq .05$ level).

Perusal of the data by region of upbringing brings out that it has a significant impact on Millennials' SF preference (see the significant F value at $p \geq .05$ level). The highest priority is given to SF by Millennial from south India (4.05), closely followed by those from north India (4.03), and central India (3.99).

## Conclusions

Analysis of Tables 2B.4a and 2B.4b have brought out the following salient conclusions regarding the influence of background variables on the Millennials' SF value priorities.

- Millennials have attached second highest priority to SF value after personal growth value with a very high mean value (4.01).
- Five of the twelve demographic variables—place of upbringing, family decision-making process (autocratic and democratic), father's style critical nurturing; rational and emotional, family risk-taking ability (low and high)—have a significant impact on SF value preference.
- The remaining seven background factors—age, prior work experience, parental occupation, parental employment status, educational stream, gender and family type—do not significantly impact SF preference.
- Families which are democratic, nurturing, emotionally inclined, and higher on risk-taking ability produce Millennials who are much higher on SF value preference.
- Millennials from south and north India also have the highest SF preference.

## Community development (CD) value

In this section Millennials' valence of SF has been examined across the 12 demographic variables. Table 2B.5a clearly brings out that of the seven demographic variables only two—father's style critical-nurturing and parents' risk-taking ability—significantly affect CD preference. Millennials whose families are high on risk taking have a very high score on CD value—3.87 compared to Millennials from low risk-taking families. Likewise Millennials whose father had been more nurturing in style also have the highest CD value preference compared to those whose fathers had been more critical.

Table 2B.5b presents the CD value across five background variables—age, prior work experience, parental occupation, parents' employment status, and place of upbringing.

It is interesting to note that those Millennials in the youngest age group have the highest score on CD value (3.82). However, age does not significantly influence CD preference as brought out by the insignificant F values at $p \geq .05$ level. Similarly, parents' employment status does not make a significant difference to the Millennials' CD mean values (see the insignificant F values at $p \geq .05$ level). Prior work experience, parental occupation and region of upbringing however do significantly influence CD value preference (see the significant F values). Further perusal of the table shows that those Millennials with highest work experience also have the highest CD mean score (3.88) while those with 3.1 years to 5 years have the least mean score (3.73). Millennials from agriculture background have a mean score of 3.98 which is significantly different from those of Millennials hailing from service as well as business background. Millennials from the south have the highest score on CD (3.90) while those from the west have the least score on CD (3.74).

## Conclusions

Analysis of the findings in Tables 2B.5a and 2B.5b bring out the following key conclusions about the influence of background variables on CD value preference:

- CD value preference is not as high as PG and SF values (3.80).
- Five of the 12 demographic variables—prior work experience, parental occupation, place of upbringing, father's style nurturing, and family with high risk-taking ability—have a significant influence on CD priority.
- Seven of the demographic variables like age, parents' employment, educational stream, gender, family type, family decision-making process, and father's style (rational and emotional) did not significantly influence CD priority.

- Those Millennials hailing from an agriculture background, hailing from south India and from families where the father shows more nurturing style and also those who come from families with high risk-taking ability, are the ones who show the highest preference for CD value.

**Progressive orientation (PO) value**

In this section Millennials' valence of progressive orientation has been examined across the 12 demographic variables. Tables 2B.6a and 2B.b present the means, SDs, and tests of significance.

Perusal of Tables 2B.6a and 2B.6b bring out very clearly that barring one variable—stream of education—none of the other 11 demographic and psycho-social variables significantly influence PO preference (see Table for the insignificant F values at $p \geq .05$ level). Those from the MBA stream of education have significantly higher PO score than those from the engineering stream as indicated by the significant $t$ value.

## *Conclusions*

Analysis of the findings in Tables 2B.6a and 2B.6b bring out the following salient conclusions regarding the impact of background variables on Progressive Orientation preference:

- Those from MBA stream have a significantly higher mean value on PO than those from engineering.
- The other 11 variables—demographic and psycho-social—have insignificant impact on PO value.

Table 2.4 presents a summary of the influence of the demographic and psycho-social factors on locus of control, achievement orientation, and the four individual level values—personal growth, community development, progressive orientation, self-fulfillment. Five of the selected attributes—educational background, parental occupation, place of upbringing, parents' risk-taking and decision-making process—influence four of the six values and personality attributes. Prior work experience and father's style (rational and emotional) influence three of the six selected attributes. Age

**Table 2.4 Background variables and personality: A comparative picture**

| S. No. | Variable | Locus of control | Achievement orientation | Personal growth | Community development | Progressive orientation | Self-fulfillment |
|---|---|---|---|---|---|---|---|
| 1. | Age | S | NS | S | NS | NS | NS |
| 2. | Prior work experience | S | NS | S | S | NS | NS |
| 3. | Educational background | S | S | S | NS | S | NS |
| 4. | Parents' occupation | S | S | S | S | NS | NS |
| 5. | Family type | NS | NS | NS | NS | NS | NS |
| 6. | Place of upbringing | NS | S | S | S | NS | S |
| 7. | Gender | NS | NS | NS | NS | NS | NS |
| 8. | Birth order | NS | NS | NS | NS | NS | NS |
| 9. | Parents' employment status | NS | S | NS | NS | NS | NS |
| 10. | Parents' style on "risk taking ability" | NS | S | S | S | NS | S |
| 11. | Father's style (rational-emotional) | NS | S | S | NS | NS | S |
| 12. | Father's style (critical-nurturing) | S | NS | S | S | NS | S |
| 13. | Family decision making process | NS | NS | S | NS | NS | S |
| 14. | Family in terms of conservative to liberal | NS | NS | NS | NS | NS | NS |

*Note:* S = Significant; NS = Not Significant.

and family decision-making process influence two of the six attributes, while parental employment status influences one of the six selected attributes. Incidentally it is interesting that gender and family type (nuclear or joint) do not significantly influence the selected values and personality attributes.

Further examination of the table brings out that personal growth value is significantly influenced by as many as nine of the twelve background variables. Only three—family type, gender, and parental employment status—have no influence on the preference for personal growth value. Community development value is influenced by five of the nine background variables—prior work experience, parental occupation, place of upbringing, parental risk-taking ability and nurturing (critical style). SF value is influenced by five of the twelve variables—place of upbringing and the four family-style variables. Progressive orientation is however influenced only by one background variable—educational background.

Locus of control is significantly influenced by five of the twelve demographic variables—age, prior work experience, educational background, parental occupation, and father's style (nurturing–critical). Achievement orientation of the respondents is influenced significantly by educational background, parental occupation, place of upbringing, parental employment status, parental risk taking and rational–emotional style.

Background variables—demographic and psychosocial—are formative and transformative for human beings. They reflect the unique life experiences and life stages of a person and provide insights to understand the respondents' psychological profile at values and personality level.

## Conclusions

The following salient conclusions emerge from the findings presented in Chapter 2:

- The four personal values—personal growth, self-fulfillment, and progressive orientation, and community development—are highly valued by the Millennials group.

- Of these, personal growth is the most important, followed by self-fulfillment and progressive orientation, in that order.
- Community development value, though important, is rated less important compared to the other three values.
- Millennials are highly achievement oriented and also have high internal control beliefs.
- Demographic and psychosocial variables do have significant impact on the value preference and personality.
- Family type (nuclear or joint), gender (male or female), birth order (first born, second born, and other), do not significantly influence the personality (locus of control and achievement) and value scores.
- Demographic and psychosocial variables thus significantly contribute to understand what makes the Millennials who they are.

# Appendix 2A: Instruments Details

## Personal Values

In order to understand the values of Millennials, we have used a questionnaire consisting of 25 items on personal values. It consists of 18 terminal values from the widely recognized Rokeach Value Survey (RVS), an instrument designed by Rokeach (1973) to measure personal and societal values. It also consisted of seven values added by the team based on literature survey. Respondents were asked to rate each of the items on a five-point Likert scale with "1" being the least important and "5" being the most important.

### Rokeach value survey

Rokeach Value Survey (RVS), the instrument designed by Rokeach to measure personal and societal values consisting of 25 items. The RVS was adapted into a Likert scale and adapted and administered in the Indian context (see Singh et al., 2011). Rokeach measured ratings of personal and societal values through a 25-item scale which yielded four usable factors, namely, self-fulfillment, personal growth, community development, and progressive orientation. These four factors have been utilized in the subsequent analysis presented in both Chapter 2 and 3.

Factor structure of the first factor indicates values which are emotionally satisfying for employees. The factor structure of the second factor consists of values which are related to individual growth and development through opportunities of learning which had the highest mean rating of 4.15. The third factor structure consists of factors which indicate concern for the development of the society and nation, which were rated as less important with an average score of 3.69. Finally, the structure of the fourth factor indicates the factors' importance for a favorable social identity of the individual. Thus, 22 out of 25 items were retained. A mean analysis of the factors revealed that personal growth was considered as most important and community-related factors as the least.

## Achievement Motivation

In this study we have adapted the questionnaire by Ying-Feng Kuo (2006) to measure achievement motivation. Respondents were asked to rate each of the items on a five-point Likert scale with "1" being strongly disagree and "5" being strongly agree.

## Work Locus of Control (WLOC)

In our study we have used Spector (1988) WLOC scale, consisting of 16 items (8 for measuring internal work locus of control and 8 for external work locus of control). The items are to be rated on a five-point Likert scale, 1 being least important and 5 being most important. Work locus of control refers to an individual's belief that work outcomes such as promotions or salary increases are controlled either by one's own actions indicating an internal locus of control, or by factors beyond the individual's control indicating an external locus of control (Spector, 1988).

# Appendix 2B: Differences in Personality by Background Factors

**Table 2B.1a  Achievement orientation by background variables (t test)**

| S. No. | Variable | Groups | N | Mean | SD | t | Sig. |
|---|---|---|---|---|---|---|---|
| 1. | Stream of education | MBA | 920 | 3.66 | 0.45 | 2.00 | 0.05* |
|  |  | Engineering | 800 | 3.62 | 0.50 |  |  |
| 2. | Gender | Male | 1,702 | 3.66 | 0.45 | 1.86 | 0.06 |
|  |  | Female | 447 | 3.61 | 0.48 |  |  |
| 3. | Family type | Nuclear | 1,496 | 3.65 | 0.47 | −0.93 | 0.35 |
|  |  | Joint | 651 | 3.67 | 0.42 |  |  |
| 4. | Family decision-making process | Autocratic | 1,265 | 3.65 | 0.46 | 0.23 | 0.82 |
|  |  | Democratic | 893 | 3.65 | 0.45 |  |  |
| 5. | Father's style (critical, nurturing) | Critical | 1,132 | 3.65 | 0.46 | −0.47 | 0.64 |
|  |  | Nurturing | 1,026 | 3.66 | 0.45 |  |  |
| 6. | Father's style (rational, emotional) | Rational | 1,571 | 3.64 | 0.46 | −2.02 | 0.04* |
|  |  | Emotional | 558 | 3.69 | 0.44 |  |  |
| 7. | Parents' "risk-taking ability" | Low | 1,348 | 3.63 | 0.45 | −2.30 | 0.02* |
|  |  | High | 810 | 3.68 | 0.46 |  |  |

*Note:* *The values are statistically significant at $p \geq 0.05$.

**Table 2B.1b  Achievement orientation by background variables (F test)**

| S. No. | Variable | Groups | N | Mean | SD | F | Sig. |
|---|---|---|---|---|---|---|---|
| 1. | Age | 1) 17–22 years | 815 | 3.62 | 0.51 | 2.20 | 0.11 |
| | | 2) 23–28 years | 1,014 | 3.67 | 0.42 | | |
| | | 3) 29–34 years | 207 | 3.65 | 0.41 | | |
| | Tukey test shows that there is no significant difference between the means of the three sub-groups of age. (See Table 2B.1c for details) | | | | | | |
| 2. | Prior work experience | 1) Nil | 893 | 3.61 | 0.50 | 2.29 | 0.08 |
| | | 2) 3 months–3 years | 284 | 3.65 | 0.45 | | |
| | | 3) 3.1 months–5 years | 470 | 3.66 | 0.42 | | |
| | | 4) 5.1 months–12 years | 215 | 3.69 | 0.34 | | |
| | Tukey test shows that there is no significant difference between the means of the three sub-groups of prior work experience. (See Table 2B.1c for details) | | | | | | |
| 3. | Parental occupation | 1) Service | 1,445 | 3.64 | 0.45 | 5.43 | 0.00* |
| | | 2) Agriculture | 150 | 3.77 | 0.49 | | |
| | | 3) Business | 462 | 3.64 | 0.49 | | |
| | Tukey test shows that the mean of group 2 is significantly different from the means of group 1 and 3. (See Table 2B.1c for details) | | | | | | |
| 4. | Parents' employment status | 1) Mother employed | 188 | 3.72 | 0.45 | 4.44 | 0.01* |
| | | 2) Father employed | 1,254 | 3.65 | 0.45 | | |
| | | 3) Both employed | 496 | 3.60 | 0.45 | | |
| | Tukey test shows that the mean of group 1 is significantly different from the mean of group 3. (See Table 2B.1c for details) | | | | | | |
| 5. | Place of upbringing | 1) North India | 808 | 3.64 | 0.45 | 2.44 | 0.05* |
| | | 2) South India | 436 | 3.67 | 0.50 | | |
| | | 3) Eastern India | 261 | 3.73 | 0.41 | | |
| | | 4) Western India | 318 | 3.63 | 0.42 | | |
| | | 5) Central India | 92 | 3.61 | 0.44 | | |
| | Tukey test shows that there is no significant difference between the means of the sub-groups of place of upbringing. (See Table 2B.1c for details) | | | | | | |

*Note:* *The values are statistically significant at $p \geq 0.05$.

**Table 2B.1c  Achievement orientation by background variables (Tukey Table)**

| Dependent variable | Background variable | Background variable (I) | Background variable (J) | Mean difference (I−J) | Standard error | Sig. |
|---|---|---|---|---|---|---|
| Achievement orientation | Age | | | | | Insignificant difference |
| | Prior work experience | | | | | Insignificant differences |
| | Parental occupation | 1) Service | 2) Agriculture | −0.13 | 3.94E-02 | 0.00* |
| | | 2) Agriculture | 1) Service | 0.13 | 3.94E-02 | 0.00* |
| | | | 3) Business | 0.13 | 4.31E-02 | 0.01* |
| | | 3) Business | 2) Agriculture | −0.13 | 4.31E-02 | 0.01* |
| | Employment status | 1) Mother employed | 3) Both Employed | 0.11 | 3.84E-02 | 0.01* |
| | | 3) Both employed | 1) Mother Employed | −0.11 | 3.84E-02 | 0.01* |
| | Place of upbringing | | | | | No significant differences found |

*Note:* *The values are statistically significant at $p \geq 0.05$.

**Table 2B.2a  Locus of control by background variables (t test)**

| S. No. | Variable | Groups | N | Mean | SD | t | Sig. |
|---|---|---|---|---|---|---|---|
| 1. | Stream of education | MBA | 920 | 3.52 | 0.46 | 4.16 | 0.00* |
| | | Engineering | 800 | 3.42 | 0.48 | | |
| 2. | Gender | Male | 1,702 | 3.48 | 0.46 | −1.21 | 0.23 |
| | | Female | 447 | 3.51 | 0.46 | | |
| 3. | Family type | Nuclear | 1,496 | 3.48 | 0.46 | 0.02 | 0.99 |
| | | Joint | 651 | 3.48 | 0.47 | | |
| 4. | Family decision-making process | Autocratic | 1,265 | 3.47 | 0.47 | −1.28 | 0.20 |
| | | Democratic | 893 | 3.50 | 0.45 | | |
| 5. | Father's style (critical, nurturing) | Critical | 1,132 | 3.46 | 0.48 | −2.61 | 0.01* |
| | | Nurturing | 1,026 | 3.51 | 0.45 | | |
| 6. | Father's style (rational, emotional) | Rational | 1,571 | 3.48 | 0.47 | −0.44 | 0.66 |
| | | Emotional | 558 | 3.49 | 0.44 | | |
| 7. | Parents' style on "risk-taking ability" | Low | 1,348 | 3.48 | 0.47 | −1.09 | 0.28 |
| | | High | 810 | 3.50 | 0.45 | | |

*Note:* *The values are statistically significant at $p \geq 0.05$.

**Table 2B.2b  Locus of control by background variables (*F* test)**

| S. No. | Variable | Groups | N | Mean | SD | F | Sig. |
|---|---|---|---|---|---|---|---|
| 1. | Age | 1) 17–22 years | 815 | 3.42 | 0.46 | 13.35 | 0.00* |
| | | 2) 23–28 years | 1,014 | 3.53 | 0.46 | | |
| | | 3) 29–34 years | 207 | 3.51 | 0.48 | | |
| | Tukey test shows that the mean of group 1 is significantly different from the means of group 2 and 3. (See Table 2B.2c for details) | | | | | | |
| 2. | Prior work experience | 1) Nil | 893 | 3.44 | 0.46 | 7.35 | 0.00* |
| | | 2) 3 months–3 years | 284 | 3.51 | 0.48 | | |
| | | 3) 3.1 years–5 years | 470 | 3.55 | 0.46 | | |
| | | 4) 5.1 years–12 years | 215 | 3.43 | 0.44 | | |
| | Tukey test shows that the mean of the group 1 is significantly different from the mean of group 3. (See Table 2B.2c for details) | | | | | | |
| 3. | Parental occupation | 1) Service | 1,445 | 3.50 | 0.46 | 7.59 | 0.00* |
| | | 2) Agriculture | 150 | 3.35 | 0.46 | | |
| | | 3) Business | 462 | 3.48 | 0.48 | | |
| | Tukey test shows that the mean of group 2 is significantly different from the means of group 1 and 3. (See Table 2B.2c for details) | | | | | | |
| 4. | Parents' employment status | 1) Mother employed | 188 | 3.51 | 0.52 | 0.67 | 0.51 |
| | | 2) Father employed | 1,254 | 3.47 | 0.46 | | |
| | | 3) Both employed | 496 | 3.49 | 0.46 | | |
| | Tukey test shows that there is no significant difference between the means of the three sub-groups of parents' employment status. (See Table 2B.2c for details) | | | | | | |
| 5. | Place of upbringing | 1) North India | 808 | 3.46 | 0.43 | 1.95 | 0.10 |
| | | 2) South India | 436 | 3.46 | 0.47 | | |
| | | 3) Eastern India | 261 | 3.50 | 0.51 | | |
| | | 4) Western India | 318 | 3.54 | 0.49 | | |
| | | 5) Central India | 92 | 3.48 | 0.46 | | |
| | Tukey test shows that there is no significant difference between the means of the sub-groups of place of upbringing. (See Table 2B.2c for details) | | | | | | |

*Note*: *The values are statistically significant at $p \geq 0.05$.

**Table 2B.2c  Locus of control by background variables (Tukey Table)**

| Dependent variable | Background variable | Background variable (I) | Background variable (J) | Mean difference (I-J) | Standard error | Sig. |
|---|---|---|---|---|---|---|
| Locus of Control | Age | 1) 17–22 years | 2) 23–28 years | -0.11 | 2.18E-02 | 0.00* |
| | | | 3) 29–34 years | -9.03E-02 | 3.60E-02 | 0.03* |
| | | 2) 23–28 years | 1) 17–22 years | 0.11 | 2.18E-02 | 0.00* |
| | | 3) 29–34 years | 1) 17–22 years | 9.03E-02 | 3.60E-02 | 0.03* |
| | Prior work experience | 1) Nil | 3) 3–5 years | -0.11 | 2.60E-02 | 0.00* |
| | | 3) 3–5 years | 1) Nil | 0.11 | 2.60E-02 | 0.00* |
| | | | 4) 5–12 years | 0.12 | 3.76E-02 | 0.01* |
| | | 4) 5–12 years | 3) 3–5 years | -0.12 | 3.76E-02 | 0.01* |
| | Parental occupation | 1) Service | 2) Agriculture | 0.15 | 3.98E-02 | 0.00* |
| | | 2) Agriculture | 1) Service | -0.15 | 3.98E-02 | 0.00* |
| | | | 3) Business | -0.13 | 4.36E-02 | 0.01* |
| | | 3) Business | 2) Agriculture | 0.13 | 4.36E-02 | 0.01* |
| | Employment status | | | | | No significant differences found |
| | Place of upbringing | | | | | No significant differences found |

*Note:* *The values are statistically significant at $p \geq 0.05$.

Table 2B.3a  Personal growth by background variables (t test)

| S. No. | Variable | Groups | N | Mean | SD | t | Sig. |
|---|---|---|---|---|---|---|---|
| 1. | Nature of education | MBA | 920 | 4.17 | 0.51 | 3.19 | 0.00* |
|  |  | Engineering | 800 | 4.09 | 0.57 |  |  |
| 2. | Gender | Male | 1,702 | 4.18 | 0.53 | 1.35 | 0.18 |
|  |  | Female | 447 | 4.14 | 0.55 |  |  |
| 3. | Family type | Nuclear | 1,496 | 4.17 | 0.53 | -0.40 | 0.69 |
|  |  | Joint | 651 | 4.18 | 0.54 |  |  |
| 4. | Family decision-making process | Autocratic | 1,265 | 4.11 | 0.53 | -6.10 | 0.00* |
|  |  | Democratic | 893 | 4.26 | 0.53 |  |  |
| 5. | Father's style (critical, nurturing) | Critical | 1,132 | 4.13 | 0.53 | -3.98 | 0.00* |
|  |  | Nurturing | 1,026 | 4.22 | 0.53 |  |  |
| 6. | Father's style (rational, emotional) | Rational | 1,571 | 4.14 | 0.53 | -4.95 | 0.00* |
|  |  | Emotional | 558 | 4.27 | 0.53 |  |  |
| 7. | Parents' style on "risk-taking ability" | Low | 1,348 | 4.14 | 0.53 | -3.86 | 0.00* |
|  |  | High | 810 | 4.23 | 0.54 |  |  |

Note: *The values are statistically significant at $p \geq 0.05$.

**Table 2B.3b  Personal growth by background variables (F test)**

| S. No. | Variable | Groups | N | Mean | SD | F | Sig. |
|---|---|---|---|---|---|---|---|
| 1. | Age | 1) 17–22 years | 815 | 4.09 | 0.56 | 22.63 | 0.00* |
| | | 2) 23–28 years | 1,014 | 4.20 | 0.51 | | |
| | | 3) 29–34 years | 207 | 4.36 | 0.53 | | |
| | Tukey test shows that the mean of group 1 is significantly different from the means of groups 2 and 3. The mean of group 2 is significantly different from the mean of group 3. (See Table 2B.3c for details) | | | | | | |
| 2. | Prior work experience | 1) Nil | 893 | 4.08 | 0.56 | 14.90 | 0.00* |
| | | 2) 3 months–3 years | 284 | 4.16 | 0.48 | | |
| | | 3) 3.1–5 years | 470 | 4.24 | 0.51 | | |
| | | 4) 5.1–12 years | 215 | 4.29 | 0.55 | | |
| | Tukey test shows that the mean of group 1 is significantly different from the means of groups 3 and 4. The mean of group 2 is significantly different from the mean of group 4. (See Table 2B.3c for details) | | | | | | |
| 3. | Parental occupation | 1) Service | 1,445 | 4.20 | 0.52 | 6.86 | 0.00* |
| | | 2) Agriculture | 150 | 4.11 | 0.57 | | |
| | | 3) Business | 462 | 4.11 | 0.55 | | |
| | Tukey test shows that the mean of group 1 is significantly different from the mean of group 3. (See Table 2B.3c for details) | | | | | | |
| 4. | Parents' employment status | 1) Mother employed | 188 | 4.20 | 0.51 | 2.26 | 0.10 |
| | | 2) Father employed | 1,254 | 4.14 | 0.54 | | |
| | | 3) Both employed | 496 | 4.19 | 0.51 | | |
| | Tukey test shows that there is no significant difference between the means of the three sub-groups of parents' employment status. (See Table 2B.3c for details) | | | | | | |
| 5. | Place of upbringing | 1) North India | 808 | 4.21 | 0.54 | 3.93 | 0.00* |
| | | 2) South India | 436 | 4.15 | 0.56 | | |
| | | 3) Eastern India | 261 | 4.13 | 0.55 | | |
| | | 4) Western India | 318 | 4.22 | 0.45 | | |
| | | 5) Central India | 92 | 4.03 | 0.56 | | |
| | Tukey test shows that the mean of group 5 is significantly different from the means of groups 1 and 5. (See Table 2B.3c for details) | | | | | | |

*Note:* *The values are statistically significant at $p \geq 0.05$.

**Table 2B.3c  Personal growth by background variables (Tukey Table)**

| Dependent variable | Background variable | Background variable (I) | Background variable (J) | Mean difference (I–J) | Std. error | Sig. |
|---|---|---|---|---|---|---|
| Personal growth | Age | 1) 17–22 years | 2) 23–28 years | −0.11 | 2.51E−02 | 0.00* |
| | | | 3) 29–34 years | −0.26 | 4.15E−02 | 0.00* |
| | | 2) 23–28 years | 1) 17–22 years | 0.11 | 2.51E−02 | 0.00* |
| | | | 3) 29–34 years | −0.16 | 4.07E−02 | 0.00* |
| | | 3) 29–34 years | 1) 17–22 years | 0.26 | 4.15E−02 | 0.00* |
| | | | 2) 23–28 years | 0.16 | 4.07E−02 | 0.00* |
| | Prior work experience | 1) Nil | 3) 3–5 years | −0.16 | 3.04E−02 | 0.00* |
| | | | 4) 5–12 years | −0.21 | 4.06E−02 | 0.00* |
| | | 2) 3 months–3 years | 4) 5–12 years | −0.13 | 4.83E−02 | 0.03* |
| | | 3) 3–5 years | 1) Nil | 0.16 | 3.04E−02 | 0.00* |
| | | 4) 5–12 years | 1) Nil | 0.21 | 4.06E−02 | 0.00* |
| | | | 2) 3 months–3 years | 0.13 | 4.83E−02 | 0.03* |
| | Parental occupation | 1) Service | 3) Business | 9.47E−02 | 2.85E−02 | 0.00* |
| | | 3) Business | 1) Service | −9.47E−02 | 2.85E−02 | 0.00* |
| | Employment status | | | | | No significant differences found |
| | Place of upbringing | 1) North India | 5) Central India | 0.18 | 5.88E−02 | 0.02* |
| | | 4) Western India | 5) Central India | 0.19 | 6.33E−02 | 0.02* |
| | | 5) Central India | 1) North India | −0.18 | 5.88E−02 | 0.02* |
| | | | 4) Western India | −0.19 | 6.33E−02 | 0.02* |

*Note:* *The values are statistically significant at $p \geq 0.05$.

Table 2B.4a  Self-fulfillment by background variables (*t* test)

| S. No. | Variable | Groups | N | Mean | SD | t | Sig. |
|---|---|---|---|---|---|---|---|
| 1. | Nature of education | MBA | 920 | 4.00 | 0.55 | 0.28 | 0.78 |
|  |  | Engineering | 800 | 3.99 | 0.59 |  |  |
| 2. | Gender | Male | 1,702 | 4.00 | 0.58 | −1.20 | 0.23 |
|  |  | Female | 447 | 4.04 | 0.63 |  |  |
| 3. | Family type | Nuclear | 1,496 | 4.00 | 0.60 | −1.04 | 0.30 |
|  |  | Joint | 651 | 4.03 | 0.57 |  |  |
| 4. | Family decision-making process | Autocratic | 1,265 | 3.98 | 0.57 | −2.04 | 0.04* |
|  |  | Democratic | 893 | 4.04 | 0.62 |  |  |
| 5. | Father's style (critical, nurturing) | Critical | 1,132 | 3.97 | 0.58 | −2.92 | 0.004* |
|  |  | Nurturing | 1,026 | 4.04 | 0.60 |  |  |
| 6. | Father's style (rational, emotional) | Rational | 1,571 | 3.99 | 0.57 | −2.45 | 0.02* |
|  |  | Emotional | 558 | 4.06 | 0.64 |  |  |
| 7. | Parents' style on "risk-taking ability" | Low | 1,348 | 3.97 | 0.57 | −3.45 | 0.00* |
|  |  | High | 810 | 4.06 | 0.61 |  |  |

*Note:* *The values are statistically significant at $p \geq 0.05$.

**Table 2B.4b Self-fulfillment by background variables (F test)**

| S. No. | Variable | Groups | N | Mean | SD | F | Sig. |
|---|---|---|---|---|---|---|---|
| 1. | Age | 1) 17–22 years | 815 | 4.01 | 0.57 | 1.07 | 0.34 |
| | | 2) 23–28 years | 1,014 | 4.00 | 0.58 | | |
| | | 3) 29–34 years | 207 | 4.07 | 0.70 | | |
| | Tukey test shows that there is no significant difference between the means of the three sub-groups of age. (See Table 2B.4c for details) | | | | | | |
| 2. | Prior work experience | 1) Nil | 893 | 4.00 | 0.58 | 2.15 | 0.09 |
| | | 2) 3 months–3 years | 284 | 3.96 | 0.55 | | |
| | | 3) 3.1–5 years | 470 | 4.01 | 0.55 | | |
| | | 4) 5.1–12 years | 215 | 4.09 | 0.66 | | |
| | Tukey test shows that there is no significant difference between the means of the three sub-groups of prior work experience. (See Table 2B.4c for details) | | | | | | |
| 3. | Parental occupation | 1) Service | 1,445 | 4.01 | 0.58 | 1.23 | 0.29 |
| | | 2) Agriculture | 150 | 4.09 | 0.63 | | |
| | | 3) Business | 462 | 4.02 | 0.59 | | |
| | Tukey test shows that there is no significant difference between the means of the three sub-groups of parental occupation. (See Table 2B.4c for details) | | | | | | |
| 4. | Parents' employment status | 1) Mother employed | 188 | 3.96 | 0.60 | 2.31 | 0.10 |
| | | 2) Father employed | 1,254 | 3.98 | 0.59 | | |
| | | 3) Both employed | 496 | 4.04 | 0.56 | | |
| | Tukey test shows that there is no significant difference between the means of the three sub-groups of parents' employment status. (See Table 2B.4c for details) | | | | | | |
| 5. | Place of upbringing | 1) North India | 808 | 4.03 | 0.59 | 4.60 | 0.00* |
| | | 2) South India | 436 | 4.05 | 0.60 | | |
| | | 3) Eastern India | 261 | 3.93 | 0.60 | | |
| | | 4) Western India | 318 | 3.90 | 0.56 | | |
| | | 5) Central India | 92 | 3.99 | 0.55 | | |
| | Tukey test shows that the mean of group 1 is significantly different from the mean of group 4 and mean of group 2 is significantly different from the mean of group 4. (See Table 2B.4c for details) | | | | | | |

*Note:* *The values are statistically significant at $p \geq 0.05$.

**Table 2B.4c  Self-fulfillment by background variables (Tukey table)**

| Dependent variable | Background variable | Background variable (I) | Background variable (J) | Mean difference (I–J) | Standard error | Sig. |
|---|---|---|---|---|---|---|
| Self-fulfillment | Age | | | | | No significant differences found |
| | Prior work experience | | | | | No significant differences found |
| | Parental occupation | | | | | No significant differences found |
| | Employment status | | | | | No significant differences found |
| | Place of upbringing | 1) North India | 4) Western India | 0.13 | 3.89E-02 | 0.01* |
| | | 2) South India | 4) Western India | 0.15 | 4.34E-02 | 0.00* |
| | | 4) Western India | 1) North India | −0.13 | 3.89E-02 | 0.01* |
| | | | 2) South India | −0.15 | 4.34E-02 | 0.00* |

*Note*: *The values are statistically significant at $p \geq 0.05$.

Table 2B.5a  Community development by background variables (t test)

| S. No. | Variable | Groups | N | Mean | SD | t | Sig. |
|---|---|---|---|---|---|---|---|
| 1. | Nature of education | MBA | 920 | 3.77 | 0.79 | −0.96 | 0.34 |
|  |  | Engineering | 800 | 3.81 | 0.77 |  |  |
| 2. | Gender | Male | 1,702 | 3.79 | 0.78 | −0.88 | 0.38 |
|  |  | Female | 447 | 3.83 | 0.83 |  |  |
| 3. | Family type | Nuclear | 1,496 | 3.79 | 0.78 | −0.72 | 0.47 |
|  |  | Joint | 651 | 3.82 | 0.81 |  |  |
| 4. | Family decision-making process | Autocratic | 1,265 | 3.81 | 0.77 | 0.87 | 0.39 |
|  |  | Democratic | 893 | 3.78 | 0.81 |  |  |
| 5. | Father's style (critical, nurturing) | Critical | 1,132 | 3.76 | 0.79 | −2.14 | 0.03* |
|  |  | Nurturing | 1,026 | 3.83 | 0.78 |  |  |
| 6. | Father's style (rational, emotional) | Rational | 1,571 | 3.78 | 0.78 | −0.94 | 0.35 |
|  |  | Emotional | 558 | 3.82 | 0.80 |  |  |
| 7. | Parents' style on "risk-taking ability" | Low | 1,348 | 3.75 | 0.77 | −3.37 | 0.00* |
|  |  | High | 810 | 3.87 | 0.80 |  |  |

*Note:* *The values are statistically significant at $p \geq 0.05$.

**Table 2B.5b Community development by background variables (F test)**

| S. No. | Variable | Groups | N | Mean | SD | F | Sig. |
|---|---|---|---|---|---|---|---|
| 1. | Age | 1) 17–22 years | 815 | 3.82 | 0.76 | 0.86 | 0.43 |
|  |  | 2) 23–28 years | 1,014 | 3.77 | 0.82 |  |  |
|  |  | 3) 29–34 years | 207 | 3.76 | 0.82 |  |  |
|  | Tukey test shows that there is no significant difference between the means of the three sub-groups of age. (See Table 2B.5c for details) | | | | | | |
| 2. | Prior work experience | 1) Nil | 893 | 3.82 | 0.77 | 2.56 | 0.05* |
|  |  | 2) 3 months–3 years | 284 | 3.75 | 0.82 |  |  |
|  |  | 3) 3.1–5 years | 470 | 3.73 | 0.79 |  |  |
|  |  | 4) 5.1–12 years | 215 | 3.88 | 0.77 |  |  |
|  | Tukey test shows that there is no significant difference between the means of the three sub-groups of prior work experience. (See Table 2B.5c for details) | | | | | | |
| 3. | Parental occupation | 1) Service | 1,445 | 3.81 | 0.77 | 4.97 | 0.01* |
|  |  | 2) Agriculture | 150 | 3.98 | 0.73 |  |  |
|  |  | 3) Business | 462 | 3.74 | 0.84 |  |  |
|  | Tukey test shows that the mean of group 2 is significantly different from the means of groups 1 and 3. (See Table 2B.5c for details) | | | | | | |
| 4. | Parents' employment status | 1) Mother employed | 188 | 3.72 | 0.79 | 0.79 | 0.45 |
|  |  | 2) Father employed | 1,254 | 3.78 | 0.79 |  |  |
|  |  | 3) Both employed | 496 | 3.81 | 0.78 |  |  |
|  | Tukey test shows that there is no significant difference between the means of the three sub-groups of parents' employment status. (See Table 2B.5c for details) | | | | | | |
| 5. | Place of upbringing | 1) North India | 808 | 3.76 | 0.78 | 2.97 | 0.02* |
|  |  | 2) South India | 436 | 3.90 | 0.78 |  |  |
|  |  | 3) Eastern India | 261 | 3.75 | 0.78 |  |  |
|  |  | 4) Western India | 318 | 3.74 | 0.78 |  |  |
|  |  | 5) Central India | 92 | 3.80 | 0.91 |  |  |
|  | Tukey test shows that the mean of the group 1 is significantly different from the mean of group 2. The mean of the group 2 is significantly different from the mean of group 4. (See Table 2B.5c for details) | | | | | | |

*Note:* *The values are statistically significant at $p \geq 0.05$.

**Table 2B.5c  Community development by background variables (Tukey table)**

| Dependent variable | Background variable | Background variable (I) | Background variable (J) | Mean difference (I–J) | Standard error | Sig. |
|---|---|---|---|---|---|---|
| Community Development | Age | | | | | No significant differences found |
| | Prior work experience | | | | | No significant differences found |
| | Parental occupation | 1) Service | 2) Agriculture | −0.16 | 6.71E-02 | 0.04* |
| | | 2) Agriculture | 3) Service | 0.16 | 6.71E-02 | 0.04* |
| | | | 3) Business | 0.23 | 7.35E-02 | 0.01* |
| | | 3) Business | 2) Agriculture | −0.23 | 7.35E-02 | 0.01* |
| | Employment status | | | | | No significant differences found |
| | Place of upbringing | 1) North India | 2) South India | −0.14 | 4.69E-02 | 0.02* |
| | | 2) South India | 1) North India | 0.14 | 4.69E-02 | 0.02* |
| | | | 4) Western India | 0.16 | 5.82E-02 | 0.04* |
| | | 4) Western India | 2) South India | −0.16 | 5.82E-02 | 0.04* |

*Note:* *The values are statistically significant at $p \geq 0.05$.

Table 2B.6a  Progressive orientation by background variables (*t* test)

| S. No. | Variable | Groups | N | Mean | SD | t | Sig. |
|---|---|---|---|---|---|---|---|
| 1. | Nature of education | MBA | 920 | 3.95 | 0.67 | 2.38 | 0.02* |
|  |  | Engineering | 800 | 3.88 | 0.69 |  |  |
| 2. | Gender | Male | 1,702 | 3.92 | 0.68 | -1.52 | 0.13 |
|  |  | Female | 447 | 3.97 | 0.64 |  |  |
| 3. | Family type | Nuclear | 1,496 | 3.94 | 0.68 | 1.13 | 0.26 |
|  |  | Joint | 651 | 3.91 | 0.64 |  |  |
| 4. | Family decision-making process | Autocratic | 1,265 | 3.95 | 0.64 | 1.43 | 0.15 |
|  |  | Democratic | 893 | 3.91 | 0.70 |  |  |
| 5. | Father's style (critical, nurturing) | Critical | 1,132 | 3.92 | 0.66 | -0.98 | 0.33 |
|  |  | Nurturing | 1,026 | 3.95 | 0.68 |  |  |
| 6. | Father's style (rational, emotional) | Rational | 1,571 | 3.92 | 0.67 | -1.00 | 0.32 |
|  |  | Emotional | 558 | 3.95 | 0.67 |  |  |
| 7. | Parents' style on "risk-taking ability" | Low | 1,348 | 3.91 | 0.67 | -1.56 | 0.12 |
|  |  | High | 810 | 3.96 | 0.67 |  |  |

*Note:* *The values are statistically significant at $p \geq 0.05$.

Table 2B.6b  Progressive orientation by background variables (F test)

| S. No. | Variable | Groups | N | Mean | SD | F | Sig. |
|---|---|---|---|---|---|---|---|
| 1. | Age | 1) 17–22 years | 815 | 3.95 | 0.66 | 0.70 | 0.50 |
|  |  | 2) 23–28 years | 1,014 | 3.92 | 0.67 |  |  |
|  |  | 3) 29–34 years | 207 | 3.96 | 0.72 |  |  |
|  | Tukey test shows that there is no significant difference between the means of the three sub-groups of age. (See Table 2B.6c for details) | | | | | | |
| 2. | Prior work experience | 1) Nil | 893 | 3.95 | 0.67 | 1.64 | 0.18 |
|  |  | 2) 3 months–3 years | 284 | 3.89 | 0.67 |  |  |
|  |  | 3) 3.1–5 years | 470 | 3.88 | 0.67 |  |  |
|  |  | 4) 5.1–12 years | 215 | 3.95 | 0.60 |  |  |
|  | Tukey test shows that there is no significant difference between the means of the three sub-groups of prior work experience. (See Table 2B.6c for details) | | | | | | |
| 3. | Parental occupation | 1) Service | 1,445 | 3.93 | 0.67 | 2.48 | 0.08 |
|  |  | 2) Agriculture | 150 | 4.04 | 0.71 |  |  |
|  |  | 3) Business | 462 | 3.90 | 0.65 |  |  |
|  | Tukey test shows that there is no significant difference between the means of the three sub-groups of parental occupation. (See Table 2B.6c for details) | | | | | | |
| 4. | Parents' employment status | 1) Mother employed | 188 | 3.96 | 0.67 | 0.26 | 0.77 |
|  |  | 2) Father employed | 1,254 | 3.92 | 0.68 |  |  |
|  |  | 3) Both employed | 496 | 3.93 | 0.64 |  |  |
|  | Tukey test shows that there is no significant difference between the means of the three sub-groups of parents' employment status. (See Table 2B.6c for details) | | | | | | |
| 5. | Place of upbringing | 1) North India | 808 | 3.97 | 0.64 | 1.96 | 0.10 |
|  |  | 2) South India | 436 | 3.93 | 0.65 |  |  |
|  |  | 3) Eastern India | 261 | 3.97 | 0.66 |  |  |
|  |  | 4) Western India | 318 | 3.89 | 0.67 |  |  |
|  |  | 5) Central India | 92 | 3.81 | 0.82 |  |  |
|  | Tukey Test shows that there is no significant difference between the means of the sub-groups of place of upbringing. (See Table 2B.6c for details) | | | | | | |

**Table 2B.6c  Progressive orientation by background variables (Tukey[4] table)**

| Dependent variable | Background variable | Background variable (I) | Background variable (J) | Mean difference (I–J) | Standard error | Sig. |
|---|---|---|---|---|---|---|
| Progressive orientation | Age |  |  |  |  | No significant differences found |
|  | Prior work experience |  |  |  |  | No significant differences found |
|  | Parental occupation |  |  |  |  | No significant differences found |
|  | Employment status |  |  |  |  | No significant differences found |
|  | Place of upbringing |  |  |  |  | No significant differences found |

---

[4] Tukey's test is a single-step multiple comparison procedure and statistical test generally used in conjunction with an ANOVA to find which means are significantly different from one another. A post-hoc test is conducted after completing an ANOVA in order to determine which groups differ from each other.

# References

Agrawal, T., & Krishnan, V. R. (2000). Relationship between leadership styles and value systems. *Management & Labor Studies*, 25 (2), 136–143.

Ali, A. J., Ahmed, A. A., & Krishnan, K. S. (1995). Expatriates and host country nationals: Managerial values and decision styles. *Leadership and Organizational Development*, 16 (6), 27–34.

Andre, R. (2009). Organizational behavior: An introduction to your life in organizations. Delhi: Pearson Education.

Argyris, C. (1973). *On organizations of the future*. Beverly Hills, California: Sage Publications.

Atkinson, J. (1974). *Motivation and achievement*. Washington, D. C.: V. H. Winston and Sons.

Atkinson, J. W. (1957). Motivational determinants of risk-taking behavior. *Psychological Review*, 64 (6/1), 359–372.

———. (ed.) (1958). *Motives in fantasy, action and society*. D. Van Nostrand Company, Inc.: Princeton.

Bains, G., & Bains, K. (2007). *Meaning Inc: The blue print for business success in the 21st century*. Profile Books: London.

Bernstein, D. A., Penner, L. A., Clarker-Stewart, A., & Roy, E. J. (2003). *Psychology*. Boston and New York: Houghton Mifflin Company.

Bilsky, W., & Schwartz, S. H. (1994). Values and personality. *European Journal of Personality*, 8 (3), 163–181, Paragraph 3.

Blau, G. (1993). Testing the relationship of locus of control to different performance dimensions. *Journal of Occupational and Organizational Psychology*, 66, 125–138.

Blegen, M. A. (1993) Nurses' job satisfaction: A meta analysis of related variables. *Nursing Research*, 42 (1), 36–41.

Boone, C. (1992). *Onderzoek naar het verband tussen de perceptie van controle van bedrijfsleiders en de strategie en de resultaten van ondernemingen in de meubelindustrie*, Unpublished doctoral dissertation. University of Antwerp (RUCA).

Boone, C., & De Brabander, B. (1992). The relationship between the locus of control of chief executive officers and the successful implementation of strategic intentions and firm performance: An empirical investigation in the furniture industry. Unpublished manuscript. University of Antwerp (RUCA).

Box, W. R., Dom, R. Y. O., & Dunn, M. G. (1991). Organizational values and value congruency and their impact on satisfaction, commitment, and cohesion: An empirical examination within the public sector. *Public Personnel Management*, 20 (2), 195–205.

Burns, T., & Stalker, G. M. (1994). *The management of innovation*. Oxford University Press.

Cassidy, T., & Lynn, R. (1989). A multi-factorial approach to achievement motivation: The development of a comprehensive measure. *Journal of Occupational Psychology*, 62, 301–312.

Chen, Po-Ju, & Choi, Y. (2008). Generational differences in work values: A study of hospitality management. *International Journal of Contemporary Hospitality*, 20 (6), 595–615.

Clugston, M., Howell, J. P., & Dorfman, P. W. (2000). Does cultural socialization predict multiple bases and foci of commitment? *Journal of Management*, 26 (1), 5–30.

Collins, J. (2009). *How the mighty fall and why some companies never give in*. London, Great Britain: Random House Business Books, Back page quote.

Connor, P. E., & Becker, B. W. (2003). Personal values systems and decision-making styles of public managers. *Public Personnel Management, 32* (1), 155–180.

Cooper, W. H. (1983). An achievement motivation nomological network. *Journal of Personality and Social Psychology, 44* (4), 841–861.

Cox, T. (Jr.). (1993). *Cultural diversity in organizations: Theory, research and practice.* San Francisco, California: Berrett-Koehler Publishing.

Dailey, R. (1980). Relationship between locus of control, task characteristics, and work attitudes. *Psychological Reports, 47*, 855–861.

Daniels, E. (1998). *There and back: Robben island, 1964–1979.* Bellville, South Africa: Mayibuye Books.

Davis, W. L., and Davis, D. E. (1972). Internal-external control and attribution of responsibility for success or failure. *Journal of Personality, 40* (1), 123–136.

Elizur, D. (1979) Assessing achievement motive of American and Israeli managers: Design and application of a three-facet measure. *Applied Psychological Measurement, 3* (2), 201–212.

———. (1986). Achievement motive and sport performance. *International Review of Applied Psychology, 35* (2), 209–224.

Feather, N. T. (1962). Cigarette smoking and lung cancer: A study of cognitive dissonance. *Australian Journal of Psychology, 14* (1), 55–64.

Finegan, J. E. (2000). The impact of person and organizational values on organizational commitment. *Journal of Occupational and Organizational Psychology, 73* (2), 149–169.

Fischer, R., & Smith, P. B. (2006). Who cares about justice? The moderating effect of values on the link between organizational justice and work behavior. *Applied Psychology: An International Review, 55*, 541–562.

Forte, A. (2005). Locus of control and the moral reasoning of managers. *Journal of Business Ethics, 58* (1), 65–77.

Friedland, N. (1992). On luck and chance: Need for control as a mediator of the attribution of luck. *Journal of Behavioral Decision Making, 5* (4), 267–282.

Fuqua, R., & Couture, K. (1986). Burnout and locus of control in child daycare staff. *Child Care Quarterly, 15* (2), 98–109.

Garson, B. E., & Stanwyck, D. J. (1997). Locus of control and incentive in self-managing teams. *Human Resource Development Quarterly, 8* (3), 247–258.

Glazer, S., Daniel, S. K., & Short, K. M. (2004). A study of the relationship between organizational commitment and human values in four countries. *Human Relations, 57* (3), 323–345.

Grote, G. F., & James, L. R. (1991). Testing behavioral consistency and coherence with the situation-response measure of achievement motivation. *Multivariate Behavioral Research, 26*, 655–691.

Hall, C. S., Lindazey, G., & Campbell, J. B. (2007). *Theories of personality* (4th ed.). Wiley India: New Delhi.

Handy, C. (1995). *The empty raincoat: Making sense of the future.* London: Arrow Business.

Harper, Douglas. (2011) "Value," Online etymology dictionary. Retrieved July 8, 2011, from http://dictionary.reference.com/browse/value.

Heckhausen, H., & Spence, D. (1995). Increasing productivity in organizations. *Harvard Business Review, 55*, 201–210.

Heintz, P. Jr., & Steele-Johnson, D. (2004). Clarifying the conceptual definitions of goal orientation dimensions: Competence, control, and evaluation. *International Journal of Organizational Analysis, 12* (1), 5–19.

Helmreich, R. L., & Spence, J. T. (1978). The work and family orientation questionnaire: An objective instrument to assess components of achievement motivation and attitudes towards family and career. *JSAS Catalogue of selected Documents in Psychology, 8* (35), 21–35.

Hofstede, G. (1980). *Cultures consequences: International differences in work related values.* Beverly Hills, California: Sage.

Hofstede, G. (2001) Culture's consequences (2nd ed). Thousand Oaks, California: Sage.

Jackson, D. N., Ahmed, S. A., & Heapy, N. A. (1976). Is achievement a unitary construct? *Journal of Research in Personality, 10* (1), 1–21.

Jha, S. S. and Nair, S. K. (2008). Influence of locus of control, job characteristics and superior–subordinate relationship on psychological empowerment. A study in five star hotels. *Journal of Management Research, 8* (3), 147–161.

Kasperson, C. (1982). Locus of control and job dissatisfaction. *Psychological Reports, 50,* 823–826.

Keast, D. A. (1996). Values in the decision-making of CEOs in public colleges. *Canadian Journal of Higher Education, 26* (1), 1–34.

Kirkman, B. L., & Sharpiro, D. L. (2001). The impact of cultural values on job satisfaction and organizational commitment in self-managing work teams: The mediating role of employee resistance. *Academy of Management Journal, 44,* 557–569.

Knoop, R. (1981). Locus of control as a moderator between job characteristics and job attitudes. *Psychological reports, 48* (2), 519–525.

Kulshrestha, U., & Sen, C. (2006). Subjective well being in relation to emotional intelligence and locus of control among executives. *Journal of the Indian Academy of Applied Psychology, 32* (2), 93–98.

Kuo, Ying-Feng (2006). Influences on employee career strategy adoption in the information service industry: Superior leadership style or employee achievement motivation? *International Journal of Management, 23* (1), 176–186.

Kundu, S. C., and Rani, S. (2004). Entrepreneurial orientation of aspiring managers: A study. *International Journal of Management and Enterprise Development, 1* (3), 233–250.

Lefcourt, H. M. (1982). *Locus of control.* Hillsdale, New Jersey: Lawrence Erlbaum.

Lenartowicz, T., & Johnson, J. P. (2003). A cross-cultural assessment of the values of Latin America managers: Contrasting hues or shades of gray. *Journal of International Business Studies, 34* (3), 787–811.

Leung, T. W., Siu, O. L., & Spector, P. E. (2000). Faculty stressors, job satisfaction, and psychological distress among university teachers in Hong Kong: The role of locus of control. *International Journal of Stress Management, 7,* 121–138.

Lunenburg, F. C., & Cadavid, V. (1992). Locus of control, pupil control ideology, and dimensions of teacher burnout. *Journal of Instructional Psychology, 19* (1), 13–22.

McClelland, D. C. (1961). *The Achieving Society.* Princeton, New Jersey: D. Van Nostrand.

——— (1965). Towards a theory of motive acquisition. *American Psychologist, 20* (5), 321–333.

McClelland, D. C., Atkinson, J. W., Clark, R. W., & Lowell, E. L. (1953). *The achievement motive.* New York: Appleton-Century-Crofts.

McGuire, D., Garavan, T. N., Saha, S. K., & O'Donnell, D. (2006). The impact of individual values on human resource decision-making by line managers. *International Journal of Manpower, 27* (3), 253, Paragraph 5.

Meglino, B. M., Ravlin, E. C., & Adkins, C. L. (1989). A work values approach to corporate culture: A field test of the value congruence process and its relationship in individual outcomes. *Journal of Applied Psychology, 74* (3), 424–432.

Merritte, K. K. (2000). A domain-specific investigation of goal orientation, related cognitive and behavioral variables and prediction model for academic achievement. Unpublished doctoral dissertation, Tulane University, New Orleans, Los Angeles.

Mitchell, T. R., Smyser, C. M., and S. E. Weed. 1975. Locus of control: Supervision and work satisfaction. *Academy of Management Journal*, 18 (September): 623–631.

Murphy, E. F., & Gordon, J. D. (2004). A preliminary study exploring the value changes taking place in the United States since the September 11, 2001 terrorist attack on the world trade center in New York, *Journal of Business Ethics*, 50 (1), 81–97.

Murray, D. (1990). The performance effects of participative budgeting: An integration of intervening and moderating variables. *Behavioral Research in Accounting*, 2, 104–123.

Murray, H. A. (1938). *Exploration in personality*. New York: Oxford University Press.

Pearson, C. A. L., & Chong J. (1997). Contributions of job content and social information on organizational commitment and job satisfaction: An exploration in a Malaysian nursing context. *Journal of Occupational and Organizational Psychology*, 70 (4), 357–374.

Phares, E. J., Wilson, K. G., & Klyver, N. W. (1971). Internal-external control and the attribution of blame under neutral and distractive conditions. *Journal of Personality and Social Psychology*, 18 (3), 285–288.

Rees, D. W., & Cooper, C. L. (1992). The occupational stress indicator locus of control scale: Should this be regarded as a state rather than trait measure? *Work and Stress*, 6 (1), 45–48.

Roe, R. A., & Ester, P. (1999). Values and work. *Applied Psychology: An International Review*, 48 (1), 1–102.

Rokeach, M. (1973). *The nature of human values*. New York: Free Press.

Rokeach, M. and Regan, J. F. (1980). The role of values in the counseling situation. *Personnel and Guidance Journal*, 58 (9), 576–583.

Rokeach, M., Miller, M., & Snyder, J. (1971). The value gap between police and policed. *Journal of Social Issues*, 27, 155–171.

Ros, M., Schwartz, S. H., & Surkiss, S. (1999). Basic Individual Values, Work Values, and the Meaning of Work. *Applied Psychology: An International Review*, 48 (1), 49–71.

Rotter, J. (1966). Generalized expectancies for internal versus external control of reinforcements. *Psychological Monographs*, 80, 609.

Sagie, A. (1994). Assessing achievement motivation: Construction and application of a new scale using Elizur's multifaceted approach. *Journal of Psychology*, 128 (1), 51–61.

Schafer, W. E., and McKenna, J. F. (1991) Perceived energy and stress resistance: A study of city managers. *Journal of Social Behavior and Personality*, 6 (2), 271–282.

Seeman, M. (1967). Powerlessness and knowledge: A comparative study of alienation and learning. *Sociometry*, 30 (1), 105–123.

Sheridan, J. E. (1992). Organizational culture and employee retention. *Academy of Management Journal*, 35 (5), 1036–1056.

Singh, P., & Bhandarker, A. (2011). *In search of change maestros*. Sage: New Delhi.

Singh, P., Bhandarker, A., & Bhatnagar, J. (2006). *Future work of mastering change: Introduction*. National HRD Network. New Delhi: Excel Books.

Singh, P., Bhandarker, A., Rai, S., & Jain, A. K. (2011). Relationship between values and workplace: An exploratory analysis. *Facilities*, 29 (11/12), 499–520.

Singh, S. K. (2006). Social work professionals' emotional intelligence, locus of control, and role efficacy: An exploratory study, *South African Journal of Human Resource Management*, 4 (2), 39–45.

Spector, P. (1982). Behavior in organizations as a function of employee's locus of control. *Psychological Bulletin*, 91 (3), 482–492.

Spector, P. E. (1988). Development of the work locus of control scale. *Journal of Occupational Psychology, 61* (4), 335–340.

Spector, P. E., Cooper, C. L., Sanchez, J. I., O'Driscoll, M., Sparks, K., Bernin, P. et al.(2002). A 24 nation/territory study of work locus of control in relation to well-being at work: How generalizable are western findings? *Academy of Management Journal, 45* (2), 453–466.

Spence, J. T., Pred, R. S., & Helmreich, R. L. (1989). Achievement strivings, scholastic aptitude and academic performance: A follow-up to "Impatience versus achievement strivings in the Type A pattern." *Journal of Applied Psychology, 74* (1), 176–178.

Stewart, W. H. Jr, Carland, J. C., Carland, J. W., Watson, W. E., & Sweo, R. (2003). Entrepreneurial dispositions and goal orientations: A comparative exploration of United States and Russian entrepreneurs. *Journal of Small Business Management, 41* (1), 27–46.

Tapscott, D. (1998). *Growing up digital: The rise of the net generation.* New York: McGraw-Hill.

Veroff, J. (1982). Assertive motivations: Achievement vs. power. In A. Stewart (Ed.), *Motivation and society* (pp. 99–132). San Francisco, California: Jossey-Bass.

Volansky, A., & Habinski, A. (1998). The emerging role of school leadership in Israel: From external to internal locus of control. *New Directions in School Leadership, 9* (Fall), 87–105.

Wasti, S. A. (2003). The influence of cultural values on antecedents of organizational commitment: An individual-level analysis. *Applied Psychology: An International Review, 52* (4), 533–554.

Watson, L. E. (Ed.) (1988) *Light from many lamps: A treasury of inspiration.* New York: Simon & Schuster.

Weiner, B. (1992). *Human Motivation: Metaphors, Theories, and Research.* Newbury Park, California: Sage Publications.

Whitebook, M., Howes, C., Darrah, R., & Friedman, J. (1982) Caring for the caregivers: Staff burnout in child care. In L. Katz (Ed.), *Current topics in early childhood education* (pp. 55–79). Norwood, New Jersey: Ablex Publishing.

Wolfe, R. N. (1972). Effects of economic threat on autonomy and perceived locus of control. *The Journal of Social Psychology, 86* (2), 233–240.

Yamauchi, H., & Li, Y. (1993). Achievement-related motives and work-related attitudes of Japanese and Chinese students. *Psychological Reports, 73* (3/1), 755–767.

Yeo, G., & Neal, A. (2004). A multilevel analysis of the relationship between effort and performance: Effects of ability, conscientiousness and goal orientation. *The Journal of Applied Psychology, 89* (2), 231–247.

Yukl, G. A., & Latham, G. P. (1978). Interrelationships among employee participation, individual differences, goal difficulty, goal acceptance, goal instrumentality, and performance. *Personnel Psychology, 31* (2), 305–323.

Zhao, J., He, N., & Lovrich, N. P. (1998). Individual value preferences among American police officers: The Rokeach theory of human values revisited. *Policing: An international Journal of Police Strategies & Management, 21,* 22–37.

———. (1999). Value change among police officers as a time of organizational reform: A follow-up study using Rokeach values. *Policing: An International Journal of Police Strategies & Management, 22* (2), 152–170.

# Meaning of Workplace

**3**

## Millennials' Valence

As highlighted earlier in Chapter 1, understanding and appreciating meaning of workplace from Millennials' lens is the core around which new forms of organization need to be architected. In fact the entire gamut of organizational strategy, structure, systems, processes, styles, and work culture need to be aligned and oriented around Millennials' workplace expectations. Fit between Millennials' expectations and workplace realities will enable the organization to unleash the potential of Millennials, heighten their motivation, tap into their innovative and entrepreneurial capabilities, and prepare organizations to compete and excel globally. The importance of fit emerges from the fact that it is considerably influential in individual level job satisfaction, performance, commitment and career related outcomes (Bretz and Judge, 1994; Cable and DeRue, 2002; Kristof-Brown, Zimmerman, and Johnson, 2005; Ostroff, Shinn, and Kinicki, 2005). Researchers on P-E fit (Caplan, 1983; French, Rodgers, and Cobb, 1974; Harrison, 1978; Locke, 1969 and Porter, 1962, 1961) have discussed, researched, and assessed fit from the perspective of its outcomes—adjustment, well-being, and satisfaction. Research has shown that P-E fit results in better psychological and physical well-being, higher job satisfaction, job performance, organization commitment, reduced turnover (Cummings and Cooper, 1979; French, Caplan, and Harrison, 1982; Hecht and Allen, 2005;

Hackman, 1980; Kulik, Oldham, and Hackman, 1987; Edwards, 1991; Kristof, 1996; Spokane, Meir, and Catalano, 2000; Verquer, Beehr, and Wagner, 2003). Congruence has been studied between personality and organizational climate (Tom, 1971; Christiansen, Villanova, and Mikulay, 1997; Ryan and Schmitt, 1996). In fact Chatman's (1989) model specifically focused on individual values and organization climate congruence.

Understanding Millennials' expectations becomes much more critical in the coming decades as the war for talent becomes more severe on a global scale. This war for talent will get worse as most of the nations, particularly advanced countries become progressively grey, leading to greater demand and lesser supply of high quality talent. Understanding MOWP has implications for many HR strategies for attracting, socializing, and retaining millennials through various workplace policies, practices, styles, and culture. For example, findings of research by Schneider and Tinsley (Schneider, 1987a, 1987b; Tinsley 2000) have confirmed that organizational values are a good predictor of job choices and that individuals preferred jobs and organizations which displayed values similar to their own. Creating this fit would in turn help organizations to attract Millennials and retain them for a longer period of time.

It would be worthwhile to reiterate that India would have a large working population until 2050 (O'Neill and Poddar, 2008) and in the graying context of the world except for Africa, become a key sourcing point for highly skilled and educated talent. In fact estimates for 2020 show that there will be 230 million in the 15–24 age group; 480 in the 25–49 age group, and 130 in the 50–59 age group (O' Neill and Poddar, 2008). In such a scenario Indian Millennials would increasingly have the luxury of multiple options both in India and globally. In view of this changing context, organizations will have to devise new approaches and strategies to continuously attract, retain talent and provide opportunity for the unleashing of their creative abilities. The importance of fostering employee creativity cannot be over-emphasized. It has been found that employee creativity can fundamentally contribute to organizational innovation, effectiveness and survival (Amabile, 1996; Shalley, Zhou, and Oldham, 2004) This would be possible only when the corporate world and recruiters understand the Millennials and their expectations from the workplace and in turn reorient organizations to align with their needs (Zhang and Bartol, 2010).

This chapter has been organized using the above context as a backdrop. The chapter is divided into three parts:

Part 1 deals with the perceived valence of workplace attributes;
Part 2 identifies major meaning of workplace factors;
Part 3 focuses on identifying the critical causal variables influencing workplace expectations.

## PART I: Valence of the Workplace Attributes (MOWP)[1]

Table 3.1 presents the means and SDs of the 49 workplaces attributes. Analysis of this table reveals that all items have been found to be relevant for the Millennials, the lowest mean being 2.66. These items have been sub grouped into four clusters for detailed analysis:

Table 3.1 Meaning of workplace—mean values

| S. No. | Items | Mean | SD |
|---|---|---|---|
| 1. | Encourages innovation and idea generation | 4.26 | 0.83 |
| 2. | Recognizes performance | 4.25 | 0.76 |
| 3. | Believes in fairness and justice | 4.19 | 0.88 |
| 4. | Recognizes contribution | 4.19 | 0.82 |
| 5. | Provides opportunities for personality development | 4.19 | 0.83 |
| 6. | Encourages learning | 4.16 | 0.82 |
| 7. | Provides opportunities to take initiatives | 4.15 | 0.81 |
| 8. | Gives autonomy and freedom to express my views | 4.14 | 0.81 |
| 9. | Encourages leadership development | 4.14 | 0.82 |
| 10. | Encourages trust and transparency | 4.11 | 0.85 |
| 11. | Values work–life balance | 4.11 | 0.91 |
| 12. | Provides constructive feedback for my development | 4.05 | 0.86 |

*Table 3.1 continued*

---

[1] The questionnaire used for the study is titled "The Meaning of Work Place." The instrument consisted of 49 (see Singh et al., 2011) expectations regarding workplace attributes including the job itself, the environment, and the physical location of the work place. A five-point scale ranging from "Least Important" to "Most Important" was used to study participants' assessments of individual attributes and values.

*Table 3.1 continued*

| S. No. | Items | Mean | SD |
|---|---|---|---|
| 13. | Encourages team work | 4.04 | 0.87 |
| 14. | Is open to suggestions for improvement | 4.03 | 0.83 |
| 15. | Provides opportunities for decision making | 4.02 | 0.76 |
| 16. | Helps me earn respect from society | 3.98 | 0.92 |
| 17. | Is ethical in dealings | 3.98 | 0.97 |
| 18. | Cares about physical and mental health of its employees | 3.97 | 0.85 |
| 19. | Has role clarity | 3.93 | 0.89 |
| 20. | Empowers people | 3.91 | 0.89 |
| 21. | Takes care of financial needs | 3.90 | 0.97 |
| 22. | Provides job security | 3.88 | 1.02 |
| 23. | Reduces fear of losing job | 3.83 | 1.01 |
| 24. | Encourages people to voice their concerns | 3.82 | 0.85 |
| 25. | Encourages experimentation | 3.79 | 0.91 |
| 26. | Has a strong brand value | 3.75 | 1.04 |
| 27. | Has high prestige | 3.74 | 0.94 |
| 28. | Has latest technology | 3.72 | 0.96 |
| 29. | Celebrate success | 3.68 | 0.96 |
| 30. | Is flexible with work timings | 3.67 | 1.09 |
| 31. | Follow rules and regulations | 3.65 | 0.99 |
| 32. | Has a well-defined "shared vision" | 3.63 | 0.93 |
| 33. | Has modern equipments to facilitate work | 3.63 | 0.92 |
| 34. | Brings discipline among its employees | 3.62 | 1.03 |
| 35. | Requires working in a planned manner | 3.61 | 0.99 |
| 36. | Contributes to the economy of the country | 3.60 | 1.02 |
| 37. | Provides sense of community | 3.58 | 0.95 |
| 38. | Provides a platform for forming life-long relationships | 3.57 | 1.02 |
| 39. | Takes initiatives for planned change | 3.53 | 0.92 |
| 40. | Has a green environment (trees, etc.) | 3.52 | 1.12 |
| 41. | Brings people closer | 3.50 | 0.99 |
| 42. | Provides opportunities to influence others | 3.47 | 1.02 |
| 43. | Provides opportunity for social networking | 3.44 | 1.04 |
| 44. | Provides opportunity to exercise power | 3.32 | 1.03 |
| 45. | Is well lit | 3.31 | 1.04 |
| 46. | Is conveniently located from my residence | 3.19 | 1.21 |
| 47. | Has wide open spaces | 3.18 | 1.11 |
| 48. | Gives freedom for many coffee breaks | 2.77 | 1.24 |
| 49. | Has a crèche | 2.66 | 1.17 |

There are 15 workplace attributes in the Very Highly Valued (VHV) category (with means ranging from 4.26 to 4.00), 26 items in the Highly Valued (HV) category (with means ranging from 3.98 to 3.5), 6 items fall in the Moderately Valued (MV) category (with means ranging from 3.49 to 3.00) and 2 are in the Least Valued (LV) category (below 3.00 mean value). In the subsequent part, only the top 15 VHV items have been discussed in detail since these appear to be the most pivotal from the Millennials' point of view. Taking care of these workplace expectations, it is assumed will create a sense of excitement, passion, and commitment among them. Organizations cannot ignore these 15 workplace attributes while designing a workplace which can keep people excited and motivated. Those items in the HV category are also important although relatively they are slightly lesser in importance as compared to the VHV items cluster.

Perusal of the means of these top 15 items (HV cluster–VHV cluster) brings out four powerful themes:

1. **Freedom to take initiative, experiment, and express views:** This seems to be a high priority workplace expectation. This is indicated by five items—"provides opportunity to take initiative" (rank 7, mean 4.15); "Gives autonomy and freedom to express my views'" (rank 8, mean 4.14); "encourages innovation and idea generation" (rk1, mean 4.26); "provides opportunity for decision making" (rank 15, mean 4.02); and "open to suggestions for improvement" (rank 14, mean 4.03)—which feature in the top 15 items. The most valued workplace attribute is encourages innovation and idea generation. The other four items mentioned above are also related to these core expectations of the Millennials.
2. **Performance-based recognition:** Another theme in this VHV cluster is performance based recognition and consists of two items, "recognizes performance" (rank 2, mean 4.25) and "recognizes contribution" (rank 3, mean 4.19).
3. **Equity and fairness:** It has also emerged as a major expectation with two items, "believes in fairness and justice" and "encourages trust and transparency" (rank 10, mean 4.11), emerging in the top 15 highly valued workplace attributes.
4. **Learning and development:** Working in an organization which provides opportunity for learning and development is another credo of the Millennials. This category consists of four items—provides opportunity for personal development (rank 5, mean 4.19), encourages learning (rank 6, mean 4.16), and encourages leadership development (rank 9, mean 4.14) and provides constructive feedback (rank 12, 4.05).

5. **Work–Life balance:** Millennials also value workplaces characterized by work–life balance (rank 11, mean 4.11) and team work (rank 13, mean 4.04).

The following salient conclusions can be drawn from the analysis of these 15 VHV items:

- Millennials crave for a workplace which provides freedom for experimentation, offers opportunities to take initiatives, and encourages idea generation and innovation;
- Millennials also desire to work in a place where their performance and contribution are amply recognized and rewarded;
- Fairness and transparency are important attractors for the Millennials;
- Millennials would like to embrace a workplace where there is plenty of opportunity for learning, growth, and development.

In a nutshell, it can be said that Millennials would not like to be associated with a workplace which is bureaucratic, mechanistic, hierarchical, status quoist, de-empowering, and non-entrepreneurial. In our experience as consultants and trainers we have found that unfortunately a large number of Indian organizations still have many shades of the above characteristics of the typical 20th century workplace, creating mismatch and disconnect of the Millennials' group with the organization.

## Part II: Major factors of Meaning of Workplace (MOWP)

Factor analysis has been utilized to reduce the 49 MOWP items into broad clusters of related items. Such an analysis can help bring clarity in the data and thus enable organizations to develop broad architectural framework conducive to develop an appropriate strategy to build the future workplace.

Table 3A.1 (Appendix 3A) presents the nine factors—innovation, process centricity with shared vision, sense of community, sense of security, conducive physical ambience, sharing and celebrating culture, techno savvy workplace, company's brand image, and ethical—which emerged from the factor analysis of the forty nine MOWP items (Table 3A.1), explaining 53.66 percent of the variance. The purpose of conducting factor analysis has been to identify underlying factors of meaning of workplace (MOWP) and, in this way also make the data more manageable for further analysis. The nine factors which emerged from Factor Analysis of the 49 items are now discussed next.

## Entrepreneurial Innovation

The most important factor as seen through the Millennials' lens is entrepreneurial innovation. This factor consists of 11 items and explains 23.20 percent of variance. Perusal of the items indicates that Millennials are looking for a workplace which provides opportunity to take initiatives, make decisions, gives autonomy and freedom to express views and encourages experimentation, innovation and idea generation, besides encouraging leadership development. Further they expect the organization to encourage employees to voice their concerns and suggestions for improvement and at the same time want the organization to give them constructive feedback for their own development. Recognition for contribution as well as performance, the fulcrum of creating an exciting, motivating and meaningful workplace, is also viewed as important.

## Process Centricity with Shared Vision

The second factor—process centricity with shared vision—explains 5.56 percent variance. This factor encompasses workplace attributes like follows rules and regulations, brings discipline among employees, requires working in a planned manner, has a well-defined shared vision. In other words, Millennials prefer to work for an organization where processes are well defined; operate in an organized way and where there is shared vision thus creating clarity and predictability and sense of direction at the workplace.

## Sense of Community

Sense of community explains 4.81 percent of the variance. This factor reveals that Millennials value the organization which provides the opportunity to build life-long relationships, creates a sense of community and also brings people closer. An organization with such characteristics needless to say, would meet the human need for connectedness and also the need to belong to a community.

## Sense of Security

This factor explains 3.95 percent of the variance and refers to the expectation that the organization provides job security and also reduces the anxiety experienced from threat of job loss. This indicates that Millennials don't like to work in an organization where there is uncertainty about their future.

## Conducive Physical Ambience

This factor explains 3.57 percent of the variance and indicates that Millennials expect a workplace where there are frequent coffee breaks, flexible work timings, and a well-lit facility set in wide open spaces. This indicates that Millennials dislike rigidity of routinized work and look for flexible workplace practices and conducive work ambience with a sense of space and light.

## Sharing and Celebrating Culture

The sixth factor explains 2.82 percent of the variance. Perusal of the items loading on this factor conveys that Millennials also attach importance to a work culture which celebrates success and has a sharing culture.

## Techno-savvy Workplace

This factor explains 2.62 percent of the variance and brings out that Millennials want technologically enabled workplaces with modern equipment and latest technology.

## Company's Brand Image

This factor explains 2.55 percent variance. It reflects that Millennials would like to work in an organization with high prestige and brand, which in turn would reflect on the employees and enhance their ability to influence others and give them a strong identity in society.

## Ethical

This factor explains 2.19 percent of the variance. The items on this factor indicate the Millennials' preference for a workplace which is ethical in its functioning as well as believes in fairness and justice.

The following salient points emerge from the preceding analysis:

- The most valued and preferred cluster of items is the first factor—entrepreneurial innovation. This indicates that Millennials value and look for organizations where entrepreneurial urge can be unleashed. In other words, they would like to work in an organization where they are empowered to take risk as well as experiment and innovate. They prefer to work in an organization where they have the freedom to express their ideas and voice their dissent;
- They prefer to work in the organization where there is equity, fairness, and justice, especially with regard to performance–reward linkage;
- They would also like to work in an organization where they are given appropriate nurturing, support and continuous feedback which helps them to blossom into leaders;
- Entrepreneurial innovation is in fact the factor accounting for almost half the explained variance indicating that this cluster is the core workplace expectations which Millennials hold.

The other eight factors are also important; however, relatively speaking, each of them is much lesser in importance as compared to entrepreneurial innovation which is indicated by the variance explained by these factors.

The eight factors—from the second factor to the ninth factor—primarily center on hygiene factors.

In a nutshell it may be concluded that the major expectation which Millennials hold from the workplace are around intrinsic work-related motivators which have clustered together in the first factor—entrepreneurial innovation.

## PART III: Variables Influencing Meaning of Workplace (MOWP)

This part brings out the impact of the causal variables on the valence of workplace expectations.

Understanding the influence of these causal factors will enable organizations to create an employee centric workplace, the assumption being that the person environment fit is key to create an exciting and meaningful workplace, which can help harness individual potential besides satisfying employee expectations. We now purport to examine the impact of selected causal variables on MOWP (for details of Cronbach's alpha and inter-scale correlations see Tables 3B.2a and 3B.2b of Appendix 3B).

Findings have been presented in two sections:

- Section 1 deals with the impact of demographic variables on MOWP.[2]
- Section 2 examines the personality predisposition, locus of control, achievement orientation, personal values, and family background on MOWP[3] to identify the major influencing factors on MOWP.

---

[2] ANOVA technique has been used. This is used to test for significance of differences between means of three or more groups. A $t$ test analysis has been used to evaluate the differences in means where the number of groups are only two (King, Rosopa, and Minium, 2010). These tests have been conducted on those important demographic variables which are hypothesized to effect MOWP, but cannot be entered in the stepwise multiple regression analysis owing to their being nominal variables.

[3] Stepwise multiple regression analysis has been utilized. This is a statistical technique that allows additional factors to enter the analysis separately so that the effect of each can be estimated. It is valuable for quantifying the impact of various simultaneous influences upon a single dependent variable (Allison, 1999).

## Section 1: Influence of Demographics on MOWP

Seven demographic variables—age, work, experience, educational background, gender, family type, family background, and place of upbringing have been utilized to examine their impact on MOWP. The impact of these factors has been studied across: (a) MOWP total score and (b) total scores of each of the nine factors (arrived at through factor analysis [see part II])

### Demographics and MOWP total score

Four of the seven demographic variables—educational background, age, work experience, and parental background significantly influence MOWP (see Appendix 3C Tables 3C.3a and 3C.3b for $t$ test and $F$ test analysis and significance levels). MBAs have significantly higher expectations as compared to Engineers. Respondents with higher work experience have significantly greater expectations from the workplace as compared to those with lesser (3 months to 3 years) or nil work experience. Respondents hailing from an agriculture background (families engaged in this activity) have significantly higher expectations from the workplace, in comparison with those from business and service backgrounds.

Other demographics like gender, family type and place of upbringing do not show significant impact on MOWP. It may be concluded from the above that MBAs, older Millennials, people with longer work experience, and those coming from an agriculture background demonstrate significantly higher valence on MOWP.

### Entrepreneurial innovation (EI)[4]

EI refers to an organization which provides the opportunity to freely express ideas, voice dissent, take risk, make decisions as well as experiment, innovate and take the unbeaten path. Four of the seven demographic variables—educational background, family type, age, and prior work experience—influence the desire to work in an organization characterized by entrepreneurial innovation as indicated by the significant $t$ values and

---

[4] See Table 3A.1 (Appendix 3A) for details of the MOWP factors.

F values (at $p \geq .05$ level [see Appendix 3C Tables 3C.4a and 3C.4b). MBAs are found to have much higher expectations that the workplace should offer them with entrepreneurial opportunity as compared to engineers. Likewise those from nuclear families have significantly greater preference for high EI compared to those from joint families. Older Millennials (aged 23–28 and 29–34) have much greater desire for an EI workplace as compared to those who are in the 17–22 age group. Likewise work experience also has a significant impact on EI expectations. Respondents with greater work experience (3–5 years and 5–12 years) have significantly higher desire for an EI workplace as compared to those with less/nil work experience. Variables like gender, parental occupation and place of upbringing have no significant impact on the EI valence.

## Process centricity with shared vision

Process centricity refers to the workplace which is well organized and planned and provides role and goal clarity. Four of the seven demographic variables—family type, age, work experience, and parental occupation—significantly influence the valence for process-centric factor as indicated by the significant (at $p \geq .05$) $t$ values and $F$ values (see Appendix 3C Tables 3C.5a and 3C.5b present the findings on this factor).

Respondents hailing from joint families have significantly greater desire for a clearly planned and defined way of working as compared to those from nuclear families. Those who are in the 29–34 years category have significantly higher preference for a process centric workplace as compared to those who are in the younger age groups (17–22 and 22–28 years). Respondents from agriculture family background have significantly higher expectations of a process centric workplace as compared to those coming from service and business family backgrounds. Gender and place of upbringing do not have much impact of MOWP preference.

## Sense of community

Sense of community refers to the desire for a workplace which brings people closer and provides opportunity to form lifelong relationships and creates a sense of belonging to a group. Five of the seven demographics—educational background, family type, parental occupation, and place of upbringing—significantly influence the clamor for a workplace which promotes a sense of community (see $t$ and $F$ values presented in Appendix 3C Tables 3C.6a and 3C.6b).

MBAs have significantly higher desire for a workplace which promotes a sense of community as compared to engineering graduates. Respondents hailing from nuclear families prefer a workplace which promotes a sense of community as compared to those coming from joint families. The youngest age group—17–22 years—has a significantly greater desire for community centric workplaces compared to the older respondents. People hailing from an agriculture family background have a significantly greater liking for a community-centric workplace as compared to those from service or business backgrounds. The highest (and significant) valence is attached to community centric workplace by respondents who grew up in south India as compared to those from other parts of the country—north, west, south, and central.

It may be concluded from the findings that a community centric workplace is highly preferred by respondents who are MBAs, who grew up in nuclear families, from agriculture backgrounds and who group up in south India. Gender, age, and prior work experience have little impact of preference for sense of community at the workplace.

## Sense of security (SS)

Sense of security refers to a workplace where there is low constant anxiety and threat of job loss. Four of the seven variables—gender, age, prior work experience, parental occupation—significantly impact the preference for SS at the workplace (See Appendix 3C Tables 3c.7a and 3c.7b for significant $t$ and $F$ values (sig. at $p \geq .05$ level).

Further perusal of this table shows that females have a significantly greater preference for a workplace providing SS compared to males. Millennials in the highest age category—29–34 years—have significantly greater expectations of SS workplace as compared to the younger Millennials. Similar findings are seen in the case of work experience where those with longest work experience also show significantly higher preference for SS. Those from agriculture backgrounds show greater preference for SS at the workplace as compared to those from service and business backgrounds.

It may be concluded from this table that females, those in the older age group among the Millennials, those respondents with longer work experience and those who hail from agriculture backgrounds have a significantly greater preference for SS at the workplace. Educational background, family type, and place of upbringing have no significant impact on preference for SS.

## Conducive physical ambience (CPA)

Conducive physical ambience refers to a desire for a workplace with freedom to have breaks, flexible work timings and with good lighting and sense of space. Three of the seven demographics—age, prior work experience and parental occupation—have a strong impact on preference for CPA (see the significant $t$ and $F$ values in Appendix 3C Tables 3c.8a and 3c.8b).

The oldest among the three Millennials' categories (29–34 years) have the highest and significantly different preference on CPA as compared to the other two younger age categories. Those with the highest work experience (5–12 years) attach the maximum importance to CPA as compared to and those with lesser work experience. Respondents from an agriculture background attach significantly greater valence to CPA compared with people from business and service class backgrounds. Educational background, gender, family type, and place of upbringing have insignificant impact on preference for CPA.

It can be concluded that older Millennials, with greater work experience and an agriculture family background have significantly higher CPA expectation as compared to the other categories. Education, gender, family type, and place of upbringing have insignificant influence on CPA preference.

## Sharing and celebrating workplace (SC)

Sharing and celebrating refers to a workplace where success is celebrated and there is a trusting and open environment. Three of the seven demographic variables—educational background, age, and prior work experience—significantly influence preference for a sharing and celebrating workplace (see Appendix 3C, Tables 3c.9a and 3c.9b for $t$ and $F$ values). MBAs have a significantly higher preference for SC culture compared to those from engineering backgrounds. Millennials aged 23–28 years (unlike those with lesser or greater work experience) and have 3.1–5 years of work experience (rather than lesser or greater) also have a significantly higher preference for a sharing and celebrating work culture (SCC). The other variables do not significantly influence MOWP preferences.

## Techno-savvy (TS)

Techno-savvy refers to a workplace with modern equipment and latest technology which would facilitate efficient working. Only three of the seven demographic variables—educational background, age, and prior work experience—significantly influence the valence attached to techno-savvy workplace (see $t$ and $F$ values in Appendix 3C, Tables 3c.10a and 3c.10b).

Engineering graduates have significantly higher preference for a techno-savvy workplace, as compared to MBAs. Those who are older Millennials—29–34 years group—have a significantly higher preference for a techno-savvy workplace compared to the other age categories. Further, those with the highest work experience—5.1–12 years—attach significantly higher value to a TS workplace unlike those with lesser work experience. The other five demographic variables—gender, family type, parental occupation, and place of upbringing—have no significant impact on MOWP valence.

## Company's brand image

Company's brand image refers to the high prestige and brand value which high end organizations enjoy which in turn contribute to the status, prestige and influence which their employees enjoy in society.

Four of the seven variables—education, age, work experience, and place of upbringing—have a significant ($p \geq .05$ level) influence on preference to work in an organization with a strong brand image (see Appendix 3C, Tables 3c.11a and 3c.11b for the $t$ and $F$ tests). Perusal of the table clearly shows that MBAs have significantly high preference for a company with a strong brand image as compared to engineering graduates. Those who are in the highest age group—29–34 years—have significantly greater preference for working in a company with a strong brand image unlike those who are in the younger age groups—17–22 years and 23–28 years. The more experienced Millennials—5.1–12 years—attach the highest valence to company's brand image. Those brought up in eastern India have the highest preference for working in a high-brand company while those from central India and south India have significantly lower preference relatively speaking, although all the means are in the above average zone ranging from 3.47 to 3.77. Gender, family type and parental occupation have an insignificant influence on preference for a workplace with a powerful brand image.

## Fair and ethical (F&E) workplace

This factor refers to the valence attached to working in an organization which is ethical in dealings and believes in fairness and justice. Six of the eight demographic variables significantly (see Appendix 3C Tables 3c.12a and 3c.12b for the $t$ test and $F$ test values) influence the desire for a fair and ethical workplace. MBAs desire a F&E workplace to a significantly higher extent than Engineers. Respondents in the older age groups 23–28 and 29–34 years have a significantly higher preference for a F&E workplace, unlike those who are really young 17–22 years. Prior work experience significantly influences the valence attached to FE workplace as indicated by the higher mean values. In fact those with "Nil" work experience attach significantly lesser valence to F&E workplace. Respondents from service families attach a significantly greater value to a fair and ethical workplace in comparison with those from agriculture and business families. Upbringing of those in north, east, west and central India seems to make them attach greater value to F&E workplace as compared to those brought up in the south.

## Summary of influence of demographic factors on meaning of workplace

Table 3.2 presents the findings schematically: age, work experience, educational background, and parental occupation have been found to have a consistent and significant impact on MOWP total score as well as MOWP factors.

Further perusal brings out that the following demographic variables significantly influenced expectations of Millennials on some factors:

**Table 3.2 Influence of demographic variables on meaning of workplace**

| S. No. | Variable | MOWP | Entrepreneurial innovation | Process centricity with shared vision | Sense of security | Conducive physical ambience | Sharing and celebrating culture | Techno-savvy workplace | Company brand image | Ethical |
|---|---|---|---|---|---|---|---|---|---|---|
| 1. | Age | S | S | S | S | S | S | S | S | S |
| 2. | Prior work experience | S | S | S | S | S | S | S | S | S |
| 3. | Educational background | S | S | S | NS | NS | S | S | S | S |
| 4. | Gender | NS | NS | NS | S | NS | NS | NS | NS | NS |
| 5. | Parents' occupation | S | NS | S | S | S | NS | NS | NS | S |
| 6. | Family type | NS | S | S | NS | NS | NS | NS | NS | NS |
| 7. | Place of upbringing | NS | NS | NS | NS | NS | NS | NS | S | S |

*Notes*: N = 2158; see Appendix 3C for a detailed analysis of the data. S = Significant; NS = Not Significant.

- Gender—whether male or female—influenced sense of security;
- Family type—whether nuclear or joint—significantly influenced preference for entrepreneurial innovation, process centricity with shared vision and sense of community; and
- Place of upbringing—whether from the north, south, east, west or central—significantly influenced sense of community, company brand image and ethical preference.

At this juncture one may like to understand the rationale behind the dominant influence of age, work experience, educational background and parental occupation on MOWP. An attempt is now made to explain the findings. Such phenomena can be explained by understanding the human life cycle and how it shifts human priorities at the workplace, in the family as well as in society depending on stage in life. In fact Erik Erikson's (1950) theory of personality development emphasized the presence of stages in human life and the challenges each stage throws up and the shift in focus which takes place in human life. Increasing age and work experience go hand in hand with rising intensity of expectations of fulfillment of different kinds of needs from the workplace. Human beings get used to what they have gained and tend to look for more than what they have, and in this sense human expectations are like a moving target and continue to grow and expand. This means that as a certain set of needs get addressed, certain others get activated. It appears natural that Millennials in the higher age group and with greater work experience would attach higher valence to MOWP. Researchers have suggested that the influence of age on work attitudes is both normative and universal (Krau, 1989; Vander velde, Feiz, and Van Emmerick, 1998). The sample chosen for this study comprises engineers and MBAs. Those who go for an MBA degree are highly ambitious and hence it is not surprising that they have much higher expectations from the workplace as compared to engineers. It may be further mentioned that MBAs possess higher and additional qualifications and they tend to value their "worth" (monetary) in the industry much higher than engineers. When MBAs enter the workplace therefore they carry much greater expectations to the workplace. The logic of higher intensity of expectations of MOWP in the case of those from agricultural family backgrounds can be understood by examining the value profile and personality disposition. Individuals who get into higher education especially into elite professional education—engineering and MBA—from an agriculture background, would have great ambition, high achievement orientation and would have developed some outstanding capabilities of learning, observing and coping. This is because unlike their urban counterparts, they would not have experienced a supportive and facilitative environment to be able to reach this level. Their struggle and striving and ultimate mastery would boost their self-efficacy (Bandura, 1997) and self-confidence and understandably they would have much greater expectations from the workplace.

The impact of seven demographic variables—educational background, gender, family type, age, work experience, parental occupation, and place of upbringing on MOWP has been studied across: (a) MOWP total score and (b) total scores of each of the nine factors. Age, work experience, educational background, and parental occupation have been found to have a powerful and consistent impact on MOWP and MOWP factors. Other demographic variables do have some influence but it is not consistent across all the MOWP factors.

## Section 2: Impact of Personality and Values on MOWP[5]

This section brings out the influence of the two personality variables—locus of control and achievement orientation, four value factors, i.e., progressive, self-fulfillment, community, and personal growth—on MOWP using stepwise regression analysis. Stepwise multiple regression analysis (see Appendix 3D for the details of beta weights, $R^2$, significance levels, and percentage of variables explained and a technical write up) has been carried out using the six predictor variables mentioned above to explain the criterion variable—MOWP total score. Similar analysis (See Table 3D.13) has also been carried out using the six predictor variables and each of the nine MOWP factors (entrepreneurial innovation, process

---

[5] Demographic variables have not been entered in the Multiple Regression Analysis model because these are not on the interval (continuous) scale. Only continuous variables can be entered into MRA (Allison, 1977).

centric, sense of community, sense of security, conducive physical ambience, sharing and celebrating culture, techno-savvy workplace, company's brand image and ethical).

Analysis brings out that the first model using the six predictor variables on MOWP total score, explained 51 percent of the variance. The other nine models—using the nine MOWP factors—explained much lesser variance ranging from .39 to .13 adjusted R². Hence Model 1 is now discussed in detail below:

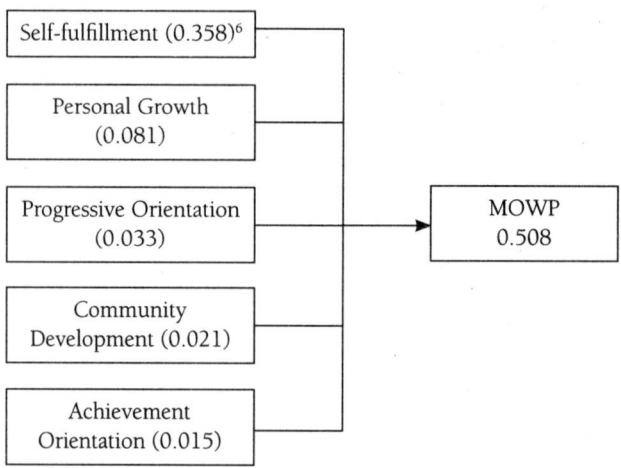

Figure 3.1 MOWP total score and six predictor variables

As Figure 3.1 reveals, the Stepwise Multiple Regression Analysis (MRA) has brought out that five of the six predictor variables—self-fulfillment value, personal growth, progressive orientation, community orientation, and achievement orientation—together explain MOWP expectation to the tune of 51 percent. Of the selected predictor variables, locus of control did not contribute to explain overall MOWP (total score). Thus it can be safely concluded that MOWP can be explained to a good extent by this figure—four value scores and one achievement score. It is interesting to note that bulk of the variance—44 percent—has been explained by two value factors, i.e., self-fulfillment and personal growth. Those with high self-fulfillment and high personal growth values would have high MOWP expectations.

---

[6] Beta value—percentage of total variance (adjusted R²) explained by each predictor variable.

In fact, this finding reinforces Chatman's (1991) research, which focused on values and brought out that the congruence of individual and organizational values predicts job satisfaction, organizational commitment, and tenure.

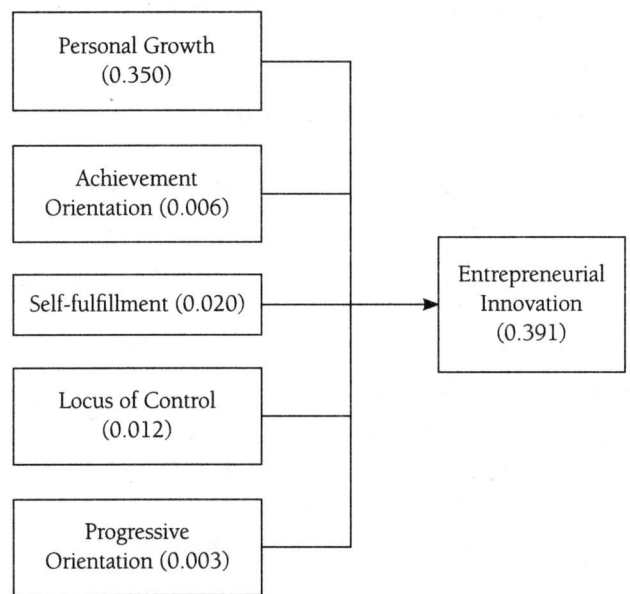

Figure 3.2  Entrepreneurial innovation and five predictor variables

In Figure 3.2, entrepreneurial innovation factor is explained to the tune of 39 percent by five personality variables: personal growth, achievement orientation, self-fulfillment, locus of control, and progressive orientation. Bulk of the variance however—36 percent—is explained by personal growth value and achievement orientation. Those who have the highest score on personal growth value and achievement orientation are the ones who have the highest expectation of entrepreneurial innovation from the workplace. Self-fulfillment, locus of control, and progressive orientation also help explain it. Thus, those Millennials who have higher personal growth, self-fulfillment, progressive orientation, achievement orientation, and internal locus of control score would be the ones with high expectations regarding entrepreneurial innovation.

## Summary and Conclusions

This chapter studied meaning of workplace from the Millennials' lens. This chapter also focused on identifying the influence of selected causal variables—background as well as personality variables on meaning of workplace. The salient findings are presented next.

### MOWP Preference of Millennials

Millennials demonstrate intense desire to work at an organization which is characterized by

- freedom for experimentation;
- opportunities to take initiatives and generate ideas and be innovative;
- fairness and transparency;
- performance centric reward system; and
- abundance of opportunity for learning, growth and self-development.

Factor analysis has thrown up the following nine MOWP factors: entrepreneurial innovation, process centricity with shared vision, sense of community, sense of security, conducive physical ambience, sharing and celebrating culture, techno-savvy workplace, company's brand image, and ethical.

- Of these nine factors, the most valued and preferred cluster of items is the first factor—entrepreneurial innovation which explained 53% of the variance. This indicates that Millennials value and look for organizations where entrepreneurial urge can be unleashed. In other words, they would like to work in an organization where they are empowered to take risk as well as experiment and innovate. They prefer to work in an organization where they have the freedom to express their ideas and voice their dissent.
- They prefer to work in the organization where there is equity, fairness, and justice especially with regard to performance–reward linkage.

- They would also like to work in an organization where they are given appropriate nurturing, support, and continuous feedback which helps them to blossom into leaders.
- The other factors mentioned above are also important. Relatively speaking however, each of them is much lesser in importance as compared to entrepreneurial innovation in explaining the meaning of workplace which the Millennials hold. In a nutshell it may be concluded that the major factor—entrepreneurial innovation—contains intrinsic work-related motivators. The remaining eight factors are primarily centering on hygiene factors interspersed with a few motivators.

In a nutshell it can be said that Millennials would not like to be associated with a workplace which is bureaucratic, mechanistic, hierarchical, status quoist, de-empowering, and non-entrepreneurial which is unfortunately still prevalent in a large number of Indian organizations creating mismatch and disconnect between the Millennials' expectations and existing workplace realities.

## Impact of Demographic Variables on MOWP

The impact of seven demographic variables—educational background, gender, family type, age, work experience, parental occupation, and place of upbringing have been studied on MOWP.

The influence of these factors has been studied across: (a) MOWP total score and (b) total scores of each of the nine factors (discussed earlier). The study revealed the following noteworthy conclusions:

- Age, work experience, educational background, and parental occupation have been found to have a powerful and consistent impact on MOWP and MOWP factors.
- Other demographic variables like place of upbringing, gender and family type do have some influence across all the MOWP factors. However the impact of these factors is not consistently found.
- Gender, family type, and place of upbringing did not significantly influence the overall MOWP total score.

- However these variables do significantly influence some of the MOWP factors.
- Gender—whether male or female—influenced sense of security.
- Family type—whether nuclear or joint—significantly influenced preference for entrepreneurial innovation, process centricity with shared vision, and sense of community.
- Place of upbringing—whether from the north, south, east, west, or central—significantly influenced preference for a workplace with a sense of community, strong company-brand-image and ethical orientation.

At this stage one may like to understand the rationale behind the dominant influence of age, work experience, educational background and parental occupation on MOWP. Such phenomena can be explained by understanding the human life cycle. Increasing age and work experience go hand in hand with rising intensity of expectations of fulfillment of different kinds of needs from the workplace. Human beings get used to what they have gained and tend to look for more than what they have, and in this sense human expectations are like a moving target continuously growing and expanding. This means that once a certain set of needs get addressed, certain other needs get activated. It appears natural that Millennials in the higher age group and with greater work experience would attach higher valence to MOWP.

The sample chosen for this study comprises engineers and MBAs. Those who go for an MBA degree are highly ambitious and hence it is not surprising that they have much higher expectations from the workplace as compared to engineers group in the sample. It may be further mentioned that MBAs possess higher and additional qualifications and they therefore tend to value their "worth" in the industry much higher than engineers. When MBAs enter the workplace therefore they carry much greater expectations to the workplace.

The logic of higher intensity of expectations of MOWP in the case of those from agriculture family backgrounds can be understood by examining their value profile and personality disposition. Individuals who get into higher education especially into elite professional education—engineering and MBA—from agriculture background, would have great ambition, high achievement orientation and would have developed some outstanding capabilities of learning, observing and coping. This is because unlike their urban counterparts, they would not have experienced a supportive and facilitative environment to be able to reach this level. Their struggle and striving and ultimate mastery would boost their sense of self-efficacy (Bandura, 1997) and self-confidence and therefore they would understandably have much greater expectations from the workplace.

## Impact of Personality and Values on MOWP

Six personality variables—self-fulfillment value, personal growth value, progressive orientation value, community orientation value, locus of control and achievement orientation—have been used to examine their impact on MOWP total score. MRA technique has been used to this end. The first model using the six personality variables explained 51% of the variance on MOWP total score.

The nine MOWP factors were examined using these six personality variables. Findings indicated that the predictive power of these personality variables is much lesser ranging from 0.39 to 0.13 adjusted $R^2$.

It may be concluded from the findings that people with high self-fulfillment value, high personal growth value, high progressive value, high community value and high achievement orientation have greater MOWP expectations.

# Appendix 3A: Rotated Component Matrix

**Table 3A.1 Meaning of workplace: Rotated component matrix**

| | \<br>Component | | | | | | | | |
|---|---|---|---|---|---|---|---|---|---|
| | 1 | 2 | 3 | 4 | 5 | 6 | 7 | 8 | 9 |
| Eigen Value | 11.37 | 2.72 | 2.36 | 1.93 | 1.75 | 1.38 | 1.28 | 1.25 | 1.07 |
| % of Variance | 23.205 | 5.559 | 4.807 | 3.946 | 3.57 | 2.819 | 2.618 | 2.549 | 2.186 |
| Cumulative % of Variance | 23.205 | 28.764 | 33.571 | 37.517 | 41.087 | 43.906 | 46.524 | 49.073 | 53.662 |
| Reliability | .86 | .69 | .67 | .74 | .61 | .64 | .70 | .59 | .54 |
| Mean | 4.08 | 3.63 | 3.55 | 3.85 | 3.39 | 3.91 | 3.68 | 3.65 | 4.09 |
| SD | .54 | .71 | .77 | .90 | .81 | .68 | .82 | .74 | .77 |

| Factors | Entrep. innovation | Process centricity | Sense of community | Sense of security | Physical ambience | Sharing and celebrating | Techno-savvy | Brand image | Ethical |
|---|---|---|---|---|---|---|---|---|---|
| No. of Items | 11 | 4 | 3 | 2 | 4 | 3 | 2 | 3 | 2 |
| provides opportunities to take initiatives | 0.723 | | | | | | | | |
| gives autonomy and freedom to express my views | 0.691 | | | | | | | | |
| encourages experimentation | 0.624 | | | | | | | | |
| is open to suggestions for improvement | 0.624 | | | | | | | | |
| encourages leadership development | 0.624 | | | | | | | | |
| recognizes contribution | 0.611 | | | | | | | | |
| provides opportunities for decision making | 0.546 | | | | | | | | |
| recognizes performance | 0.538 | | | | | | | | |
| encourages people to voice their concerns | 0.526 | | | | | | | | |
| encourages innovation and idea generation | 0.468 | | | | | | | | |

| Item | F1 | F2 | F3 | F4 | F5 | F6 | F7 | F8 | F9 |
|---|---|---|---|---|---|---|---|---|---|
| provides constructive feedback for my development | 0.453 | | | | | | | | |
| follow rules and regulations | | 0.685 | | | | | | | |
| brings discipline among its employees | | 0.679 | | | | | | | |
| requires working in a planned manner | | 0.597 | | | | | | | |
| has a well-defined "shared vision" | | 0.487 | | | | | | | |
| provides a platform for forming life-long relationships | | | 0.654 | | | | | | |
| provides sense of community | | | 0.61 | | | | | | |
| brings people closer | | | 0.583 | | | | | | |
| provides job security | | | | 0.752 | | | | | |
| reduces fear of losing job | | | | 0.731 | | | | | |
| gives freedom for many coffee breaks | | | | | 0.608 | | | | |
| is flexible with work timings | | | | | 0.594 | | | | |
| is well lit | | | | | 0.551 | | | | |
| has wide open spaces | | | | | 0.526 | | | | |
| celebrate success | | | | | | 0.633 | | | |
| encourages trust and transparency | | | | | | 0.59 | | | |
| has role clarity | | | | | | 0.52 | | | |
| has modern equipments to facilitate work | | | | | | | 0.763 | | |
| has latest technology | | | | | | | 0.678 | | |
| has high prestige | | | | | | | | 0.73 | |
| has a strong brand value | | | | | | | | 0.631 | |
| provides opportunities to influence others | | | | | | | | 0.531 | |
| is ethical in dealings | | | | | | | | | 0.641 |
| believes in fairness and justice | | | | | | | | | 0.522 |

*Note:* N = 2158; Extraction Method: Principal Component Analysis; Rotation Method: Varimax with Kaiser Normalization; Rotation converged in 15 iterations.

# Appendix 3B: Psychometric Properties of the Scales

**Table 3B.2a  Cronbach alpha values of the psychometric scales**

| S. No. | Scales | Items | Alpha value |
|---|---|---|---|
| 1. | Meaning of Workplace | 49 | .9255 |
| 2. | Values Scale | 25 | .9001 |
| 3. | Achievement Motivation | 9 | .5736 |
| 4. | Work Locus of Control | 16 | .7648 |
| 5. | Values factors | 4 | .7814 |

**Table 3B.2b  Inter-scale correlations**

| | MOWP | Achievement orientation | Locus of control | Self-fulfillment | Personal growth | Community development | Progressive orientation |
|---|---|---|---|---|---|---|---|
| MOWP | 1.000 | | | | | | |
| Achievement Orientation | .375** | 1.000 | | | | | |
| Locus of Control | .118** | .162** | 1.000 | | | | |
| Self-fulfillment | .598** | .242** | .102** | 1.000 | | | |
| Personal Growth | .560** | .343** | .220** | .531** | 1.000 | | |
| Community Development | .513** | .246** | .109** | .602** | .378** | 1.000 | |
| Progressive Orientation | .526** | .334** | .039 | .557** | .425** | .430** | 1.000 |

*Note:* ** Correlation is significant at the 0.01 level (2-tailed).

# Appendix 3C: Differences in MOWP by Background Factors

Table 3C.3a  Overall MOWP by selected demographic variables (*t* test)

| S. No. | Variable | Groups | N | Mean | SD | t | Sig. |
|---|---|---|---|---|---|---|---|
| 1. | Educational background | MBA | 920 | 3.79 | 0.42 | 3.47 | 0.00* |
|  |  | Engineering | 800 | 3.72 | 0.44 |  |  |
| 2. | Gender | Male | 1,702 | 3.76 | 0.44 | −1.06 | 0.29 |
|  |  | Female | 447 | 3.78 | 0.47 |  |  |
| 3. | Family Type | Nuclear | 1,496 | 3.77 | 0.44 | 1.33 | 0.18 |
|  |  | Joint | 651 | 3.74 | 0.44 |  |  |

Table 3C.3b  Overall MOWP by selected demographic variables (*F* test)

| S. No. | Variable | Groups | N | Mean | SD | F | Sig. |
|---|---|---|---|---|---|---|---|
| 1. | Age | 1) 17–22 yrs | 815 | 3.73 | 0.44 | 4.89 | 0.01* |
|  |  | 2) 23–28 yrs | 1,014 | 3.78 | 0.43 |  |  |
|  |  | 3) 29–34 yrs | 207 | 3.83 | 0.52 |  |  |

Tukey test shows that the mean of group 1 is significantly different from the mean of group 3. (See Table 3C.3c for details)

| 2. | Prior work experience | 1) Nil | 893 | 3.72 | 0.44 | 11.04 | 0.00* |
|---|---|---|---|---|---|---|---|
|  |  | 2) 3 Mo–3 yrs | 283 | 3.72 | 0.38 |  |  |
|  |  | 3) 3.1–5 yrs | 471 | 3.80 | 0.45 |  |  |
|  |  | 4) 5.1–12 yrs | 403 | 3.86 | 0.47 |  |  |

Tukey test shows that the mean of group 1 is significantly different from the mean of group 3 and 4 and the mean of group 2 is significantly different from the mean of group 4. (See Table 3C.3c for details)

| 3. | Parental occupation | 1) Service | 1,445 | 3.77 | 0.44 | 4.23 | 0.01* |
|---|---|---|---|---|---|---|---|
|  |  | 2) Agriculture | 150 | 3.84 | 0.43 |  |  |
|  |  | 3) Business | 462 | 3.72 | 0.45 |  |  |

The mean of group 2 is significantly different from the mean of group 3. (See Table 3C.3c for details)

| 4. | Place of upbringing | 1) North India | 808 | 3.76 | 0.44 | 0.72 | 0.58 |
|---|---|---|---|---|---|---|---|
|  |  | 2) South India | 436 | 3.76 | 0.46 |  |  |
|  |  | 3) Eastern India | 261 | 3.79 | 0.44 |  |  |
|  |  | 4) Western India | 318 | 3.76 | 0.42 |  |  |
|  |  | 5) Central India | 92 | 3.70 | 0.48 |  |  |

Tukey test shows that there are no significant differences in the means of the sub-groups of "place of upbringing" variable. (See Table 3C.3c for details)

*Note:* *The values are statistically significant at $p \geq 0.05$.

### Table 3C.3c  Overall MOWP by selected demographic variables (Tukey test)

| Dependent Variable | Background variable | Background variable (I) | Background variable (J) | Mean difference (I–J) | Std. error | Sig. |
|---|---|---|---|---|---|---|
| MOWP | Age | 1) 17–22 yrs | 3) 29–34 yrs | −9.70E-02 | 3.45E-02 | 0.01* |
|  |  | 3) 29–34 yrs | 1) 17–22 yrs | 9.70E-02 | 3.45E-02 | 0.01* |
|  | Prior work experience | 1) Nil | 3) 3.1–5 yrs | −7.99E-02 | 2.44E-02 | 0.01* |
|  |  |  | 4) 5.1–12 yrs | −0.11 | 3.26E-02 | 0.01* |
|  |  | 2) 3 Mo–3 yrs | 3) 3.1–5 yrs | −8.32E-02 | 3.22E-02 | 0.05* |
|  |  |  | 4) 5.1–12 yrs | −0.11 | 3.88E-02 | 0.02* |
|  |  | 3) 3.1–5 yrs | 1) Nil | 7.99E-02 | 2.44E-02 | 0.01* |
|  |  |  | 2) 3 mo–3 yrs | 8.32E-02 | 3.22E-02 | 0.05* |
|  |  | 4) 5.1–12 yrs | 1) Nil | 0.11 | 3.26E-02 | 0.01* |
|  |  |  | 2) 3 mo–3 yrs | 0.11 | 3.88E-02 | 0.02* |
|  | Parental occupation | 2) Agriculture | 3) Business | 0.12 | 4.17E-02 | 0.02* |
|  |  | 3) Business | 2) Agriculture | −0.12 | 4.17E-02 | 0.02* |
|  | Place of upbringing |  |  |  |  | No significant differences found |

Note: *The values are statistically significant at $p \geq 0.05$.

### Table 3C.4a  Entrepreneurial innovation factor by selected demographic variables (t test)

| S. No. | Variable | Groups | N | Mean | SD | t | Sig. |
|---|---|---|---|---|---|---|---|
| 1. | Nature of education | MBA | 920 | 4.13 | 0.52 | 4.51 | 0.00* |
|  |  | Engineering | 800 | 4.01 | 0.53 |  |  |
| 2. | Gender | Male | 1,702 | 4.08 | 0.53 | 0.33 | 0.74 |
|  |  | Female | 447 | 4.07 | 0.56 |  |  |
| 3. | Family type | Nuclear | 1,496 | 4.09 | 0.54 | 2.29 | 0.02* |
|  |  | Joint | 651 | 4.04 | 0.53 |  |  |

Note: *The values are statistically significant at $p \geq 0.05$.

**Table 3C.4b  Entrepreneurial innovation factor by selected demographic variables (F test)**

| S. No. | Variable | Groups | N | Mean | SD | F | Sig. |
|---|---|---|---|---|---|---|---|
| 1. | Age | 1) 17–22 yrs | 815 | 4.00 | 0.54 | 15.09 | 0.00* |
| | | 2) 23–28 yrs | 1,014 | 4.13 | 0.53 | | |
| | | 3) 29–34 yrs | 207 | 4.12 | 0.52 | | |
| | Tukey test shows that the mean of the group 1 is significantly different from the means of the 2 and 3 groups. (See Table 3C.4c for details) | | | | | | |
| 2. | Prior work experience | 1) Nil | 893 | 4.00 | 0.54 | 16.82 | 0.00* |
| | | 2) 3 Mo–3 yrs | 283 | 4.04 | 0.52 | | |
| | | 3) 3.1–5 yrs | 471 | 4.17 | 0.54 | | |
| | | 4) 5.1–12 yrs | 403 | 4.17 | 0.52 | | |
| | Tukey test shows that the mean of the group 1 is significantly different from the means of groups 3 and 4. The mean of the group 2 is significantly different from the means of the groups 3 and 4. (See Table 3C.4c for details) | | | | | | |
| 3. | Parental occupation | 1) Service | 1,445 | 4.09 | 0.53 | 2.32 | 0.10 |
| | | 2) Agriculture | 150 | 4.04 | 0.50 | | |
| | | 3) Business | 462 | 4.04 | 0.58 | | |
| | Tukey test shows that there are no significant differences in the means of the sub-groups of parental occupation variable. (See Table 3C.4c for details) | | | | | | |
| 4. | Place of upbringing | 1) North India | 808 | 4.07 | 0.52 | 1.22 | 0.30 |
| | | 2) South India | 436 | 4.03 | 0.57 | | |
| | | 3) Eastern India | 261 | 4.08 | 0.53 | | |
| | | 4) Western India | 318 | 4.11 | 0.53 | | |
| | | 5) Central India | 92 | 4.01 | 0.56 | | |
| | Tukey test shows that there are no significant differences in the means of the sub-groups of place of upbringing variable. (See Table 3C.4c for details) | | | | | | |

*Note:* *The values are statistically significant at $p \geq 0.05$.

Table 3C.4c  Entrepreneurial innovation factor by selected demographic variables (Tukey test)

| Dependent variable | Background variable | Background variable (I) | Background variable (J) | Mean difference (I-J) | Std. error | Sig. |
|---|---|---|---|---|---|---|
| Entrepreneurial innovation | Age | 1) 17–22 yrs | 2) 23–28 yrs | -0.13 | 2.51E-02 | 0.00* |
| | | | 3) 29–34 yrs | -0.12 | 4.16E-02 | 0.01* |
| | | 2) 23–28 yrs | 1) 17–22 yrs | 0.13 | 2.51E-02 | 0.00* |
| | | 3) 29–34 yrs | 1) 17–22 yrs | 0.12 | 4.16E-02 | 0.01* |
| | Prior work experience | 1) Nil | 3) 3.1–5 yrs | -0.17 | 3.01E-02 | 0.00* |
| | | 2) 3 mo–3 yrs | 3) 3.1–5 yrs | -0.14 | 3.98E-02 | 0.00* |
| | | 3) 3.1–5 yrs | 1) Nil | 0.17 | 3.01E-02 | 0.00* |
| | | | 2) 3 mo–3 yrs | 0.14 | 3.98E-02 | 0.00* |
| | Parental occupation | | | | | No significant differences found |
| | Place of upbringing | | | | | No significant differences found |

Note: *The values are statistically significant at $p \geq 0.05$.

**Table 3C.5a  Process centricity with shared vision factor by selected demographic variables (*t* test)**

| S. No. | Variable | Groups | N | Mean | SD | t | Sig. |
|---|---|---|---|---|---|---|---|
| 1. | Educational background | MBA | 920 | 3.59 | 0.71 | 1.03 | 0.30 |
|  |  | Engineering | 800 | 3.55 | 0.73 |  |  |
| 2. | Gender | Male | 1,702 | 3.63 | 0.70 | –0.55 | 0.58 |
|  |  | Female | 447 | 3.65 | 0.74 |  |  |
| 3. | Family type | Nuclear | 1,496 | 3.61 | 0.72 | –2.08 | 0.04* |
|  |  | Joint | 651 | 3.68 | 0.67 |  |  |

*Note:* *The values are statistically significant at $p \geq 0.05$.

**Table 3C.5b  Process centricity with shared vision factor by selected demographic variables (*F* test)**

| S. No. | Variable | Groups | N | Mean | SD | F | Sig. |
|---|---|---|---|---|---|---|---|
| 1. | Age | 1) 17–22 yrs | 815 | 3.56 | 0.73 | 15.38 | 0.00* |
|  |  | 2) 23–28 yrs | 1,014 | 3.62 | 0.69 |  |  |
|  |  | 3) 29–34 yrs | 207 | 3.86 | 0.70 |  |  |
|  | \multicolumn{7}{l}{Tukey test shows that the mean of the group 3 is significantly different from the means of the 1 and 2 groups. (See Table 3C.5c for details)} |
| 2. | Prior work experience | 1) Nil | 893 | 3.55 | 0.75 | 14.05 | 0.00* |
|  |  | 2) 3 Mo–3 yrs | 284 | 3.62 | 0.65 |  |  |
|  |  | 3) 3.1–5 yrs | 470 | 3.6 | 0.67 |  |  |
|  |  | 4) 5.1–12 yrs | 215 | 3.79 | 0.61 |  |  |
|  | \multicolumn{7}{l}{Tukey test shows that the mean of the group 4 is significantly different from the means of groups 1, 2 and 3. (See Table 3C.5c for details)} |
| 3. | Parental occupation | 1) Service | 1,445 | 3.62 | 0.69 | 11.79 | 0.00* |
|  |  | 2) Agriculture | 150 | 3.88 | 0.63 |  |  |
|  |  | 3) Business | 462 | 3.57 | 0.76 |  |  |
|  | \multicolumn{7}{l}{Tukey test shows that the mean of the group 1 is significantly different from the mean of group 2 and the mean of group 2 is also significantly different from the mean of group 3. (See Table 3C.5c for details)} |
| 4. | Place of upbringing | 1) North India | 808 | 3.62 | 0.69 | 0.55 | 0.70 |
|  |  | 2) South India | 436 | 3.62 | 0.76 |  |  |
|  |  | 3) Eastern India | 261 | 3.68 | 0.71 |  |  |
|  |  | 4) Western India | 318 | 3.62 | 0.70 |  |  |
|  |  | 5) Central India | 92 | 3.57 | 0.70 |  |  |
|  | \multicolumn{7}{l}{Tukey test shows that there are no significant differences in the means of the sub-groups of place of upbringing variable. (See Table 3C.5c for details)} |

*Note:* *The values are statistically significant at $p \geq 0.05$.

**Table 3C.5c  Process centricity with shared vision factor by selected demographic variables (Tukey test)**

| Dependent Variable | Background variable | Background variable (I) | Background variable (J) | Mean difference (I–J) | Std. error | Sig. |
|---|---|---|---|---|---|---|
| Process Centricity | Age | 1) 17–22 yrs | 3) 29–34 yrs | −0.30 | 5.49E-02 | 0.00* |
| | | 2) 23–28 yrs | 3) 29–34 yrs | −0.24 | 5.38E-02 | 0.00* |
| | | 3) 29–34 yrs | 1) 17–22 yrs | 0.30 | 5.49E-02 | 0.00* |
| | | | 2) 23–28 yrs | 0.24 | 5.38E-02 | 0.00* |
| | Prior work experience | 1) Nil | 4) 5.1–12 yrs | −0.24 | 5.32E-02 | 0.00* |
| | | 2) 3 Mo–3 yrs | 4) 5.1–12 yrs | −0.17 | 6.33E-02 | 0.04* |
| | | 3) 3.1–5 yrs | 4) 5.1–12 yrs | −0.18 | 5.77E-02 | 0.01* |
| | | 4) 5.1–12 yrs | 1) Nil | 0.24 | 5.32E-02 | 0.00* |
| | | | 2) 3 Mo–3 yrs | 0.17 | 6.33E-02 | 0.04* |
| | | | 3) 3.1–5 yrs | 0.18 | 5.77E-02 | 0.01* |
| | Parental occupation | 1) Service | 2) Agriculture | −0.26 | 6.04E-02 | 0.00* |
| | | 2) Agriculture | 1) Service | 0.26 | 6.04E-02 | 0.00* |
| | | | 3) Business | 0.32 | 6.62E-02 | 0.00* |
| | | 3) Business | 2) Agriculture | −0.32 | 6.62E-02 | 0.00* |
| | Place of upbringing | | | | | No significant differences found |

*Note:* *The values are statistically significant at $p \geq 0.05$.

**Table 3C.6a  Sense of community factor by selected demographic variables (t test)**

| S. No. | Variable | Groups | N | Mean | SD | t | Sig. |
|---|---|---|---|---|---|---|---|
| 1. | Educational background | MBA | 920 | 3.62 | 0.74 | 2.98 | 0.00* |
| | | Engineering | 800 | 3.51 | 0.79 | | |
| 2. | Gender | Male | 1,702 | 3.56 | 0.77 | 0.82 | 0.41 |
| | | Female | 447 | 3.52 | 0.76 | | |
| 3. | Family type | Nuclear | 1,496 | 3.58 | 0.77 | 2.50 | 0.01* |
| | | Joint | 651 | 3.49 | 0.76 | | |

*Note:* *The values are statistically significant at $p \geq 0.05$.

**Table 3C.6b  Sense of community factor by selected demographic variables (F test)**

| S. No. | Variable | Groups | N | Mean | SD | F | Sig. |
|---|---|---|---|---|---|---|---|
| 1. | Age | 1) 17–22 yrs | 815 | 3.57 | 0.77 | 2.88 | 0.06 |
|  |  | 2) 23–28 yrs | 1,014 | 3.56 | 0.74 |  |  |
|  |  | 3) 29–34 yrs | 207 | 3.43 | 0.92 |  |  |
|  | Tukey test shows that the mean of the group 1 is significantly different from the mean of group 3. (See Table 3C.6c for details) | | | | | | |
| 2. | Prior work experience | 1) Nil | 893 | 3.54 | 0.79 | 1.88 | 0.13 |
|  |  | 2) 3 Mo–3 yrs | 284 | 3.51 | 0.70 |  |  |
|  |  | 3) 3.1–5 yrs | 470 | 3.62 | 0.74 |  |  |
|  |  | 4) 5.1–12 yrs | 215 | 3.51 | 0.67 |  |  |
|  | Tukey test shows that there are no significant differences in the means of the sub-groups of prior work experience variable. (See Table 3C.6c for details) | | | | | | |
| 3. | Parental occupation | 1) Service | 1,445 | 3.54 | 0.76 | 6.64 | 0.01* |
|  |  | 2) Agriculture | 150 | 3.76 | 0.75 |  |  |
|  |  | 3) Business | 462 | 3.50 | 0.80 |  |  |
|  | Tukey test shows that the mean of the group 2 is significantly different from the mean of group 1 and 3. (See Table 3C.6c for details) | | | | | | |
| 4. | Place of upbringing | 1) North India | 808 | 3.50 | 0.77 | 5.33 | 0.00* |
|  |  | 2) South India | 436 | 3.67 | 0.75 |  |  |
|  |  | 3) Eastern India | 261 | 3.56 | 0.78 |  |  |
|  |  | 4) Western India | 318 | 3.47 | 0.77 |  |  |
|  |  | 5) Central India | 92 | 3.39 | 0.75 |  |  |
|  | Tukey test shows that the mean of the group 2 is significantly different from the mean of groups 1, 4 and 5. (See Table 3C.6c for details) | | | | | | |

*Note:* *The values are statistically significant at $p \geq 0.05$.

Table 3C.6c  Sense of community factor by selected demographic variables (Tukey test)

| Dependent variable | Background variable | Background variable (I) | Background variable (J) | Mean difference (I–J) | Std. error | Sig. |
|---|---|---|---|---|---|---|
| Sense of community | Age | 1) 17–22 yrs | 3) 29–34 yrs | 0.14 | 6.00E-02 | 0.05* |
| | | 3) 29–34 yrs | 1) 17–22 yrs | −0.14 | 6.00E-02 | 0.05* |
| | Prior work experience | | | | | No significant differences found |
| | Parental occupation | 1) Service | 2) Agriculture | −0.22 | 6.61E-02 | 0.00* |
| | | 2) Agriculture | 1) Service | 0.22 | 6.61E-02 | 0.00* |
| | | | 3) Business | 0.26 | 7.24E-02 | 0.00* |
| | | 3) Business | 2) Agriculture | −0.26 | 7.24E-02 | 0.00* |
| | Place of upbringing | 1) North India | 2) South India | −0.17 | 4.54E-02 | 0.00* |
| | | 2) South India | 1) North India | 0.17 | 4.54E-02 | 0.00* |
| | | | 4) Western India | 0.20 | 5.63E-02 | 0.00* |
| | | | 5) Central India | 0.28 | 8.76E-02 | 0.01* |
| | | 4) Western India | 2) South India | −0.20 | 5.63E-02 | 0.00* |
| | | 5) Central India | 2) South India | −0.28 | 8.76E-02 | 0.01* |

Note: *The values are statistically significant at $p \geq 0.05$.

Table 3C.7a  Sense of security factor by selected demographic variables (t test)

| S. No. | Variable | Groups | N | Mean | SD | t | Sig. |
|---|---|---|---|---|---|---|---|
| 1. | Educational background | MBA | 920 | 3.79 | 0.92 | −1.23 | 0.22 |
| | | Engineering | 800 | 3.84 | 0.90 | | |
| 2. | Gender | Male | 1,702 | 3.81 | 0.90 | −4.48 | 0.00* |
| | | Female | 447 | 4.03 | 0.89 | | |
| 3. | Family type | Nuclear | 1,496 | 3.85 | 0.91 | −0.32 | 0.75 |
| | | Joint | 651 | 3.87 | 0.89 | | |

Note: *The values are statistically significant at $p \geq 0.05$.

**Table 3C.7b** Sense of security factor by selected demographic variables (*F* test)

| S. No. | Variable | Groups | N | Mean | SD | F | Sig. |
|---|---|---|---|---|---|---|---|
| 1. | Age | 1) 17–22 yrs | 815 | 3.84 | 0.89 | 11.55 | 0.00* |
|  |  | 2) 23–28 yrs | 1,014 | 3.81 | 0.92 |  |  |
|  |  | 3) 29–34 yrs | 207 | 4.14 | 0.80 |  |  |
|  | Tukey test shows that the mean of the group 3 is significantly different from the mean of group 1 and 2. (See Table 3C.7c for details) | | | | | | |
| 2. | Prior work experience | 1) Nil | 893 | 3.87 | 0.90 | 10.86 | 0.00* |
|  |  | 2) 3 Mo–3 yrs | 283 | 3.74 | 0.90 |  |  |
|  |  | 3) 3.1–5 yrs | 471 | 3.74 | 0.90 |  |  |
|  |  | 4) 5.1–12 yrs | 403 | 4.05 | 0.87 |  |  |
|  | Tukey test shows that there are no significant differences in the means of the sub-groups of prior work experience variable. (See Table 3C.7c for details) | | | | | | |
| 3. | Parental occupation | 1) Service | 1,445 | 3.88 | 0.88 | 3.791 | 0.02* |
|  |  | 2) Agriculture | 150 | 3.94 | 0.88 |  |  |
|  |  | 3) Business | 462 | 3.76 | 0.96 |  |  |
|  | Tukey test shows that the mean of the group 1 is significantly different from the mean of group 3. (See Table 3C.7c for details) | | | | | | |
| 4. | Place of upbringing | 1) North India | 808 | 3.88 | 0.86 | 1.37 | 0.24 |
|  |  | 2) South India | 436 | 3.83 | 0.92 |  |  |
|  |  | 3) Eastern India | 261 | 3.93 | 0.85 |  |  |
|  |  | 4) Western India | 318 | 3.78 | 0.94 |  |  |
|  |  | 5) Central India | 92 | 3.83 | 0.95 |  |  |
|  | Tukey test shows that there are no significant differences in the means of the sub-groups of place of upbringing variable. (See Table 3C.7c for details) | | | | | | |

*Note:* *The values are statistically significant at $p \geq 0.05$.

Table 3C.7c  Sense of security factor by selected demographic variables (Tukey test)

| Dependent variable | Background variable | Background variable (I) | Background variable (J) | Mean difference (I-J) | Std. error | Sig. |
|---|---|---|---|---|---|---|
| Sense of security | Age | 1) 17–22 yrs | 3) 29–34 yrs | −0.3 | 6.97E-02 | 0.00* |
| | | 2) 3 Mo–3 yrs | 3) 29–34 yrs | −0.33 | 6.83E-02 | 0.00* |
| | | 3) 29–34 yrs | 1) 17–22 yrs | 0.3 | 6.97E-02 | 0.00* |
| | | | 2) 3 Mo–3 yrs | 0.33 | 6.83E-02 | 0.00* |
| | Prior work experience | | | | | No significant differences found |
| | Parental occupation | 1) Service | 3) Business | 0.12 | 4.81E-02 | 0.03* |
| | | 3) Business | 1) Service | −0.12 | 4.81E-02 | 0.03* |
| | Place of upbringing | | | | | No significant differences found |

Note: *The values are statistically significant at $p \geq 0.05$.

Table 3C.8a  Conducive physical ambience factor by selected demographic variables (t test)

| S. No. | Variable | Groups | N | Mean | SD | t | Sig. |
|---|---|---|---|---|---|---|---|
| 1. | Educational background | MBA | 920 | 3.36 | 0.77 | 0.31 | 0.75 |
| | | Engineering | 800 | 3.34 | 0.80 | | |
| 2. | Gender | Male | 1,702 | 3.38 | 0.82 | −1.14 | 0.25 |
| | | Female | 447 | 3.43 | 0.77 | | |
| 3. | Family type | Nuclear | 1,496 | 3.40 | 0.80 | 1.25 | 0.21 |
| | | Joint | 651 | 3.36 | 0.83 | | |

Table 3C.8b  Conducive physical ambience factor by selected demographic variables (*F* test)

| S. No. | Variable | Groups | N | Mean | SD | F | Sig. |
|---|---|---|---|---|---|---|---|
| 1. | Age | 1) 17–22 yrs | 815 | 3.39 | 0.78 | 7.69 | 0.00* |
|  |  | 2) 23–28 yrs | 1,014 | 3.35 | 0.78 |  |  |
|  |  | 3) 29–34 yrs | 207 | 3.60 | 1.05 |  |  |
|  | Tukey test shows that the mean of the group 3 is significantly different from the mean of group 1 and 2. (See Table 3C.8c for details) |||||||
| 2. | Prior work experience | 1) Nil | 893 | 3.36 | 0.79 | 10.62 | 0.00* |
|  |  | 2) 3 Mo–3 yrs | 283 | 3.23 | 0.74 |  |  |
|  |  | 3) 3.1–5 yrs | 471 | 3.42 | 0.79 |  |  |
|  |  | 4) 5.1–12 yrs | 403 | 3.57 | 0.91 |  |  |
|  | Tukey test shows that the mean of the group 1 is significantly different from the mean of group 4. The mean of the group 2 is significantly different from the mean of group 3 and 4 and the mean of the group 3 is significantly different from the mean of the (See Table 3C.8c for details) |||||||
| 3. | Parental occupation | 1) Service | 1,445 | 3.41 | 0.82 | 4.04 | 0.02* |
|  |  | 2) Agriculture | 150 | 3.51 | 0.73 |  |  |
|  |  | 3) Business | 462 | 3.31 | 0.80 |  |  |
|  | Tukey test shows that the mean of the group 2 is significantly different from the mean of group 3. (See Table 3C.8c for details) |||||||
| 4. | Place of upbringing | 1) North India | 808 | 3.40 | 0.85 | 1.72 | 0.14 |
|  |  | 2) South India | 436 | 3.44 | 0.78 |  |  |
|  |  | 3) Eastern India | 261 | 3.30 | 0.80 |  |  |
|  |  | 4) Western India | 318 | 3.37 | 0.77 |  |  |
|  |  | 5) Central India | 92 | 3.28 | 0.86 |  |  |
|  | Tukey test shows that there are no significant differences in the means of the sub-groups of place of upbringing variable. (See Table 3C.8c for details) |||||||

*Note:* *The values are statistically significant at $p \geq 0.05$.

Table 3C.8c  Conducive physical ambience factor by selected demographic variables (Tukey test)

| Dependent variable | Background variable | Background variable (I) | Background variable (J) | Mean difference (I-J) | Std. error | Sig. |
|---|---|---|---|---|---|---|
| Conducive physical ambience | Age | 1) 17–22 yrs | 3) 29–34 yrs | −0.21 | 6.32E-02 | 0.00* |
| | | 2) 3 Mo–3 yrs | 3) 29–34 yrs | −0.24 | 6.20E-02 | 0.00* |
| | | 3) 29–34 yrs | 1) 17–22 yrs | 0.21 | 6.32E-02 | 0.00* |
| | | | 2) 3 Mo–3 yrs | 0.24 | 6.20E-02 | 0.00* |
| | Prior work experience | 1) Nil | 4) 5.1–12 yrs | −0.26 | 5.98E-02 | 0.01* |
| | | 2) 3 mo–3 yrs | 3) 3.1–5 yrs | −0.19 | 5.92E-02 | 0.01* |
| | | | 4) 5.1–12 yrs | −0.38 | 7.12E-02 | 0.00* |
| | | 3) 3.1–5 yrs | 2) 3 Mo–3 yrs | 0.19 | 5.92E-02 | 0.01* |
| | | | 4) 5.1–12 yrs | −0.20 | 6.49E-02 | 0.01* |
| | | 4) 5.1–12 yrs | 1) Nil | 0.26 | 5.98E-02 | 0.00* |
| | | | 2) 3 mo–3 yrs | 0.38 | 7.12E-02 | 0.00* |
| | | | 3) 3.1–5 yrs | 0.20 | 6.49E-02 | 0.01* |
| | Parental occupation | 2) Agriculture | 3) Business | 0.19 | 7.63E-02 | 0.03* |
| | | 3) Business | 2) Agriculture | −0.19 | 7.63E-02 | 0.03* |
| | Place of upbringing | | | | | No significant differences found |

Note: *The values are statistically significant at $p \geq 0.05$.

Table 3C.9a  Sharing and celebrating culture factor by selected demographic variables ($t$ test)

| S. No. | Variable | Groups | N | Mean | SD | $t$ | Sig. |
|---|---|---|---|---|---|---|---|
| 1. | Educational background | MBA | 920 | 3.99 | 0.63 | 5.63 | 0.00* |
| | | Engineering | 800 | 3.81 | 0.70 | | |
| 2. | Gender | Male | 1,702 | 3.90 | 0.67 | −0.99 | 0.32 |
| | | Female | 447 | 3.94 | 0.73 | | |
| 3. | Family type | Nuclear | 1,496 | 3.92 | 0.66 | 1.16 | 0.25 |
| | | Joint | 651 | 3.88 | 0.72 | | |

Note: *The values are statistically significant at $p \geq 0.05$.

**Table 3C.9b  Sharing and celebrating culture factor by selected demographic variables (F test)**

| S. No. | Variable | Groups | N | Mean | SD | F | Sig. |
|---|---|---|---|---|---|---|---|
| 1. | Age | 1) 17–22 yrs | 815 | 3.84 | 0.69 | 9.05 | 0.00* |
| | | 2) 23–28 yrs | 1,013 | 3.97 | 0.67 | | |
| | | 3) 29–34 yrs | 207 | 3.84 | 0.72 | | |
| | Tukey test shows that the mean of the group 2 is significantly different from the mean of group 1 and 3. (See Table 3C.9c for details) | | | | | | |
| 2. | Prior work experience | 1) Nil | 893 | 3.82 | 0.69 | 10.52 | 0.00* |
| | | 2) 3 mo–3 yrs | 283 | 3.93 | 0.61 | | |
| | | 3) 3.1–5 yrs | 470 | 4.02 | 0.68 | | |
| | | 4) 5.1–12 yrs | 403 | 3.96 | 0.71 | | |
| | Tukey test shows that the mean of the group 1 is significantly different from the mean of group 3. (See Table 3C.9c for details) | | | | | | |
| 3. | Parental occupation | 1) Service | 1,445 | 3.91 | 0.69 | 0.09 | 0.92 |
| | | 2) Agriculture | 150 | 3.89 | 0.65 | | |
| | | 3) Business | 462 | 3.92 | 0.66 | | |
| | Tukey test shows that there are no significant differences in the means of the sub-groups of family background (parental occupation) variable. (See Table 3C.9c for details) | | | | | | |
| 4. | Place of upbringing | 1) North India | 808 | 3.84 | 0.70 | 2.16 | 0.07 |
| | | 2) South India | 436 | 3.91 | 0.71 | | |
| | | 3) Eastern India | 261 | 3.94 | 0.66 | | |
| | | 4) Western India | 318 | 3.96 | 0.63 | | |
| | | 5) Central India | 92 | 3.86 | 0.63 | | |
| | Tukey test shows that there are no significant differences in the means of the sub-groups of place of upbringing variable. (See Table 3C.9c for details) | | | | | | |

*Note:* *The values are statistically significant at $p \geq 0.05$.

**Table 3C.9c  Sharing and celebrating culture factor by selected demographic variables (Tukey test)**

| Dependent variable | Background variable | Background variable (I) | Background variable (J) | Mean difference (I-J) | Std. error | Sig. |
|---|---|---|---|---|---|---|
| Sharing and celebrating culture | Age | 1) 17–22 yrs | 2) 23–28 yrs | −0.13 | 3.21E-02 | 0.00* |
| | | 2) 23–28 yrs | 1) 17–22 yrs | 0.13 | 3.21E-02 | 0.00* |
| | | | 3) 29–34 yrs | 0.13 | 5.21E-02 | 0.04* |
| | | 3) 29–34 yrs | 2) 23–28 yrs | −0.13 | 5.21E-02 | 0.04* |
| | Prior work experience | 1) Nil | 3) 3.1–5 yrs | −0.20 | 3.85E-02 | 0.00* |
| | | 3) 3.1–5 yrs | 1) Nil | 0.20 | 3.85E-02 | 0.00* |
| | Parental occupation | | | | | No significant differences found |
| | Place of upbringing | | | | | No significant differences found |

*Note:* *The values are statistically significant at $p \geq 0.05$.

**Table 3C.10a  Technology savvy workplace factor by selected demographic variables (t test)**

| S. No. | Variable | Groups | N | Mean | SD | t | Sig. |
|---|---|---|---|---|---|---|---|
| 1. | Educational background | MBA | 981 | 3.59 | 0.83 | −3.60 | 0.00* |
| | | Engineering | 737 | 3.74 | 0.84 | | |
| 2. | Gender | Male | 1,702 | 3.69 | 0.83 | 1.58 | 0.12 |
| | | Female | 447 | 3.63 | 0.80 | | |
| 3. | Family type | Nuclear | 1,496 | 3.67 | 0.81 | −0.45 | 0.65 |
| | | Joint | 651 | 3.69 | 0.84 | | |

*Note:* *The values are statistically significant at $p \geq 0.05$.

**Table 3C.10b  Technology savvy workplace factor by selected demographic variables (F test)**

| S. No. | Variable | Groups | N | Mean | SD | F | Sig. |
|---|---|---|---|---|---|---|---|
| 1. | Age | 1) 17–22 yrs | 815 | 3.73 | 0.83 | 10.54 | 0.00* |
|  |  | 2) 23–28 yrs | 1,014 | 3.59 | 0.82 |  |  |
|  |  | 3) 29–34 yrs | 207 | 3.81 | 0.86 |  |  |
|  | Tukey test shows that the mean of the group 2 is significantly different from the mean of group 1 and 3. (See Table 3C.10c for details) | | | | | | |
| 2. | Prior work experience | 1) Nil | 893 | 3.73 | 0.85 | 10.05 | 0.00* |
|  |  | 2) 3 Mo–3 yrs | 283 | 3.49 | 0.83 |  |  |
|  |  | 3) 3.1–5 yrs | 471 | 3.59 | 0.79 |  |  |
|  |  | 4) 5.1–12 yrs | 403 | 3.78 | 0.80 |  |  |
|  | Tukey test shows that the mean of the group 1 is significantly different from the mean of group 2 & 3. The mean of the group 4 is significantly different from the mean of group 2 and 3. (See Table 3C.10c for details) | | | | | | |
| 3. | Parental occupation | 1) Service | 1,445 | 3.67 | 0.83 | 2.12 | 0.12 |
|  |  | 2) Agriculture | 150 | 3.81 | 0.77 |  |  |
|  |  | 3) Business | 462 | 3.66 | 0.82 |  |  |
|  | Tukey test shows that there are no significant differences in the means of the sub-groups of family background (parental occupation) variable. (See Table 3C.10c for details) | | | | | | |
| 4. | Place of upbringing | 1) North India | 808 | 3.71 | 0.82 | 1.09 | 0.36 |
|  |  | 2) South India | 436 | 3.65 | 0.81 |  |  |
|  |  | 3) Eastern India | 261 | 3.78 | 0.82 |  |  |
|  |  | 4) Western India | 318 | 3.71 | 0.78 |  |  |
|  |  | 5) Central India | 92 | 3.73 | 0.82 |  |  |
|  | Tukey test shows that there are no significant differences in the means of the sub-groups of place of upbringing variable. (See Table 3C.10c for details) | | | | | | |

*Note:* *The values are statistically significant at $p \geq 0.05$.

**Table 3C.10c  Technology savvy workplace factor by selected demographic variables (Tukey test)**

| Dependent Variable | Background Variable | Background Variable (I) | Background Variable (J) | Mean difference (I-J) | Std. error | Sig. |
|---|---|---|---|---|---|---|
| Technology Savvy Workplace | Age | 1) 17–22 yrs | 2) 23–28 yrs | 0.15 | 3.90E-02 | 0.00* |
| | | 2) 23–28 yrs | 1) 17–22 yrs | −0.15 | 3.90E-02 | 0.00* |
| | | | 3) 29–34 yrs | −0.23 | 6.32E-02 | 0.00* |
| | | 3) 29–34 yrs | 2) 23–28 yrs | 0.23 | 6.32E-02 | 0.00* |
| | Prior work experience | 1) Nil | 2) 3 Mo –3 yrs | 0.24 | 5.64E-02 | 0.00* |
| | | | 3) 3.1–5 yrs | 0.14 | 4.72E-02 | 0.02* |
| | | 2) 3 mo–3 yrs | 1) Nil | −0.24 | 5.64E-02 | 0.00* |
| | | | 4) 5.1–12 yrs | −0.32 | 7.49E-02 | 0.00* |
| | | 3) 3.1–5 yrs | 1) Nil | −0.14 | 4.72E-02 | 0.02* |
| | | | 4) 5.1–12 yrs | −0.22 | 6.82E-02 | 0.01* |
| | | 4) 5.1–12 yrs | 2) 3 mo–3 yrs | 0.32 | 7.49E-02 | 0.00* |
| | | | 3) 3.1–5 yrs | 0.22 | 6.82E-02 | 0.01* |
| | Parental occupation | | | | | No significant differences found |
| | Place of upbringing | | | | | No significant differences found |

Note: *The values are statistically significant at $p \geq 0.05$.

**Table 3C.11a  Company's brand image factor by selected demographic variables ($t$ test)**

| S. No. | Variable | Groups | N | Mean | SD | t | Sig. |
|---|---|---|---|---|---|---|---|
| 1. | Educational background | MBA | 920 | 3.67 | 0.71 | 2.37 | 0.02* |
| | | Engineering | 800 | 3.59 | 0.78 | | |
| 2. | Gender | Male | 1,702 | 3.65 | 0.74 | −0.11 | 0.91 |
| | | Female | 447 | 3.66 | 0.72 | | |
| 3. | Family type | Nuclear | 1,496 | 3.64 | 0.74 | −1.73 | 0.09 |
| | | Joint | 651 | 3.70 | 0.73 | | |

Note: *The values are statistically significant at $p \geq 0.05$.

**Table 3C.11b  Company's brand image factor by selected demographic variables (F test)**

| S. No. | Variable | Groups | N | Mean | SD | F | Sig. |
|---|---|---|---|---|---|---|---|
| 1. | Age | 1) 17–22 yrs | 815 | 3.63 | 0.76 | 6.10 | 0.00* |
| | | 2) 23–28 yrs | 1,014 | 3.65 | 0.71 | | |
| | | 3) 29–34 yrs | 207 | 3.82 | 0.78 | | |
| | Tukey test shows that the mean of the group 3 is significantly different from the mean of group 1 and 2. (See Table 3C.11c for details) | | | | | | |
| 2. | Prior work experience | 1) Nil | 893 | 3.62 | 0.76 | 5.46 | 0.00* |
| | | 2) 3Mo–3 yrs | 283 | 3.68 | 0.68 | | |
| | | 3) 3.1–5 yrs | 471 | 3.62 | 0.74 | | |
| | | 4) 5.1–12 yrs | 403 | 3.79 | 0.73 | | |
| | Tukey test shows that the mean of the group 4 is significantly different from the mean of group 1 and 3. (See Table 3C.11c for details) | | | | | | |
| 3. | Parental occupation | 1) Service | 1,445 | 3.66 | 0.74 | 1.09 | 0.34 |
| | | 2) Agriculture | 150 | 3.71 | 0.75 | | |
| | | 3) Business | 462 | 3.62 | 0.76 | | |
| | Tukey test shows that there are no significant differences in the means of the sub-groups of family background (parental occupation) variable. (See Table 3C.11c for details) | | | | | | |
| 4. | Place of upbringing | 1) North India | 808 | 3.73 | 0.72 | 5.46 | 0.00* |
| | | 2) South India | 436 | 3.60 | 0.77 | | |
| | | 3) Eastern India | 261 | 3.77 | 0.68 | | |
| | | 4) Western India | 318 | 3.65 | 0.72 | | |
| | | 5) Central India | 92 | 3.47 | 0.80 | | |
| | Tukey test shows that the mean of the group 1 is significantly different from the mean of group 2 and 5. The mean of group 2 is significantly different from the mean of group 3. The mean of the group 3 is significantly different from the mean of group 5. (See Table 3C.11c for details) | | | | | | |

*Note:* *The values are statistically significant at $p \geq 0.05$.

**Table 3C.11c  Company's brand image factor by selected demographic variables (Tukey test)**

| Dependent variable | Background variable | Background variable (I) | Background variable (J) | Mean difference (I–J) | Std. error | Sig. |
|---|---|---|---|---|---|---|
| Company's Brand Image | Age | 1) 17–22 yrs | 3) 29–34 yrs | −0.20 | 5.76E-02 | 0.00* |
| | | 2) 3 Mo–3 yrs | 3) 29–34 yrs | −0.18 | 5.64E-02 | 0.01* |
| | | 3) 29–34 yrs | 1) 17–22 yrs | 0.2 | 5.76E-02 | 0.00* |
| | | | 2) 3 Mo–3 yrs | 0.18 | 5.64E-02 | 0.01* |
| | Prior work experience | 1) Nil | 4) 5.1–12 yrs | −0.18 | 5.67E-02 | 0.01* |
| | | 3) 3.1–5 yrs | 4) 5.1–12 yrs | −0.19 | 6.15E-02 | 0.01* |
| | | 4) 5.1–12 yrs | 1) Nil | 0.18 | 5.67E-02 | 0.01* |
| | | | 3) 3.1–5 yrs | 0.19 | 6.15E-02 | 0.01* |
| | Parental occupation | | | | | No significant differences found |
| | Place of upbringing | 1) North India | 2) South India | 0.13 | 4.33E-02 | 0.02* |
| | | | 5) Central India | 0.26 | 8.02E-02 | 0.01* |
| | | 2) South India | 1) North India | −0.13 | 4.33E-02 | 0.02* |
| | | | 3) Eastern India | −0.18 | 5.71E-02 | 0.02* |
| | | 3) Eastern India | 2) South India | 0.18 | 5.71E-02 | 0.02* |
| | | | 5) Central India | 0.30 | 8.84E-02 | 0.01* |
| | | 5) Central India | 1) North India | −0.26 | 8.02E-02 | 0.01* |
| | | | 3) Eastern India | −0.30 | 8.84E-02 | 0.01* |

*Note:* *The values are statistically significant at $p \geq 0.05$.

**Table 3C.12a  Fair and ethical factor by selected demographic variables (t test)**

| S. No. | Variable | Groups | N | Mean | SD | t | Sig. |
|---|---|---|---|---|---|---|---|
| 1. | Educational background | MBA | 920 | 4.16 | 0.73 | 6.51 | 0.00* |
| | | Engineering | 800 | 3.92 | 0.83 | | |
| 2. | Gender | Male | 1,702 | 4.08 | 0.76 | −0.84 | 0.40 |
| | | Female | 447 | 4.11 | 0.77 | | |
| 3. | Family type | Nuclear | 1,496 | 4.08 | 0.78 | −0.66 | 0.51 |
| | | Joint | 651 | 4.10 | 0.75 | | |

*Note:* *The values are statistically significant at $p \geq 0.05$.

**Table 3C.12b  Fair and ethical factor by selected demographic variables (F test)**

| S. No. | Variable | Groups | N | Mean | SD | F | Sig. |
|---|---|---|---|---|---|---|---|
| 1. | Age | 1) 17–22 yrs | 815 | 3.92 | 0.81 | 28.56 | 0.00* |
| | | 2) 23–28 yrs | 1,014 | 4.18 | 0.74 | | |
| | | 3) 29–34 yrs | 207 | 4.19 | 0.64 | | |
| | Tukey test shows that the mean of the group 1 is significantly different from the mean of group 2 and 3. (See Table 3C.12c for details) | | | | | | |
| 2. | Prior work experience | 1) Nil | 893 | 3.91 | 0.81 | 27.58 | 0.00* |
| | | 2) 3 Mo–3 yrs | 283 | 4.18 | 0.70 | | |
| | | 3) 3.1–5 yrs | 471 | 4.22 | 0.75 | | |
| | | 4) 5.1–12 yrs | 403 | 4.23 | 0.68 | | |
| | Tukey test shows that the mean of the group 1 is significantly different from the mean of group 2, 3 and 4. (See Table 3C.12c for details) | | | | | | |
| 3. | Parental occupation | 1) Service | 1,445 | 4.12 | 0.75 | 4.03 | 0.02* |
| | | 2) Agriculture | 150 | 4.03 | 0.79 | | |
| | | 3) Business | 462 | 4.01 | 0.81 | | |
| | Tukey test shows that the mean of the group 1 is significantly different from the mean of group 3. (See Table 3C.12c for details) | | | | | | |
| 4. | Place of upbringing | 1) North India | 808 | 4.09 | 0.74 | 2.55 | 0.04* |
| | | 2) South India | 436 | 3.97 | 0.81 | | |
| | | 3) Eastern India | 261 | 4.07 | 0.80 | | |
| | | 4) Western India | 318 | 4.13 | 0.76 | | |
| | | 5) Central India | 92 | 4.01 | 0.83 | | |
| | Tukey test shows that the mean of the group 2 is significantly different from the mean of group 4. (See Table 3C.12c for details) | | | | | | |

*Note:* *The values are statistically significant at $p \geq 0.05$.

Table 3C.12c  Fair and ethical factor by selected demographic variables (F test)

| Dependent variable | Background variable | Background variable (I) | Background variable (J) | Mean difference (I-J) | Std. error | Sig. |
|---|---|---|---|---|---|---|
| Company's brand image | Age | 1) 17–22 yrs | 2) 23–28 yrs | −0.26 | 3.58E-02 | 0.00* |
| | | | 3) 29–34 yrs | −0.27 | 5.92E-02 | 0.00* |
| | | 2) 23–28 yrs | 1) 17–22 yrs | 0.26 | 3.58E-02 | 0.00* |
| | | 3) 29–34 yrs | 1) 17–22 yrs | 0.27 | 5.92E-02 | 0.00* |
| | Prior work experience | 1) Nil | 2) 3 Mo–3 yrs | −0.27 | 5.19E-02 | 0.00* |
| | | | 3) 3.1–5 yrs | −0.31 | 4.34E-02 | 0.00* |
| | | | 4) 5.1–12 yrs | −0.27 | 5.79E-02 | 0.00* |
| | | 2) 3 mo–3 yrs | 1) Nil | 0.27 | 5.19E-02 | 0.00* |
| | | 3) 3.1–5 yrs | 1) Nil | 0.31 | 4.34E-02 | 0.00* |
| | | 4) 5.1–12 yrs | 1) Nil | 0.27 | 5.79E-02 | 0.00* |
| | Parental occupation | 1) Service | 3) Business | 0.11 | 4.09E-02 | 0.02* |
| | | 3) Business | 1) Service | −0.11 | 4.09E-02 | 0.02* |
| | Place of upbringing | 2) South India | 4) Western India | −0.16 | 5.68E-02 | 0.04* |
| | | 4) Western India | 2) South India | 0.16 | 5.68E-02 | 0.04* |

Note: *The values are statistically significant at $p \geq 0.05$.

# Appendix 3D: Stepwise Multiple Regression Analysis

**Table 3D.1** Summary of stepwise multiple regression analysis with the dimensions of personality and values predicting the meaning of workplace

**Criterion variable: MOWP**

| S. No. | Predictor variables | β | t | p (exact) | Adj. R² | Overall F |
|---|---|---|---|---|---|---|
| 1. | Self-fulfillment | 0.235 | 10.677 | 0.00 | 0.358 | |
| 2. | Personal growth | 0.253 | 13.593 | 0.00 | 0.439 | $F_{(5,2152)} = 445.843$ |
| 3. | Progressive orientation | 0.170 | 8.919 | 0.00 | 0.472 | $p = .000$ |
| 4. | Community development | 0.170 | 8.839 | 0.00 | 0.493 | |
| 5. | Achievement orientation | 0.133 | 8.038 | 0.00 | 0.508 | |

**Criterion variable: Entrepreneurial innovation**

| S. No. | Predictor variables | β | t | p (exact) | Adj. R² | Overall F |
|---|---|---|---|---|---|---|
| 1. | Personal growth | 0.397 | 18.879 | 0.00 | 0.350 | |
| 2. | Achievement orientation | 0.135 | 7.291 | 0.00 | 0.356 | $F_{(5,2152)} = 277.508$ |
| 3. | Self-fulfillment | 0.143 | 6.491 | 0.00 | 0.376 | $p = .000$ |
| 4. | Locus of control | 0.116 | 6.654 | 0.00 | 0.388 | |
| 5. | Progressive orientation | 0.071 | 3.374 | 0.00 | 0.391 | |

**Criterion variable: Process centricity with shared vision**

| S. No. | Predictor variables | β | t | p (exact) | Adj. R² | Overall F |
|---|---|---|---|---|---|---|
| 1. | Community development | 0.332 | 15.586 | 0.00 | 0.195 | |
| 2. | Achievement orientation | 0.172 | 8.440 | 0.00 | 0.237 | $F_{(4,2153)} = 180.785$ |
| 3. | Progressive orientation | 0.097 | 4.362 | 0.00 | 0.247 | $p = .000$ |
| 4. | Personal growth | 0.068 | 3.116 | 0.00 | 0.250 | |

### Criterion variable: Sense of community

| S. No. | Predictor variables | $\beta$ | t | p (exact) | Adj. $R^2$ | Overall F |
|---|---|---|---|---|---|---|
| 1. | Self-fulfillment | 0.240 | 8.974 | 0.00 | 0.221 | |
| 2. | Community development | 0.214 | 9.159 | 0.00 | 0.259 | $F_{(5,2152)} = 165.057$ $p = .000$ |
| 3. | Progressive orientation | 0.108 | 4.660 | 0.00 | 0.270 | |
| 4. | Achievement orientation | 0.056 | 2.763 | 0.04 | 0.274 | |
| 5. | Personal growth | 0.055 | 2.445 | 0.01 | 0.276 | |

### Criterion variable: Sense of security

| S. No. | Predictor variables | $\beta$ | t | p (exact) | Adj. $R^2$ | Overall F |
|---|---|---|---|---|---|---|
| 1. | Self-fulfillment | 0.216 | 8.908 | 0.00 | 0.098 | |
| 2. | Progressive orientation | 0.192 | 7.951 | 0.00 | 0.124 | $F_{(3,2154)} = 109.873$ $p = .000$ |
| 3. | Locus of control | −0.089 | −4.418 | 0.00 | 0.132 | |

### Criterion Variable: Conducive Physical Ambience

| S. No. | Predictor variables | $\beta$ | t | p (exact) | Adj. $R^2$ | Overall F |
|---|---|---|---|---|---|---|
| 1. | Self-fulfillment | 0.353 | 14.458 | 0.00 | 0.220 | |
| 2. | Personal growth | 0.150 | 6.570 | 0.00 | 0.234 | $F_{(4,2153)} = 178.694$ $p = .000$ |
| 3. | Locus of control | −0.099 | −5.159 | 0.00 | 0.244 | |
| 4. | Progressive orientation | 0.077 | 3.607 | 0.00 | 0.248 | |

### Criterion variable: Sharing and celebrating culture

| S. No. | Predictor variables | $\beta$ | t | p (exact) | Adj. $R^2$ | Overall F |
|---|---|---|---|---|---|---|
| 1. | Self-fulfillment | 0.162 | 5.895 | 0.00 | 0.160 | $F_{(6,2151)} = 110.574$ $p = .000$ |
| 2. | Personal growth | 0.183 | 7.772 | 0.00 | 0.205 | |
| 3. | Community development | 0.107 | 4.442 | 0.00 | 0.216 | |
| 4. | Achievement orientation | 0.076 | 3.655 | 0.00 | 0.224 | |
| 5. | Locus of control | 0.082 | 4.196 | 0.00 | 0.229 | |
| 6. | Progressive orientation | 0.091 | 3.804 | 0.00 | 0.234 | |

### Criterion variable: Technology savvy workplace

| S. No. | Predictor variables | $\beta$ | t | p (exact) | Adj. $R^2$ | Overall F |
|---|---|---|---|---|---|---|
| 1. | Self-fulfillment | 0.080 | 2.745 | 0.01 | 0.085 | $F_{(6,2151)} = 61.658$ |
| 2. | Personal growth | 0.150 | 6.024 | 0.00 | 0.107 | $p = .000$ |
| 3. | Community development | 0.138 | 5.437 | 0.00 | 0.122 | |
| 4. | Achievement orientation | 0.105 | 4.776 | 0.00 | 0.131 | |
| 5. | Locus of control | 0.106 | 5.141 | 0.00 | 0.142 | |
| 6. | Progressive orientation | 0.062 | 2.468 | 0.01 | 0.144 | |

### Criterion variable: Company's brand image

| S. No. | Predictor variables | $\beta$ | t | P (exact) | Adj. $R^2$ | Overall F |
|---|---|---|---|---|---|---|
| 1. | Progressive orientation | 0.340 | 15.636 | 0.00 | 0.182 | $F_{(4, 2153)} = 143.428$ |
| 2. | Personal growth | 0.137 | 6.180 | 0.00 | 0.199 | $p = .000$ |
| 3. | Achievement orientation | 0.095 | 4.497 | 0.00 | 0.205 | |
| 4. | Locus of control | –0.071 | –3.593 | 0.00 | 0.209 | |

### Criterion variable: Ethical

| S. No. | Predictor variables | $\beta$ | t | p (exact) | Adj. $R^2$ | Overall F |
|---|---|---|---|---|---|---|
| 1. | Community development | 0.271 | 11.114 | 0.00 | 0.133 | $F_{(6,2151)} = 94.821$ |
| 2. | Locus of control | 0.170 | 8.557 | 0.00 | 0.177 | $p = .000$ |
| 3. | Personal growth | 0.141 | 5.875 | 0.00 | 0.197 | |
| 4. | Achievement orientation | 0.087 | 4.132 | 0.00 | 0.201 | |
| 5. | Progressive orientation | –0.096 | –3.964 | 0.00 | 0.205 | |
| 6. | Self-fulfillment | 0.070 | 2.517 | 0.01 | 0.207 | |

## Stepwise Multiple Regression Analysis

From Table 3D.1, it is clear that personality variables are found to be significant positive predictors of MOWP. The overall results as depicted in Figure 3.1 shows that personality had significant and positive impact on the perception of the organizational culture. Personality variables together explain 40% variances in the construct meaning of workplace.

## Regression Analysis

The results of MRA conducted on MOWP (overall) as well as the nine dimensions—entrepreneurial innovation, process centricity, sense of community, sense of security, conducive physical ambience, sharing and celebrating culture, techno-savvy workplace, company's brand and image and ethical—showed that overall stepwise regression was significant [$F_{(5,2152)}$ = 445.843, $p$ =.0000; $F_{(5,2152)}$ = 277.508, $p$ =.0000; $F_{(4,2153)}$ = 180.785, $p$ =.0000; $F_{(5,2152)}$ = 165.057, $p$ =.0000; $F_{(3,2154)}$ = 109.873, $p$ =.0000; $F_{(4,2153)}$ = 178.694, $p$ =.0000; $F_{(6,2151)}$ = 110.574, $p$ = .0000; $F_{(6,2151)}$ = 61.658; $F_{(4,2153)}$ = 143.428; $F_{(6,2151)}$ = 94.821, $p$ = .0000] respectively.

In the case of Entrepreneurial Innovation out of the six predictor variables, five variables were retained into the stepwise regression equation that explained 39% of variance in total (Adjusted $R^2$ = .391). The variables labeled self-fulfillment, personal growth, progressive orientation, achievement orientation and locus of control were found to be positive predictors of the criterion variable entrepreneurial innovation.

In the case of process centric, out of the six predictor variables, three variables were retained into the stepwise regression equation that explained 25% of variance in total (Adjusted $R^2$ = .250). Community, progressive orientation, personal growth, and achievement orientation were found to be the positive predictors of Process Centric factor.

In the case of Sense of Community, out of the six predictor variables, five variables were retained into the stepwise regression equation that explained 28% of variance in total (Adjusted $R^2$ = .276). Self-fulfillment, community development, progressive orientation, personal growth, and achievement orientation were found to be positive predictors of sense of community.

In the case of Sense of Security, out of the six predictor variables, three variables were retained into the stepwise regression equation that explained 13% of variance in total (Adjusted $R^2$ =.132). The variables labeled as self-fulfillment, progressive orientation, and locus of control were found to be the positive predictors of sense of security as the criterion.

In the case of Physical Ambience out of the six predictor variables, four variables were retained into the stepwise regression equation that explained .25% of variance in total (Adjusted $R^2$ = .248). The variables labeled as People Centricity was found to be the positive predictor of the criterion variable—physical ambience.

All six predictor variables—self-fulfillment, personal growth, community development, achievement orientation, locus of control and progressive orientation—have been retained in the stepwise regression to explain the criterion variable Sharing and Celebrating Culture. They cumulatively explain 23% of the variance (Adjusted $R^2$ = .234).

Techno-savvy factor of MOWP has through stepwise regression been explained using all six predictor variables: self-fulfillment, personal growth, community development, achievement orientation, locus of control and progressive orientation. However, they have together explained .14 of the criterion variable techno-savvy (Adjusted $R^2$ = .144).

Stepwise regression on the criterion variable Company Brand and Image using the six predictor variables resulted in resulted in four variables—Progressive Orientation, Personal Growth, Achievement Orientation and Locus of Control—cumulatively contributing to explain 21% of the explained variance (Adjusted $R^2$ = .209).

Stepwise multiple regression was conducted using Fair and ethical factor as the criterion variable using the six predictor variables and these together explained 21% of the variance (Adjusted $R^2$ = .207).

The Overall Meaning of Workplace (total score) has been explained by five independent variables—self-fulfillment, personal growth, progressive orientation, community development and achievement orientation—to the tune of 51% (Adjusted $R^2$ =.508). Two other models using process centricity and sense of community factors as the criterion variables have some explanatory power. The rest of the models explain too little of the variance to be useful.

# References

Allison, P. D. (1977). Testing for interaction in multiple regression. *The American Journal of Sociology, 83* (1), 144–153.

Allison, P. D. (1999). *Multiple regression: A primer*. Thousand Oaks, California: Pine Forge Press.
Amabile, T. M. (1996). *Creativity in context: Update to the social psychology of creativity*. Boulder, Colorado: Westview Press.
Bandura, A. (1997). *Self-efficacy: The exercise of control*. W. H. Freeman and Company.
Bretz, R. D., & Judge, T. A. (1994). Person-organization fit and the theory of work adjustment: Implications for satisfaction, tenure, and career success. *Journal of Vocational Behavior, 44*, 32–54.
Cable, D. M., & DeRue, D. S. (2002). The convergent and discriminant validity of subjective fit perceptions. *Journal of Applied Psychology, 87*, 875–884.
Caplan, R. (1983). Person-environment fit: Past, present and future. In C. Cooper (Ed.), *Stress research's issues for the eighties* (pp. 34–74). Chichester, England: Wiley.
Chatman, J. A. (1989). Improving interactional organizational research: A model of person-organization fit. *Academy of Management Review, 14* (Special Issue), 333–349.
Chatman, J. A. (1991). Matching people and organizations: Selection and socialization in public accounting firms. *Administrative Science Quarterly, 36*, 459–484.
Christiansen, N., Villanova, P., & Mikulay, S. (1997). Political influence compatibility: Fitting the person to the climate. *Journal of Organizational Behavior, 18*, 709–730.
Cummings, T. G., & Cooper, C. L. (1979). Cybernetic framework for studying occupational stress. Minneapolis, Minnesota: Minnesota Press.
Edwards, J. R. (1991). Person-job fit: A conceptual integration, literature review, and methodological critique. In C. L. Cooper & I. T. Robertson (Eds.), *International review of industrial and organizational psychology* (vol. 6, pp. 283–357). New York: Wiley.
Erikson, E. (1950). *Childhood and society*. New York: Norton.
French, J. R. P., Jr., Caplan, R. D., & Harrison, R. V. (1982). *The mechanisms of job stress and strain*. London: Wiley.
French, J. R. P., Jr., Rodgers, W., & Cobb, S. (1974). Adjustment as person-environment fit. In G. Coelho, D. Hamburg, & J. Adams (Eds.), *Coping and adaptation* (pp. 316–333). New York: Basic Books.
Hackman, J. R. (1980). Work redesign and motivation. *Professional Psychology, 11*, 445–455.
Harrison, R. V. (1978). Person-environment fit and job stress. In C. L. Cooper & R. Payne (Eds.), *Stress at work* (pp. 175–205). New York: John Wiley and Sons.
Hecht, T. D., & Allen, N. J. (2005). Person-job fit on the dimension of polychronicity: Examining links with well-being and performance. *Organizational Behavior and Human Decision Process, 98*, 155–178.
King, B. M., Rosopa, P. & Minium, E. W. (2010). Statistical reasoning in the behavioral sciences (6th ed.). New Jersey: John Wiley & Sons Inc.
Krau, E. (1989). The transition in life domain salience and the modifications of work values between high school and adult employment. *Journal of Vocational Behavior, 34*, 100–116.
Kristof, A. L. (1996). Person-organization fit: An integrative review of its conceptualizations, measurement, and implications. *Personnel Psychology, 49*, 1–49.
Kristof-Brown, A. L., Zimmerman, R. D., & Johnson, E. C. (2005). Consequences of individuals' fit at work: A meta-analysis of person-job, person-organization, person-group, and person-supervisor fit. *Personnel Psychology, 58*, 281–342.
Kulik, C. T., Oldham, G. R., & Hackman, J. R. (1987). Work design as an approach to person–environment fit. *Journal of Vocational Behavior, 31*, 278–296.
Locke, E. A. (1969). What is job satisfaction? *Organizational Behavior & Human Decision Processes, 4*, 309–336.

O'Neill, J. & Poddar, T. (2008). Ten things for India to achieve its 2050 Potential. *Global Economics Paper No: 169*, Goldman Sachs. GS Global Economic Website, Economic Research from the GS Institutional Portal. Retrieved from https://portal.gs.com

Ostroff, C., Shinn, Y. Y., & Kinicki, A. J. (2005). Multiple perspectives of congruence: Relationships between value congruence and employee attitudes. *Journal of Organizational Behavior, 26*, 591–623.

Porter, L. W. (1961). A study of perceived need satisfactions in bottom and middle management jobs. *Journal of Applied Psychology, 45*, 1–10.

———. (1962). Job attitudes in management: Perceived deficiencies in need fulfillment as a function of job level. *Journal of Applied Psychology*, December, 375–384.

Ryan, A. M., & Schmit, M. J. (1996). An assessment of organizational climate and P-E fit: A tool for organizational change. *The International Journal of Organizational Analysis, 4* (1), 75–95.

Schneider, B. (1987a). The people make the place. *Personnel Psychology, 40*, 437–453.

———. (1987b). E= f(P, B): The road to a radical approach to person-environment fit. *Journal of Vocational Behavior, 31*, 353–361.

Shalley, C. E., Zhou, J., & Oldham, G. R. 2004. The effects of personal and contextual characteristics on creativity: Where should we go from here? *Journal of Management, 30* (6): 933–958.

Singh, P., Bhandarker, A., Rai, S., & Jain, A. K. (2011). Relationship between values and workplace: An exploratory analysis, *Facilities, 29* (11/12).

Spokane, A. R., Meir, E. I., & Catalano, M. (2000). Person-environment congruence and Holland's theory: A review and reconsideration. *Journal of Vocational Behavior, 57*, 137–187.

Tinsley, H. A. (2000). The congruence myth: An analysis of the efficacy of person-environment fit model, *Journal of Vocational Behavior, 56*, 147–179.

Tom, V. R. (1971). The role of personality and organizational images in the recruiting process. *Organizational Behavior and Human Performance, 6*, 573–592.

Van der Velde, M., Feiz, J., & Van Emmerick, H. (1998). Change in work values and norms among Dutch young adults: Ageing or societal trends? *International Journal of Behavioral Development, 22* (1), 55–76.

Verquer, M. L., Beehr, T. A., & Wagner, S. H. 2003. A meta-analysis of relations between person-organization fit and work attitudes. *Journal of Vocational Behavior, 63*, 473–489.

Zhang, X. M., & Bartol, K. M. (2010). Linking empowering leadership and employee creativity: The influence of psychological empowerment, intrinsic motivation, and creative process engagement. *Academy of Management Journal, 53* (1), 107–128.

# Meaning of Workplace

**4**

## Expectations vs Reality of Workplace Attributes

This chapter is designed to identify the extent of gap between MOWP expectations and availability of the same in the industry. Such an analysis is critical since the extent of match/mismatch will have a powerful impact on Millennials' predisposition, attitudes, and workplace behaviors. Greater congruence between expectations and reality results in higher motivation, involvement, commitment, and engagement (Dansereau, Graen, and Haga, 1975; Dienesch and Liden, 1986; Graen and Cashman, 1975; Graen and Schiemann, 1978). In contrast, the weaker the match between expectations and reality, the higher will be the levels of demoralization, dissatisfaction and consequently lower involvement, engagement, and desire to stay (Dansereau et al., 1975; Dienesch and Liden, 1986; Liden and Graen, 1980; Gerstner and Day, 1997). P-E fit has been connected with stress disorders, low job satisfaction, and other occupational dependent variables (Holland, 1985, 73; Furnham and Schaeffer, 1984). A recent study of Indian software professionals brought out that turnover is particularly high among the young newcomers (Ng and Feldman 09).

Another important factor of Millennials' workplace expectations which is presented here is their relationship with the immediate boss/senior/

supervisor.[1] In fact research (Dansereau et al., 1975; Graen, 1976; Graen and Scandura, 1987; Gerstner and Day, 1997; Ferris, 1985; Graen, Liden, and Hoel, 1982) seems to suggest that this relationship influences one's attitude towards the organization especially the intent to leave.

One of the important outcomes of gap between expectations and reality—intent to leave—has also been examined in this work, in order to understand the key push factors predisposing Millennials to look out for opportunities to move to other jobs. A recent study (Yiu and Saner, 2011) on Indian organizations brought out that there has been a rise in turnover across all categories of employees regardless of professional qualifications with younger people and highly qualified persons changing jobs more often. Knowledge workers (engineers, researchers, and professionals) exhibited the highest tendency for voluntary job change (between 10 and 20 percent) across different categories of employees. Further it was found that the highest turnover occurred between 1 and 4 years of employment. Findings bring out that the major cause of turnover refers to the relationship between the employee and the direct supervisor/boss. Relationship with the boss followed by lack of recognition is among the top four reasons for changing jobs along with salary and career advancement. Participation in decision making by the employees has been cited by the sample as the major requirement to help reduce turnover rates.

Perceptions of HR professionals regarding the Millennials have also been examined in this chapter. This data has been gathered because HR professionals are key actors at the workplace in influencing and developing policies related to employees at the workplace.

This chapter is presented in three parts.

Part 1 examines the expectations of the millennials from the workplace, their experience of workplace realities, and the gap between the two.

Part 2 brings out the findings on two work related attitudes: (a) expectations which people have from their immediate supervisor; and (b) intent to leave the organization.

Part 3 highlights the findings regarding perception of Millennials through the lens of the HR professionals.

---

[1] These terms have been used interchangeably.

## Part 1: Expectations of Millennials from the Workplace, Availability, and Gap

Part 1 presents:

- Expectations of Millennials from the workplace, availability and the gap between expectations and availability (quantitative data).
- Expectations from the workplace—insights from interview data.
- Comparisons of questionnaire and interview data on expectations of Millennials regarding workplace attributes.
- Comparisons of questionnaire and interview data on availability of desired workplace attributes.

## Expectations of Millennials from the Workplace, Availability, and Gap

As discussed in Chapter 3, the salient points which emerge at the top in MOWP expectations (Table 4.1) are the following:

- Millennials crave for a workplace which provides freedom for experimentation, offers opportunities to take initiatives, and encourages idea generation and innovation.
- Millennials also desire to work in a place where their performance and contribution are amply recognized and rewarded.
- Fairness and transparency are important attractors for Millennials to join an organization.
- Millennials would like to embrace a workplace where there is plenty of opportunity for learning, growth, and development.

The findings on meaning of workplace of Millennials have been reiterated here in order to facilitate comparison with findings on availability of factors at the workplace, as experienced by Millennials with work experience (Table 4.2).

Table 4.2 shows the availability of workplace characteristics as experienced by the Millennials sample (567). Perusal of the top ten work-related elements brings out the following:

**Table 4.1  Means and standard deviations of MOWP items (expectations)**

| S. No. | Items | Mean | SD |
|---|---|---|---|
| 1. | Encourages innovation and idea generation | 4.26 | 0.83 |
| 2. | Recognizes performance | 4.25 | 0.76 |
| 3. | Believes in fairness and justice | 4.19 | 0.88 |
| 4. | Recognizes contribution | 4.19 | 0.82 |
| 5. | Provides opportunities for personality development | 4.19 | 0.83 |
| 6. | Encourages learning | 4.16 | 0.82 |
| 7. | Provides opportunities to take initiatives | 4.15 | 0.81 |
| 8. | Gives autonomy and freedom to express my views | 4.14 | 0.81 |
| 9. | Encourages leadership development | 4.14 | 0.82 |
| 10. | Encourages trust and transparency | 4.11 | 0.85 |
| 11. | Values work–life balance | 4.11 | 0.91 |
| 12. | Provides constructive feedback for my development | 4.05 | 0.86 |
| 13. | Encourages team work | 4.04 | 0.87 |
| 14. | Is open to suggestions for improvement | 4.03 | 0.83 |
| 15. | Provides opportunities for decision making | 4.02 | 0.76 |
| 16. | Helps me earn respect from society | 3.98 | 0.92 |
| 17. | Is ethical in dealings | 3.98 | 0.97 |
| 18. | Cares about physical and mental health of its employees | 3.97 | 0.85 |
| 19. | Has role clarity | 3.93 | 0.89 |
| 20. | Empowers people | 3.91 | 0.89 |
| 21. | Takes care of financial needs | 3.90 | 0.97 |
| 22. | Provides job security | 3.88 | 1.02 |
| 23. | Reduces fear of losing job | 3.83 | 1.01 |
| 24. | Encourages people to voice their concerns | 3.82 | 0.85 |
| 25. | Encourages experimentation | 3.79 | 0.91 |
| 26. | Has a strong brand value | 3.75 | 1.04 |
| 27. | Has high prestige | 3.74 | 0.94 |
| 28. | Has latest technology | 3.72 | 0.96 |
| 29. | Celebrate success | 3.68 | 0.96 |
| 30. | Is flexible with work timings | 3.67 | 1.09 |
| 31. | Follow rules and regulations | 3.65 | 0.99 |
| 32. | Has a well-defined "shared vision" | 3.63 | 0.93 |
| 33. | Has modern equipments to facilitate work | 3.63 | 0.92 |
| 34. | Brings discipline among its employees | 3.62 | 1.03 |
| 35. | Requires working in a planned manner | 3.61 | 0.99 |
| 36. | Contributes to the economy of the country | 3.60 | 1.02 |
| 37. | Provides sense of community | 3.58 | 0.95 |
| 38. | Provides a platform for forming life long relationships | 3.57 | 1.02 |
| 39. | Takes initiatives for planned change | 3.53 | 0.92 |
| 40. | Has a green environment (trees, etc.) | 3.52 | 1.12 |
| 41. | Brings people closer | 3.50 | 0.99 |
| 42. | Provides opportunities to influence others | 3.47 | 1.02 |
| 43. | Provides opportunity for social networking | 3.44 | 1.04 |
| 44. | Provides opportunity to exercise power | 3.32 | 1.03 |
| 45. | Is well lit | 3.31 | 1.04 |

*Table 4.1 continued*

*Table 4.1 continued*

| S. No. | Items | Mean | SD |
|---|---|---|---|
| 46. | Is conveniently located from my residence | 3.19 | 1.21 |
| 47. | Has wide open spaces | 3.18 | 1.11 |
| 48. | Gives freedom for many coffee breaks | 2.77 | 1.24 |
| 49. | Has a crèche | 2.66 | 1.17 |

Notes: N = 2158; SD = Standard Deviation.

**Table 4.2 Means and standard deviations of MOWP items (availability)**

| S. No. | Items | Mean | SD |
|---|---|---|---|
| 1. | Has a strong brand value | 4.29 | 0.93 |
| 2. | Gives freedom for many coffee breaks | 4.19 | 1.04 |
| 3. | Is well lit | 4.18 | 0.82 |
| 4. | Has modern equipments to facilitate work | 4.05 | 0.89 |
| 5. | Has high prestige | 3.97 | 0.89 |
| 6. | Is ethical in dealings | 3.91 | 1.15 |
| 7. | Has latest technology | 3.89 | 1.00 |
| 8. | Follows rules and regulations | 3.86 | 0.88 |
| 9. | Encourages team work | 3.86 | 0.89 |
| 10. | Contributes to the economy of the country | 3.79 | 0.97 |
| 11. | Provides job security | 3.78 | 1.17 |
| 12. | Encourages learning | 3.78 | 0.88 |
| 13. | Celebrates success | 3.75 | 0.88 |
| 14. | Helps me to earn respect from society | 3.73 | 0.86 |
| 15. | Reduces fear of losing job | 3.67 | 1.13 |
| 16. | Provides a sense of community | 3.62 | 0.98 |
| 17. | Gives autonomy and freedom to express my views | 3.56 | 0.99 |
| 18. | Provides opportunities for personality development | 3.55 | 0.93 |
| 19. | Is flexible with work timings | 3.53 | 1.44 |
| 20. | Requires working in a planned manner | 3.53 | 0.91 |
| 21. | Recognizes contribution | 3.51 | 0.98 |
| 22. | Brings people closer | 3.51 | 0.94 |
| 23. | Has wide open spaces | 3.50 | 1.18 |
| 24. | Provides opportunities to take initiatives | 3.49 | 0.96 |
| 25. | Encourages trust and transparency | 3.49 | 1.02 |
| 26. | Encourages innovation and idea generation | 3.46 | 1.00 |
| 27. | Believes in fairness and justice | 3.45 | 1.05 |
| 28. | Recognizes performance | 3.45 | 1.00 |
| 29. | Is open to suggestions for improvement | 3.42 | 0.94 |
| 30. | Cares about physical and mental health of its employees | 3.42 | 1.10 |
| 31. | Has a well defined "shared vision" | 3.41 | 1.03 |
| 32. | Has role clarity | 3.39 | 1.00 |
| 33. | Encourages leadership development | 3.39 | 0.93 |
| 34. | Encourages people to voice their concerns | 3.37 | 0.99 |

*Table 4.1 continued*

| S. No. | Items | Mean | SD |
|---|---|---|---|
| 35. | Provides a platform for forming lifelong relationships | 3.34 | 1.15 |
| 36. | Brings discipline among its employees | 3.33 | 0.99 |
| 37. | Provides opportunity for social networking | 3.30 | 1.12 |
| 38. | Has a green environment (trees, etc) | 3.30 | 1.38 |
| 39. | Provides constructive feedback for my development | 3.30 | 1.13 |
| 40. | Takes initiatives for planned change | 3.30 | 0.87 |
| 41. | Empowers people | 3.30 | 0.91 |
| 42. | Takes care of financial needs | 3.26 | 1.10 |
| 43. | Provides opportunities to influence others | 3.24 | 0.95 |
| 44. | Values work–life balance | 3.22 | 1.25 |
| 45. | Provides opportunities for decision-making | 3.20 | 1.00 |
| 46. | Is conveniently located from my residence | 3.18 | 1.44 |
| 47. | Provides opportunity to exercise power | 3.03 | 0.99 |
| 48. | Encourages experimentation | 3.02 | 1.00 |
| 49. | Has a crèche | 2.05 | 1.30 |

*Note:* N = 567 students (with at least two years of work experience).

- They work with companies that have strong brand value; where the physical ambience of the workplace is good (well lit, modern equipment, latest technology) and there is freedom for coffee breaks.
- They also work for high prestige companies, which are ethical in dealings, follow rules and regulations and contribute to the economy.
- They have also experienced good team work.

Table 4.3 compares the two sets of ranks and brings out that there is a significant difference between what is expected at the workplace and what is available at the workplace. Comparison of the top fifteen items across the two groups clearly brings out the large gap which exists between expectations and actual availability of desired attributes at the workplace.

A comparison of the top 15 expectations versus available MOWP attributes (Table 4.3) brings out the following picture:

- The two rank sets are significantly different from each other as indicated by the rho value of 0.07.[2] Clearly there is a gap between what people look for at the workplace and what they actually get.

---

[2] Spearman rank coefficient of correlation = .07 not significant at table value .36 ≥ 0.05 level, indicating that the two rank sets are significantly different from each other (Glenberg and Andrzejewski, 2008: 541).

Table 4.3 Means and standard deviations of MOWP items (expectations and availability)

| S. No. | Item | MOWP expectations mean | MOWP expectations SD | Rank | MOWP availability mean | MOWP availability SD | Rank |
|---|---|---|---|---|---|---|---|
| 1. | Encourages innovation and idea generation | 4.26 | 0.83 | 1 | 3.46 | 1.00 | 26 |
| 2. | Recognizes performance | 4.25 | 0.76 | 2 | 3.45 | 1.00 | 28 |
| 3. | Believes in fairness and justice | 4.19 | 0.88 | 3 | 3.45 | 1.05 | 27 |
| 4. | Recognizes contribution | 4.19 | 0.82 | 4 | 3.51 | 0.98 | 21 |
| 5. | Provides opportunities for personality development | 4.19 | 0.83 | 5 | 3.55 | 0.93 | 18 |
| 6. | Encourages learning | 4.16 | 0.82 | 6 | 3.78 | 0.88 | 12 |
| 7. | Provides opportunities to take initiatives | 4.15 | 0.81 | 7 | 3.49 | 0.96 | 24 |
| 8. | Gives autonomy and freedom to express my views | 4.14 | 0.81 | 8 | 3.56 | 0.99 | 17 |
| 9. | Encourages leadership development | 4.14 | 0.82 | 9 | 3.39 | 0.93 | 33 |
| 10. | Encourages trust and transparency | 4.11 | 0.85 | 10 | 3.49 | 1.02 | 25 |
| 11. | Values work–life balance | 4.11 | 0.91 | 11 | 3.22 | 1.25 | 44 |
| 12. | Provides constructive feedback for my development | 4.05 | 0.86 | 12 | 3.30 | 1.13 | 39 |
| 13. | Encourages team work | 4.04 | 0.87 | 13 | 3.86 | 0.89 | 9 |
| 14. | Is open to suggestions for improvement | 4.03 | 0.83 | 14 | 3.42 | 0.94 | 29 |
| 15. | Provides opportunities for decision making | 4.02 | 0.76 | 15 | 3.20 | 1.00 | 45 |
| 16. | Helps me earn respect from society | 3.98 | 0.92 | 16 | 3.73 | 0.86 | 14 |
| 17. | Is ethical in dealings | 3.98 | 0.97 | 17 | 3.91 | 1.15 | 6 |
| 18. | Cares about physical and mental health of its employees | 3.97 | 0.85 | 18 | 3.42 | 1.10 | 30 |
| 19. | Has role clarity | 3.93 | 0.89 | 19 | 3.39 | 1.00 | 32 |
| 20. | Empowers people | 3.91 | 0.89 | 20 | 3.30 | 0.91 | 41 |
| 21. | Takes care of financial needs | 3.90 | 0.97 | 21 | 3.26 | 1.10 | 42 |
| 22. | Provides job security | 3.88 | 1.02 | 22 | 3.78 | 1.17 | 11 |

|  |  |  |  |  |  |  |
|---|---|---|---|---|---|---|
| 23. | Reduces fear of losing job | 3.83 | 1.01 | 23 | 3.67 | 1.13 | 15 |
| 24. | Encourages people to voice their concerns | 3.82 | 0.85 | 24 | 3.37 | 0.99 | 34 |
| 25. | Encourages experimentation | 3.79 | 0.91 | 25 | 3.02 | 1.00 | 48 |
| 26. | Has a strong brand value | 3.75 | 1.04 | 26 | 4.29 | 0.93 | 1 |
| 27. | Has high prestige | 3.74 | 0.94 | 27 | 3.97 | 0.89 | 5 |
| 28. | Has latest technology | 3.72 | 0.96 | 28 | 3.89 | 1.00 | 7 |
| 29. | Celebrate success | 3.68 | 0.96 | 29 | 3.75 | 0.88 | 13 |
| 30. | Is flexible with work timings | 3.67 | 1.09 | 30 | 3.53 | 1.44 | 19 |
| 31. | Follow rules and regulations | 3.65 | 0.99 | 31 | 3.86 | 0.88 | 8 |
| 32. | Has a well-defined "shared vision" | 3.63 | 0.93 | 32 | 3.41 | 1.03 | 31 |
| 33. | Has modern equipments to facilitate work | 3.63 | 0.92 | 33 | 4.05 | 0.89 | 4 |
| 34. | Brings discipline among its employees | 3.62 | 1.03 | 34 | 3.33 | 0.99 | 36 |
| 35. | Requires working in a planned manner | 3.61 | 0.99 | 35 | 3.53 | 0.91 | 20 |
| 36. | Contributes to the economy of the country | 3.60 | 1.02 | 36 | 3.79 | 0.97 | 10 |
| 37. | Provides sense of community | 3.58 | 0.95 | 37 | 3.62 | 0.98 | 16 |
| 38. | Provides a platform for forming lifelong relationships | 3.57 | 1.02 | 38 | 3.34 | 1.15 | 35 |
| 39. | Takes initiatives for planned change | 3.53 | 0.92 | 39 | 3.30 | 0.87 | 40 |
| 40. | Has a green environment (trees, etc.) | 3.52 | 1.12 | 40 | 3.30 | 1.38 | 38 |
| 41. | Brings people closer | 3.50 | 0.99 | 41 | 3.51 | 0.94 | 22 |
| 42. | Provides opportunities to influence others | 3.47 | 1.02 | 42 | 3.24 | 0.95 | 43 |
| 43. | Provides opportunity for social networking | 3.44 | 1.04 | 43 | 3.30 | 1.12 | 37 |
| 44. | Provides opportunity to exercise power | 3.32 | 1.03 | 44 | 3.03 | 0.99 | 47 |
| 45. | Is well lit | 3.31 | 1.04 | 45 | 4.18 | 0.82 | 3 |
| 46. | Is conveniently located from my residence | 3.19 | 1.21 | 46 | 3.18 | 1.44 | 46 |
| 47. | Has wide open spaces | 3.18 | 1.11 | 47 | 3.50 | 1.18 | 23 |
| 48. | Gives freedom for many coffee breaks | 2.77 | 1.24 | 48 | 4.19 | 1.04 | 2 |
| 49. | Has a crèche | 2.66 | 1.17 | 49 | 2.05 | 1.30 | 49 |

*Notes*: Expectations Sample: N = 2158; Availability Sample: N = 567 graduates with at least 2 years' work experience.

- While the top fifteen attributes in the expectations list had very high intensity (4.00 and above), however, only two of these workplace expectations feature in the top 15 available list—encourages team work (rank 9) and encourages learning (rank 12).
- The other 13 of the top 15 expectations—encourages innovation and idea generation (rank 1), recognizes performance (rank 2), believes in fairness and justice (rank 3), recognizes contribution (rank 4), provides opportunity for personality development (rank 5), provides opportunity to take initiatives (rank 7); gives autonomy and freedom to express my views (rank 8); encourages leadership development (rank 9); encourages trust and transparency (rank 11) provides constructive feedback for my development (rank 12), open to suggestions for improvement (rank 14) and provides opportunities for decision making (rank 15)—range from rank 17 to 45 in the available list. This is much lower than what is desired by the Millennials in the sample.
- Thus, it is clear that what is highly valued as a workplace characteristic by Millennials is not available at the workplace.
- The items which have topped the available list—strong brand value (rank 1), freedom for coffee breaks (rank 2), is well lit (rank 3), has modern equipments to facilitate work (rank 4), has high prestige (rank 5)—are actually much lower in the expectation list being ranked 26, 48, 45, 33, and 27, respectively. Thus, the respondents with work experience found that their high-priority expectations were hardly met as compared to low-priority expectations.

## Millennials' Workplace Expectations: Further Insights from Interview Data

Findings from the interview data[3] conducted on 100 Millennials with work experience have been content analyzed[4] to derive greater insight into their

---

[3] One hundred respondents were selected randomly out of 567 (with at least 2 years of work experience) and interviewed. They were mostly MBA students with work experience in public sector, private sector, MNCs, anufacturing, service, and sales. The purpose of these interviews has been to develop further insights into the rating given by the sample, in the questionnaires.

[4] The method of *content analysis* was used in processing the interview data. It is a research technique for the objective, systematic, and quantitative description of manifest content of

### Table 4.4 Millennials' workplace expectations

| S. No. | I would like to join a workplace for | N | % |
|---|---|---|---|
| 1. | A platform to grow and actualize myself | 92 | 92.00 |
| 2. | Identity and social status | 90 | 90.00 |
| 3. | Opportunity to experiment and express my creativity | 88 | 88.00 |
| 4. | Money and material comforts | 62 | 62.00 |
| 5. | Meaningful engagement | 58 | 58.00 |
| 6. | Becoming part of a community | 51 | 51.00 |
| 7. | Contributing to society | 32 | 32.00 |
| 8. | Sense of security and safety | 30 | 30.00 |

*Note:* N = 100.

expectations and availability. Through the content analysis process emergent themes were identified, quantified, and are presented below in Table 4.4 (see Figure 4.1 for graphical representation).

The eight salient[5] themes which emerged from the content analysis of the interview data regarding Millennials' expectations from the workplace are discussed in this section. Some of the salient quotes which typify each of the eight themes are cited under each head in order to illustrate the spirit and views characterizing each category. An exhaustive list of quotes has however not been presented in order to reduce repetition and maintain readability.

The most frequently cited expectation is to "join an organization to grow and actualize myself" (92%). This is followed by social status and identity (90%); opportunity to experiment and express my creativity (88%); money and material comforts (62%); meaningful engagement (58%); becoming a part of the community (51%); contributing to society (32%) and having a sense of security and safety (30%). Analysis of the present table clearly establishes the preponderance of psychosocial needs over money, material needs and security needs. Interestingly altruistic needs to make a meaningful contribution to society and align with a larger social purpose and make a difference, is valued much lower than the social-psychological

---

communications (Berelson, 1952). It involved systematically identifying properties of the large amount of textual information, using the frequencies of most used keywords, thereby detecting the more important structures of the communication content. The information was then categorized for analysis, providing at the end a meaningful reading of content.

[5] Interviewees were asked to mention five workplace expectations which were then content analyzed. Responses will not total to 100 since people gave multiple responses.

**Figure 4.1** Graphical representation of Millennials' expectations from workplace

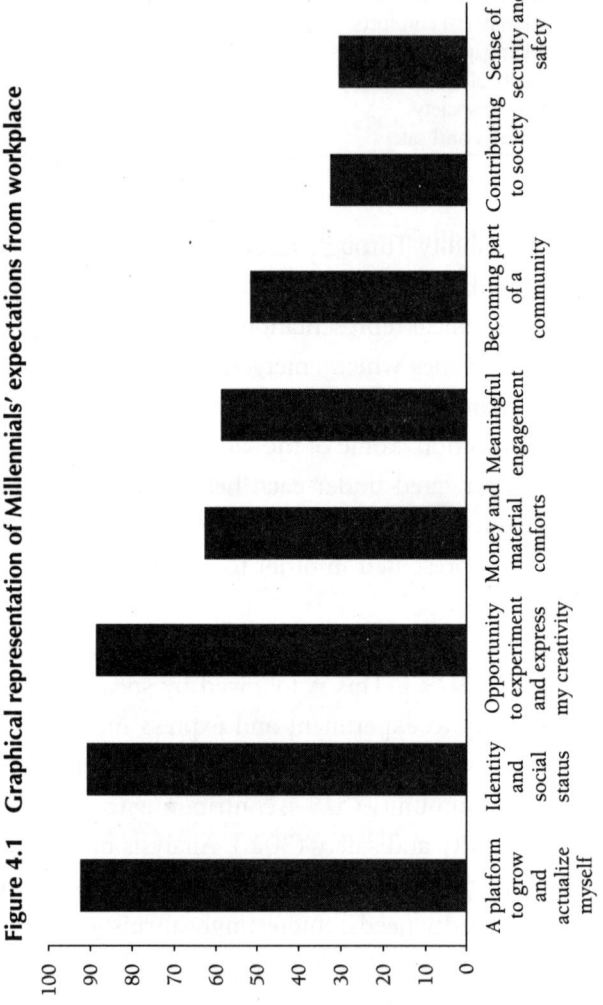

needs. This phenomenon reveals low idealism and high self-orientation. This also correlates with the value preferences and priorities presented in Chapter 2, where personal growth value was the highest closely followed by self-fulfillment value. Community development value featured as being the least important in the list. The findings clearly bring out that this is the "Me" generation, with preeminent and unabashed focus on "I," "Me," and "My". These results support the findings emerging from the work of other researchers (Twenge, 2006; Twenge et al., 2008; Twenge and Foster, 2008, 2010; Twenge and Campbell, 2009).

We now bring out the salient quotes and expressions by the Millennials around the eight MOWP themes.

## Platform to grow and actualize myself

The interviewees mentioned learning opportunity and they said this in the following ways: "I would like to work in a company where I can get plenty of learning opportunity;" "I would like to work in a place which provides good opportunity for learning because without learning one cannot grow in life;" "I would like to work at a place where there is a chance to constantly improve myself;" "I would like to join a place where I can get a lot of inputs and learning that I can use later on;" "I don't feel that drive inside me to go and work, unless I am like a student who is going to learn….;" "getting good assignments is very important for learning and development and I will work where I can get good assignments which will increase my growth and development;" "If you are getting good assignments and valuable experience then you may forego good salary for some time, because you know that at a later stage you can earn much more."

They also expressed that they would like to work in organizations where they get a chance to use their skills and abilities and actualize their potential—"I would like to work at a place which reaffirms my trust in my own capabilities and helps me develop them further;" "I would like to work in a place where I can make maximum use of my academic/professional capabilities;" "I would like to work to get the chance to put my knowledge to good use;" "I would like to work at a place where I get a chance to express myself, put to use my learning, helping me to develop my own self over time;" "The organization should give me the chance to use my talent;" "After so much education, if my capabilities are not used it will be very difficult to work in that organization;" "work is the place where I feel we can realize our potential provided we get the opportunity' to continuously learn and develop ourselves."

From the above it is clear that Millennials value learning opportunities to continuously develop themselves. They value mental stimulation. In fact they want to see the organization as a university where learning is promoted, valued, and rewarded. Further they also consider it important to get the opportunity to apply their knowledge in contributing to organizational thinking, learning, and improvement. Above all, they view learning as the most potent tool for self-actualization. Similar findings have been reported by other researchers (Lipkin and Perrymore, 2009; Johnson Controls, 2010).

## Identity and social status

Identity and social status has emerged as the second most important expectation from the workplace. Most of the respondents have said: "I would like to work in a company which helps me earn respect, position and status in society;" "I would like to work where I can get a sense of achievement which leads to social recognition and respect;" "It is important to work in a good company to get respect in society, among family and friends, everywhere;" "I would like to work at a place which can give me name and fame in life;" "I would like to work at a place where I can get a high sense of self worth and self esteem;" "I would like to work at a place where Ican get social and professional recognition." These statements very clearly bring out that Millennials view work as instrumental in being valued, recognized and appreciated by society. This theme provides insights into the perceived relationship between one's job as well as organization and the derived respect, status, and social identity thereon. Despite being the "Me" generation, Millennials highly value esteem and recognition by society and family indicating that society continues to be a reference point for self-evaluation. Other researchers have also stated that society is an important reference point for self-evaluation for the Millennials (Burke and Eddy, 2006; Ros et al., 1999; Leonard et al., 1999; Erez and Earley, 1993; Tajfel and Turner, 1986; Morin, 2004).

The high level of importance given to identity and social status brings out that Millennials are extremely conscious of their identity and image.

In contemporary society as various identity markers—community, region, family, caste, and class—steadily erode, Millennials look for alternate institutions which provide sense of identity and social image. Today it is increasingly observed that who you are is primarily linked with where you work and which profession you belong to.

## Opportunity to experiment and express creativity

The following quotes give an insight into Millennials' expectation around this theme.

Majority of them very clearly articulated that they would like to work at a place which provides them autonomy, personal space, and freedom to work experiment and innovate, indicating high entrepreneurial spirit among Millennials. This has been expressed in the following ways.

"I would like 'autonomy' to do things, 'freedom' to experiment and work, get 'independent charge' of something;" "I would like to work in a company where I am free to try and seniors intervene only if I fail;" "I would like to work in a place where I can do things in my own way;" "I want to work where I get a chance to express my own ideas and creativity;" "I need a work environment where I am encouraged to think differently, to think out of the box;" "I would like to be able to do things differently;" "The company which has out of box thinkers would be really attractive for me because it is contagious and you get influenced by others ideas;" "I need mental stimulation and places which are open and encourage thinking differently would be the kind of place that I would like to join;" "I would like to work in a company which provides me plenty of challenges and responsibilities, where I can show my creativity;" "I would like to work in a company where there is freedom, autonomy and personal space to experiment, take risk and create something exciting and meaningful;" "I would like to work for a company where being entrepreneurial is encouraged."

Millennials have also referred to the needed larger organizational culture where they would feel comfortable. Many of them said, "I would like to work at a place where there are less procedures and systems. If something is not ok we should be able to change it;" "The place should not have many rules and guidelines for everything; it will be difficult to work in a place where all your moves have to be according to rules;" "I would like to work in the system where I have to report weekly or fortnightly and not daily." "The company atmosphere should not be formal and rigid. It should not be a 'Yes Sir' kind of organization;" "I would like to work in company which has more open culture, more open door policy, where you can go and talk to anyone in the company;". "The culture should be vibrant and lively. It should not be very formal;" "I would never like to work for a company where people breathe down my neck, and curb my need to experiment and innovate."

The dominant theme emerging from these quotes seem to a strong preference for a workplace characterized by a culture of freedom, informality, with plenty of opportunity to explore and experiment; high empowerment leading to thinking differently, being creative. There is also a clear aversion for formal, rule and procedure bound organizations which are rigid and slow to change (Lyons, 2004; Smith, 2008; Smola and Sutton, 2002; Zemke et al., 2000).

## Money and material comforts

"Money" has emerged as the fourth most important theme in terms of expectations from work. Millennials said that money is important for them because financial stability is very important in life; and also because money is important to satisfy needs of self and parents as well as to make one's family feel happy. Millennials gave the following reasons why they consider money to be important:

"The more I get paid the more worthy I would feel;" "Money is a tangible, quantifiable proof of recognition and differentiation and luxury leads to happiness;" "Money gives a sense of security and freedom;" "Money is important because the world rates you on the basis of tangible value addition. It is also important to give good experiences to family;" "Money is a big motivator and is a quantifiable measure of your worth relative to others;" "Money provides status in society;" "Money is important as it gives you status and power; "Money gives power and importance;" "Money and happiness are highly correlated; "Happiness is very much related to money;" "Money buys things which make us and family happy;" "Money follows hard work; Money is needed to maintain the lifestyle and social status that I am used to;" "according to me a minimum threshold of money is required beyond which nature of job becomes more important."

In summary money is valued by Millennials for various reasons- for earning status in society, recognition for work done, maintaining a good lifestyle and for keeping the family happy. Thus money is viewed as the major instrument through which many human needs both physical and psychological are met (Agarwal, 1993; Kanungo, 1983; Vos and Meganck, 2007).

## Meaningful engagement

The fifth theme refers to work as a way to spend time meaningfully. Millennials linked work with their psychological satisfaction and growth. This has been expressed in the following ways:

"Work is not just about money; it is a reflection of my personality and an opportunity for continuous growth. Without challenging and creative work, I will never grow in my life;" "Work is important for mental stimulation;" "Apart from earning money, work is important to spend time constructively;" "Work is very important for me to pursue my ambition;" "I would stay in an organization where I will find engaging work and good people."

They said that work has to be engaging because of the amount of time Millennials have to spend at work. This has been expressed as in the following paragraphs.

"Work is how we spend majority of our time in life and it should keep us busy and engaged;" "Work is where you spend a large part of your day and it has to be stimulating;" "Work should be interesting and it should engage me for the large part of my day;" "Work is a way to spend my time well;" "Work is an important way to use one's time and so it should be fun and interesting;" "Work is an important means of engaging myself, keeping myself busy and active apart from earning money."

Work continues to be viewed as being at the centre of one's life and one's day and hence Millennials have demands from the work and workplace where they can feel meaningfully engaged, excited, challenged, and involved. Work is viewed as a source of satisfaction of one's psychological needs and the workplace as a place where one spends much of one's waking time, thus making it important that work and workplace keep people meaningfully engaged.

From the above it can be concluded that workplace is viewed by the Millennials as central to their lives (Bernstein, 1997; Harding and

Hikspoors, 1995; Ruiz-Quintanilla and Wilpert, 1991; Smola and Sutton, 2002; Twenge et al., 2010; Burke and Eddy, 2006; Shamir, 1091; Harpaz, 1990, 1999; Mannhein, 1993; Brief and Nord, 1990; England and Misumi, 1986; MOW International Research team, 1987; Kaplan and Tausky, 1974; Morse and Weiss, 1955; Parker, 1971; Warr, 1982).

## Sense of community

Millennials also look to the workplace for experiencing a sense of community. They seek cordial relations with colleagues and seniors, and consider the team rapport to be important to create an exciting workplace. This has been expressed as follows:

"People working with me should be friendly. If you don't have anybody to talk to in the organization and you are all alone, then it will be hell to go to work every day;" "There should be good rapport amongst employees, otherwise a person may get isolated and feel lonely;" "Relationship with colleagues matters, there should be people around me with whom I can relate;" "It is important for me to be with people with whom I am comfortable, so the team relationship is very important. There should be cordial relations in the team;" "If every morning you wake up and you have to go to a hellish workplace where your boss is ruthless, your employees are all out there to pull you down, so even if you have a high pay, you would not be wanting to go back there. No matter how high you are paid, if the environment is not good, the best does not come out of you, you won't be able to give in your best... it might be like fighting a losing battle."

The need for community is so strong that they feel the need to go beyond their actual teams and connect with people across functions, departments, and divisions. This has been expressed as in the following paragraphs.

"There should be good scope to network across functions;" "We should have opportunity to meet new people from our organization;" "There should be fun, there should be celebration, and there should be more opportunities to get together."

The above statements bring out the need of the Millennials to belong, to be accepted, and to have a friendly work atmosphere rather than working in an unfriendly, politicized, and suffocating environment. In fact preferred quality of relationships at work and their second order combinations jointly predicted job satisfaction, mental and physical well being, and turnover intention (Yang et al., 2008).

### Chance to contribute to society

Millennials (albeit a smaller percentage) view work as an opportunity to contribute to and serve society. This has been expressed by the Millennials in the following manner:

"At the end of the day, it gives me tremendous feeling of satisfaction for having contributed something towards society and my organization;" "It provides me the opportunity to contribute to society through my learning and experiences;" "Contribution to society is also important in life;" "It is a means of giving back to society;" "It is fulfilling to do something good for people around me."

This brings out that there are people in the Millennials group who view work from an idealistic perspective and draw a broader sense of meaning from their work. Research (Borg, 1990) has brought out that people experience a sense of satisfaction, they feel good to give back and they feel fulfilled when they contribute to others.

### Sense of security and safety

Responses which were converted into this theme have been fairly straightforward. People actually mentioned these phrases: "provides security," "provides safety," and "source of livelihood."

In conclusion, Millennials assign high importance to work as brought out by the various levels of individual needs which they believe the workplace fulfills ranging from economic to social to psychological.

## Comparing Questionnaire and Interview Data Findings on Expectations

Comparison of the two data sets on MOWP expectations brings out that there is a good amount of overlap in the case of statements from questionnaire data with the themes which emerged from the interview data. The interview data has in fact provided insights which reinforced findings from the questionnaire data.

## Group A[6]

(1) Platform to grow and actualize myself (interview data theme) conceptually matches the following items which feature in the top 15 ranks from the questionnaire data—provides opportunities for personality development (rank 5); encourages learning (rank 6); provides opportunities to take initiatives (rank 7); provides constructive feedback for my development (rank 12).

The other major theme from the interview data is "Opportunity to experiment and express my creativity" (interview data theme). This matches with encourages innovation and idea generation (rank 1) and is open to suggestions for improvement (rank 14) from the questionnaire data.

Two of the top-ranked statements: "gives autonomy and freedom to express my views" (rank 8) and "encourages trust and transparency" (rank 10) are relevant in both interview based categories—platform to grow and actualize myself as well as opportunity to experiment and express my creativity.

The third emergent theme is becoming part of the community under which the following two top statements can be subsumed—encourages team work (rank 13); values work–life balance (rank 11).

## Group B

Five items from the questionnaire data (means ranging from 3.86 to 3.98)—"helps me earn respect from society" (rank 16), "cares about physical and mental health of its employees" (rank 18), "takes care of financial needs" (rank 21), "provides job security" (rank 22), and "reduces fear of losing job" (rank 23)—also match with three of the interview-based themes: identity and social status, money and material comfort, and sense of safety and security.

Based on the above we can conclude that the interview data has amply supported the questionnaire data and provided deeper insights into the expectations of the Millennials.

---

[6] Group A consists of items which have featured in the top 15 ranks and have 4.00 and above mean, while Group B consists of items within the mean score range of 3.86 to 3.98.

## Experienced Organizational Reality

Interview findings regarding the experienced organizational reality at the workplace are now presented below:[7]

**Table 4.5   Experienced organizational reality**

| S. No. | My organization… | Frequency | % |
|---|---|---|---|
| 1. | is hierarchical and top-down | 86 | 86.00 |
| 2. | is conformity centric | 81 | 81.00 |
| 3. | pays inadequate attention to unleash human creative potential | 75 | 75.00 |
| 4. | has silo functioning | 60 | 60.00 |
| 5. | is less sensitive to people development | 54 | 54.00 |
| 6. | obsessed with ROI | 48 | 48.00 |
| 7. | is responsive to market and customer | 42 | 42.00 |
| 8. | is ambitious to grow | 40 | 40.00 |
| 9. | is a good place to work | 38 | 38.00 |
| 10. | is learning and innovating | 22 | 22.00 |

*Note:* N = 100.

Table 4.5 (see Figure 4.2 for graphical representation) presents the major themes and issues which emerged from the content analysis of the interview data regarding Millennials' experienced reality at the workplace. Ten[8] themes emerged clearly from the data. Millennials with work experience have brought out that organizations are mostly "hierarchical and top-down" (86 percent), conformity centric (81 percent), pays inadequate attention to unleash human creative potential (75 percent), Silo functioning (60 percent), less sensitive to people development (54 percent), and over obsessed with ROI (48 percent). Some of the Millennials brought out positive aspects of organizations—responsive to market and customer (42 percent), ambitious to grow (40 percent), good place to work (38 percent), and learning and innovating (22 percent).

---

[7] One hundred respondents were selected randomly out of 567 (with 2 plus years of work experience) and interviewed. They are mostly MBA students across public and private sector, MNCs, manufacturing, service, and sales. The purpose of these interviews has been to get further insights into the questionnaire data which the respondents have filled up.

[8] Interviewees were asked to identify their experiences of the organizational reality.

**Figure 4.2** Graphical representation of "experienced organizational reality"

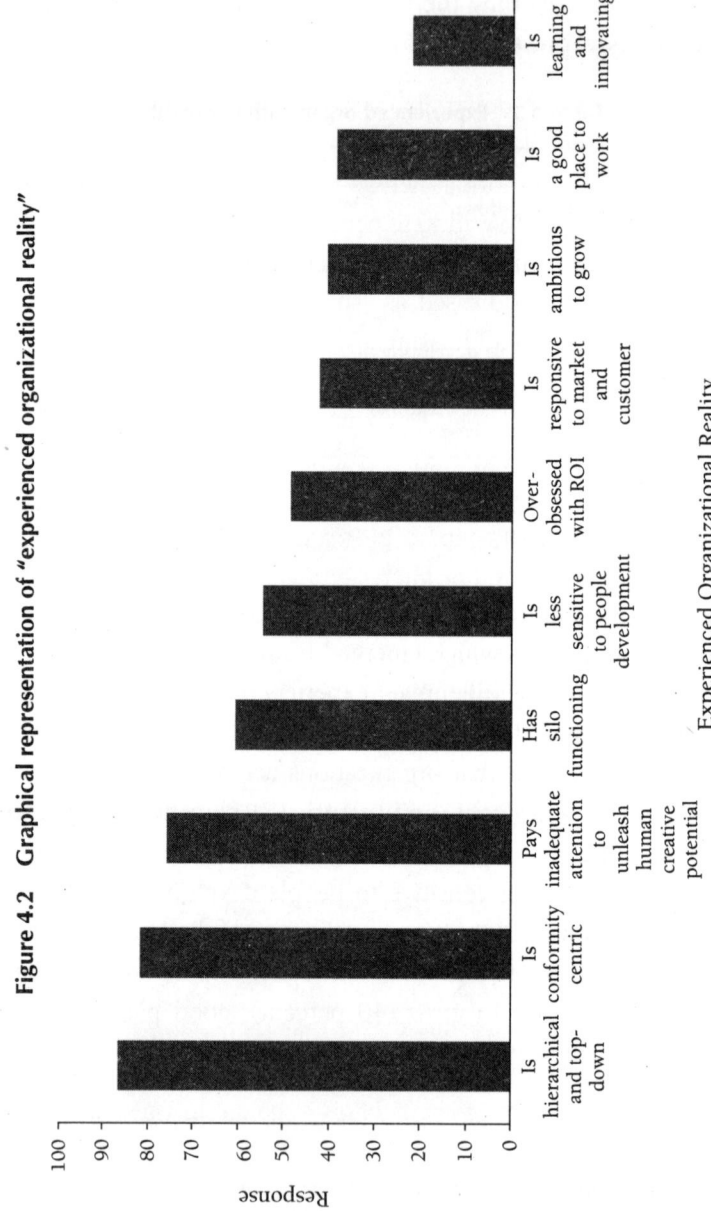

The detailed responses of the Millennials under each category are now presented in the following sections.

## Hierarchical/top-down

The hierarchical and top-down character of organizations has been deduced from statements like the following:

"Relationships are very formal here;" "People are very conscious about seating in the meetings;" "We address people as sir;" "I tried to use the first name but it was not liked; this is not the culture of the company I work for;" "If people are not addressed as "sir"/"ma'am" they show their displeasure;" "I can't think of addressing anyone in a higher position by first name; it may be seen as disrespectful;" "People feel good when addressed formally, because they feel they are being respected." "People in senior positions talk more and listen less;" "Seniors speak and we have to listen;" "We are not expected to speak;" "We have to listen all the time ... at meetings, at get-togethers, they (seniors) speak and we listen;" "When we speak seniors don't listen, they are not interested;" "Communication is one way here;" "They share about the company plans and performance, but the reverse communication rarely happens."

Many Millennials said that because of the top-down nature of organizations, there is a feeling of helplessness, suffocation, and irritation at not being able to speak out. There are moments according to many when there is a sense of apathy, disengagement, reduced involvement, and low inclination to make valuable contributions. "So we end up becoming mindless robots, doing what we are told."

## Conformity centric

A large number of the interviewees said that their company has a high preference for conformity from employees. Frequently occurring words during the interviews were "obey," "follow," "go along without questioning." These were seen as an essential requirement for success and career growth. The statements given in the following lines give a feel of how they view the work culture.

"Those in higher positions love followers!" "In this company *chamchas* are valued;" "If i say anything at the group meetings which is different from the view of the head, it is snubbed;" "If i ask questions it is not appreciated;" "Here a good employee is one who asks few questions;" "A good employee is one who agrees with the boss;" "They don't say it directly, but if you say 'yes sir, yes sir' then you can become their blue-eyed boy;" "Seniors in this company like to surround themselves with yes men;" "It is not very blatant but you can make out when you check who gets the promotions, who gets the plum postings, and who gets the rewards."

Compliance is expected in everything, in the name of process centricity and elaborately evolved norms, procedures and systems. There is no space for unconventional ideas and out-of-the-box thinking. Unless ideas fit into the framework, they are rejected.

### Pays less attention to unleash human creative potential

This is among the top three themes which have emerged from the interviews and one of the important areas of concern in building a future workplace. The view has been expressed in the following ways.

"No one is bothered about good ideas here;" "There is no scope for good suggestions here, although we have a suggestion scheme;" "The organization keeps us tightly bound to execute;" "Target achievement matters the most here;" "Meetings here are mostly about planning and chasing deadlines;" "All are too busy with the present to bother about the future;" "I was excited with a good idea recently—mind you, I am in R&D—my senior didn't even respond properly to the idea;" "Feel caged here, the air is so stale, no scope for fresh thoughts;" "Creativity is a flower which dies very quickly without care… Who cares in the company? Yet, in all the speeches the CEO speaks about creativity and innovation;" "We talk about creativity, but don't know how to harness it;" "It feels terrible when your idea is not even acknowledged;" "Company hierarchy interferes with everything; does not allow good ideas to be expressed;" "We can contribute so much more with ideas, but get no chance. Sometimes it is frustrating".

From the above quotes it can be inferred that the quest for novelty, newness, entrepreneurial innovation, are generally overlooked and assigned low priority in the frenzied obsession with execution. Thus the focus is more on managing today rather than preparing the organization for tomorrow. It also indicates that what is urgent gets greater precedence over what is important.

## Silo functioning

Silo functioning has emerged as the fourth most frequently experienced work place reality. People expressed their views as follows:

"We are pretty good at working together within our department, but across departments, there is no opportunity to meet or discuss;" "It is sometimes strange that we belong to the same company, we may work on the same floor and not know many of our own colleagues;" "There is very little chance to socialize with people across divisions." "I don't know much about related departments in my organization. Sometimes it would be helpful to know;" "All the focus is on departmental targets and we are busy with reaching them. Even related departments rarely meet;" "We need more opportunity to meet across departments." "Formal and informal meetings with colleagues from other teams will be really good;" "Never had an opportunity to learn from other departments;" "Other departments, who knows what they are doing?" "We have CFTs but the spirit of exchange is missing;" "We see work in a narrow department centric sense. We don't get the holistic picture of the organization;" "Even if I want to discuss with my counterparts in other departments, it's not so easy. I have to go through my boss;" "My organization has as many chieftains as the number of departments and verticals."

The above reflects that organizations are fragmented into fiefdoms and people working within departments have to owe allegiance to the chief and not necessarily to the organization. Such a phenomenon can create problems because work flows horizontally while coordination flows vertically. This results in low synergistic functioning in the organization.

## Less sensitive to people development

This refers to the extent to which the company is experienced by Millennials as concerned about people development. The sensitivity and concern for people seems to be experienced as less than desired as brought out in the following quotes from the interviews with the Millennials:

"The company is not very concerned about human potential. All are subjected to the same rules here, whether you are a horse or an ass the treatment is the same;" "We are chased by our seniors for target achievement but we have to chase them for getting the rewards;" "When bosses need something from us talk to us, say, 'How are you?' but when we need something from them and we approach them, they respond, 'Who are you?';" "Companies must realize that training is not equal to people development. Companies should take more interest in people;" "Mentoring and coaching and developing younger people is missing here;" "The mentor assigned to me did not meet me even once;" "Appraisal is used here for promotion, and not for developing, building, and grooming people;" "Immediate seniors are not concerned about younger people;" "Who cares for me as a person. Even HR does not know people, they rarely meet us, and they don't understand our problems and needs." "I wonder what I am ... do I matter. Am I just a resource to be used?;" "I wish seniors would help us develop into our roles;" "I have hopped across two jobs and have found that it's the same story in both companies;" "When I share the situation with friends from other organizations, I realize that it's the same story everywhere;" "My company does not have the right processes for development of talent."

The above quotes powerfully reveal that the desired attention to develop people is not present to the needed extent at the workplace. Mentoring, coaching, and counseling—the most potent tools for building and grooming people—are not taken seriously. The focus in organizations is primarily towards work and more work and in this state less attention is paid to building human beings and to harness their potential.

## Obsessed with ROI

Organizations appear to be pushing results, bottom lines, and ROI to a good extent as indicated by interviewees' responses. The following statements bring out the views of the interviewed Millennials:

"Deadlines rule in this company;" "Everyone is paranoid here, chasing his own tail, too busy to chill;" "ROI and market capitalization is everything here;" "Most reviews are about achieving targets and meeting deadlines, I wish they would spend more time planning;" "Sometimes I feel companies are so short sighted in their thinking and the people here are like blinkered horses, single mindedly cutting costs and chasing ROI;" "I have seen that the ROI focus is very high while people focus is not high enough;" "Company should bother about ROI but can they also bother more about people about building the organization for the future?;" "Why ROI at any cost?" "Company sometimes gets short sighted with their ROI-centric approach." These statements clearly bring out that these Millennials have experienced workplaces as driving results, chasing targets, operating with high cost consciousness, investing less in preparing the organization for the future, combined with lower sensitivity toward people.

## Is responsive to market and customer

Concern for the customer has emerged as an important organizational reality experienced by the interviewed Millennials. This has been expressed by them in the following ways:

"Customer delight is very highly valued by my company;" Customer is king here;" "Company makes all out effort to identify and address customer complaints;" "Customer complaints are very important for us;" "Make no mistake, here customer rules;" "I am amazed at the amount of effort my company puts into understanding the market and the customer;" "We don't allow a customer to go away dissatisfied;" "In my company market trends are watched very carefully;" "In my company we are sensitive to market requirements. Any changes are closely tracked by us."

It is possible to conclude from these statements that the experienced reality for Millennials is of an organization which puts customer at the centre and keeps track of the market.

## Ambitious to grow

Millennials view organizations as highly ambitious, competitive and growth oriented. This has been brought out by the following statements:

"My company is highly competitive;" "We are expected to push hard for growth;" "If company grows we grow;" "The top drives the company very hard so that growth is achieved."

They also raised concerns about the way growth strategy is pushed: "Company should push but this is not enough for fulfilling their growth ambitions. They will have to involve more and more people in the management;" "They will have to use people's creativity and ideas;" "Achieving high growth in growing markets is possible only if they empower people and make them part of the growth strategy and decision making and about the way growth strategy is pushed;" "The company wants to grow but waits for other competitors to take the lead; does not like to take a chance;" "We are ambitious but not bold;" "We desire to be at the top but don't have the courage to take a chance;" "We have high ambitions but want to control people;" "Company doesn't realize that employees can do so much to bring growth but they don't because of control, hierarchy, slow procedures."

## Good place to work

Only a small percentage has said that their organization is a "Good place to Work." Given here are the typical statements that the Millennials made.

The organization has been described as "A good company;" "Good company to work;" "Takes good care of our needs;" "Caring company;" "Can't think of a better organization to work for;" "Takes care of all employees especially the younger crowd;" "Has many programs to bring people together;" "Informal place." Other statements were as follows: "Team lead is very considerate;" "People are friendly and nice;" "Team relations are good here;" "I can walk into any senior's office;" "We are on first-name basis"; "It's an informal place;" " It's a great place to work, we have so much flexibility about work timings;" "I like my company because they don't believe in typical 9 to 5 pm working;" "I stay working late sometimes and then the next day I can come as I please;" "Seniors have a very positive attitude towards juniors in this company;" "People are nice here;" "Seniors are not stiff and rigid here."

The descriptions of what Millennials consider a good place to work has brought out that Millennials like to work for a caring, considerate, friendly, informal and flexible organization where experimentation and exploration are valued, where there is empowerment, autonomy, and freedom as well as the spirit of entrepreneurship, where team relations are good and seniors have a positive attitude.

## Learning and innovating organization

Some of the interviewed Millennials have viewed their organizations as learning organizations. This has emerged through statements like the following.

"Company has many systems for improvement;" "Company believes in continuous improvement;" "Company has a good suggestion scheme;" "This company believes in continuous improvement;" "We get recognized for giving good suggestions;" "New ideas are rewarded here;" "Ideas are valued here no matter who gives them;" "I feel good when my idea is accepted and implemented;" "Feel that the company is interested in taking good ideas for improvement;" "We are encouraged to find better solutions to problems;" "There is sharing and discussion on ideas;" "If I make a mistake I am not penalized, I am encouraged to learn from my mistakes;" "Company is restless and feverishly trying to become better because they have global plans;" "Company encourages and rewards people who innovate;" "I have even heard the CEO say, 'I don't know about this, can you tell me more?'"

## Comparing Questionnaire and Interview Data Findings on MOWP Availability

Questionnaire and Interview data findings on MOWP Availability are now discussed. Items which emerged in the top fifteen ranks (with a mean value above 3.50) in the case of MOWP expectations have slid down beyond rank fifteen in the MOWP availability list (and below 3.50). Comparison of these item ranks with the MOWP availability interview findings show that there is a good convergence between the two:

Themes like "hierarchical and top-down," "conformity centric," "pays inadequate attention to unleash human creative potential," "less sensitive to people development and learning and innovating" (interview based) are the antithesis of the following items: "encourages experimentation" (rank 48), "provides opportunity for decision making" (rank 45), "provides opportunities to influence others" (rank 43), "empowers people" (rank 41); "provides constructive feedback for my development" (rank 39); "encourages people to voice their concerns" (rank 34); "encourages leadership development" (rank 33); "open to suggestions for improvement" (rank 29), "encourages innovation and idea generation" (rank 26), "encourages trust and transparency" (rank 25), "provides opportunities to take initiatives" (24), which are less available at the workplace according to those millennials with some work experience.

The interview findings have thus clearly supported the outcomes from the questionnaire on MOWP availability.

Comparison of the Millennials (with work experience) expectations versus reality (based on the interview data presented above) brings out a gap. On the one hand they have many higher order self-related developmental expectations, as indicated by the fact that five of the eight expectations are of this nature, viz., "look for opportunities to actualize experiment and express their creativity," "be meaningfully engaged," become part of the community and contribute to society." On the other hand, Millennials are faced with the workplace realities which are anathema for self-development and creative self-expression, viz., they are bogged down by work culture characterized by hierarchical and top-down approach, drive for conformity, less attention to unleash human potential and less sensitivity to people development, all of which dampen the human spirit.

Research has shown that incongruence between expectations and reality can lead to stress disorders, low job-satisfaction (Furnham and Walsh, 1990; Holland, 1985, 1973; Furnham and Schaeffer, 1984); and negatively affect mental health (Furnham and Schaeffer, 1984). It is therefore not surprising if there is disenchantment, disconnect, and propensity to leave organizations (Cummings and Cooper, 1979; French et al., 1982; Hecht and Allen, 2005; Holland, 1985, 1973).

## Part II: Work-related Attitudes

Findings on two work-related attitudes have been presented here: (a) expectations from the immediate boss and (b) intent to leave.

### Expectations from the Immediate Boss

The leader–follower relationship has been one of the most fascinating themes of inquiry in the field of management. This is rightly so because the "boss" is a critical element in the work–life of the followers and subordinates. There is a plethora of literature available on how the leader affects the work attitudes, motivation and commitment (Horwitz et al., 2003;

Roehling et al., 2000; Turnley and Feldman, 2000; Dansereau et al., 1975; Graen, 1976; Graen and Scandura, 1987; Fiedler, 1967; Jablin and Sussman, 1983; Katz and Kahn, 1966, 1978) of the followers and subordinates. Successful seniors have been found to significantly affect the levels of job satisfaction of their subordinates in India, especially when they are perceived to be unethical (Visweswaran and Deshpande, 1996).

People tend to use their experiences with the boss to generalize about the organizational realities. If they get a toxic boss, they view the organization through a negative lens; if on the other hand they get a positive boss, they tend to view the organization in a positive light—exciting, inspiring, meaningful, great place to work, etc. In fact the well-known book, *First break all the rules: What the world's greatest managers do differently* (Buckingham and Coffman, 1999), powerfully highlights that people leave their bosses and not their organizations further substantiating that the organizational reality for an employee depends on his experience with the boss. It is in this perspective that the type of boss preferred by the Millennials has been probed in depth.

**Table 4.6 Expectations from a good leader**

| S. No. | | Frequency | % |
|---|---|---|---|
| 1. | Humility and listening | 86 | 86.00 |
| 2. | Inspiring and empowering | 82 | 82.00 |
| 3. | Just and fair | 79 | 79.00 |
| 4. | Gives honest feedback for performance improvement | 78 | 78.00 |
| 5. | Man of ideas | 70 | 70.00 |
| 6. | Mentor and guide | 67 | 67.00 |
| 7. | Open and approachable | 65 | 65.00 |
| 8. | Team builder | 62 | 62.00 |

*Note:* N = 100.

The most preferred quality in a leader, according to the interviewed Millennials in the study (see Table 4.6 and Figure 4.3), is that s/he should be Humble and Listening (86%), followed by empowering and inspiring (82%); and then just and fair (79%). The next three important characteristics which Millennials look for are: gives honest feedback for performance (78%), man of ideas (70%); mentor and guide (67%). The last two attributes are "open and approachable" (65%) and "team builder" (62%). It is

**Figure 4.3** Graphical representation of the "expectations from a good leader"

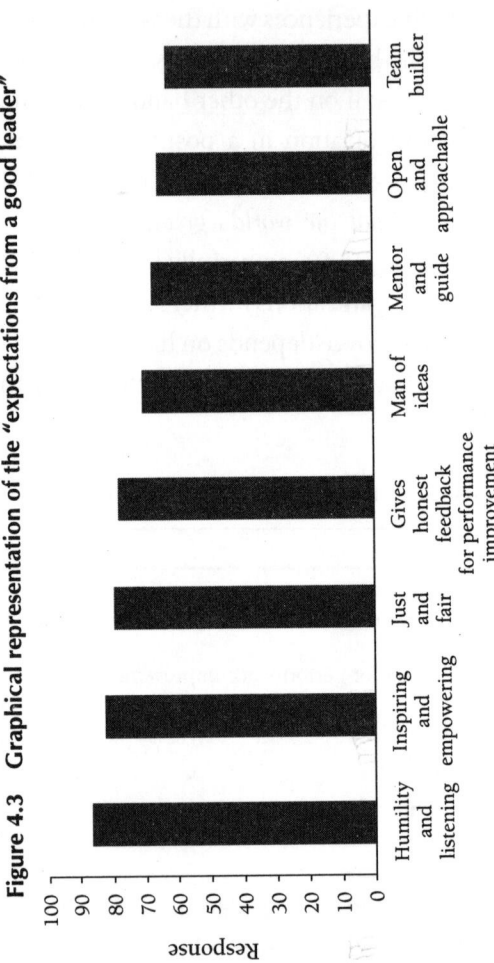

important to note that the minimum percentage of expected behavior is 62 percent, i.e., more than half of the interviewed sample has mentioned all of these attributes. This clearly shows that all the eight expectations from the leader are considered to be important by the Millennials, although relatively speaking, some are more important than others.

## Humble and listening

Millennials made the following statements that brought out the theme of "Humility" and "Listening" as the important requirement in a leader:

"I would like to work with a leader who is interested in what I have to say;" "The leader should not be bossy;" "I would like to work with a leader who respects us;" "By listening a boss becomes a leader;" "I have seen that good CEOs listen, why not our immediate superiors?" "When the leader listens, you feel valued and important;" "I would love to work with someone who pays attention when employees speak;" "I would enjoy working with a leader who is himself learning, curious and listening;" "I cannot work with someone who is arrogant;" "Sometimes I get angry. What do they think of themselves? Why are they so arrogant?" "The worst kind of leader is an arrogant boss;" "I would not like to work with someone who ignores me when I say something."

## Inspiring and empowering

The following quotes indicate the qualities which have been clustered under the theme of "Inspiring and Empowering":

"I would like to work with a leader who is highly empowering"; "I would like to work with a superior who believes in involving people;" "A boss who involves people would be very inspiring for me and I would love to work with such a person;" "I would like to work with an inspiring and empowering boss so that I feel involved and motivated;" "I would like to work with a Boss who involves all the team mates in discussion and takes view points of all;" "If I go to my boss with an idea and he says, great lets examine it, this will encourage me to think "out of the box," so that mentality should be there throughout every superior-subordinate relationship;" "The boss should have the drive and should also create conditions for me to deliver well;" "A good boss is one who lets me loose and allows me to pave my own path."

"A good boss is one who gives me space to think;" "I would love to work with a trusting boss who gives me the freedom to work;" "A boss who does not breathe down my neck, that's what I need;" "A leader who tells me what to do, not how to do … I would enjoy working with such a man;" "He should have an encouraging style, when I go wrong he should not show extreme disappointment and discouragement; rather he must tell me how I can improve;" "If the senior criticizes me all the time, what can be worse than this?! I would hate it and not stay long in the company;" "Even if a person has done 100 good things boss does not appreciate but if he makes one mistake, he is reprimanded for it … then there is no point in working for such a company;" "Boss should encourage us, whenever we introduce an idea, he should encourage us."

## Just and fair

Statements made by Millennials regarding the preferred Leader in terms of the Fairness orientation are presented in the subsequent paragraphs:

"I would like to work with a boss who is perceived to be fair not just by me but by everyone in the organization, someone who is not against or in favor of anyone in particular;" "A good leader is one who is rational in his judgment, giving fair appreciation as well as criticism;" "I would prefer to work with a boss who is fair in giving appreciation and feedback;" "For me it is important that there is no discrimination nor favoring of anyone in the behavior of the boss;" "It would be great to work with a senior who is frank in evaluation and feedback; "I would like to work with a boss who treats everyone equally;" Boss should not very bossy. I would like to work with a boss who rates me on the basis of my performance and not on my relationship; "I would like to work with a senior who pays attention to and values all the team members;" "I would like to work with a boss who gives us fair share of appraisal and recognition;" "There should not be partiality in behavior of the leader with all team members;" "The leader should be fair and just and base rewards on performance rather than relationships;" "The leader must be able to differentiate between good and bad, and performance should be rewarded and recognized for healthy competition."

## Gives valid and honest feedback

Statements made by the Millennials indicating the importance of valid and honest feedback from the leader are now presented below:

"I would like to work with a leader who tries to criticize you positively and helps you out throughout your career;" "I would like to work with a leader who gives me honest and frank feedback;" "I would love to work with a boss who appreciates me when I deserve it;" "I would love to work with a senior who give me prompt and honest feedback (not flowery criticism);" "I think a good boss for me is someone who is balanced in his approach and gives me constant feedback, both appreciation and criticism;" "I would prefer to work with a boss who constructively criticizes me and tells me how to work on my weaknesses;" "A good boss is one who gives me feedback about my performance and not leave me wondering if I am performing well enough or not;" "A good boss is one who gives me a firsthand review on my performance."

## Smart and clear thinker

Given below are some of the expressions which indicated that they would like to work with a leader who is a smart and clear thinker:

"The leaders should be smart; they should be focused and we should be able to see the direction in which we are going. If there is no clarity on this, then I would leave;" "Leader should be aware and clear thinking;" "I would like to work with a leader who can think differently, think out of the box;" "It would be great fun working with someone who can appreciate good ideas;" "Leader should be quick in understanding;" "It is difficult to respect someone who cannot appreciate good ideas;" "Only someone who can think differently can appreciate good ideas. I would like to work with such a person."

## Nurturing mentor and guide

The statements made by the interviewees from which the theme nurturing mentor and guide emerged are presented below:

"I would like to work with a leader who is a good mentor, because if you work with an experienced hand who is there to actually mentor you throughout, molding you for a better tomorrow, your career can go places;"

"I feel like the boss's role should be that of a mentor where in you give enough guidance when needed but then at the same time he is not completely autocratic and gives you the freedom to work in your own manner;" "A boss should be a good guide, because especially in the initial years of your career, you will not flourish unless your immediate boss recognizes your strengths and helps you work on them;" "A good leader is one who is motivating and trusting. The person should understand my predicament and shortcomings. He should be aware of my progress and be able to tell me where I am going wrong and how I can improve;" "I would love to work with a leader who can teach me and help me grow in my career;" "I believe the leader is the one who guides us. He should be good mentor. He should be an example setter for other people."

## Open and approachable

This theme has been arrived at on the basis of the following and similar statements made by the interviewees:

"You should be able to talk to him freely and share your ideas with him;" "The leader should not be somebody I am scared of. An assertive leader is okay but he should have a personality that makes me comfortable to share my views with him;" "The leader should not be autocratic, he should have a more flexible approach so that I can communicate comfortably with him;" "The leader should be someone I can talk to freely anytime I want;" I would like to work with a senior who makes an effort to encourage communication from subordinates;" "I would like to work with someone who is approachable; "I can work well with a leader who is approachable;" "I would like to work with a leader who can accept feedback about himself from employees;" "I would like to work with someone who can facilitate effective communication among employees and guide them to attain their goals;" "A boss is someone whom you look up to. It's not always about taking orders. He should treat us as co-workers as we are working for the same company;" "He should be open, friendly, and a good communicator."

## Team builder

"I would like to work with someone who can bring people together;" "I would love to be part of a team where there is lot of bonding;" "I look forward to work with someone who discourages infighting;" "The best leader is one who carries the team with him;" "I would love to work with a leader who believes in collaboration, where we all have good relations with each other;" "It would be really nice to work where people are positive and motivated to work together and that's what a leader can create."

It is clear from the above that Millennials consider only those organizations as learning institutions where they have personal space, empowerment, freedom to take risks, experiment and are allowed to pursue entrepreneurial innovation.

It may be concluded that Millennials prefer to work with an immediate supervisor one whose style has to be more nurturing, mentoring, and coaching, who is open to meet people, who brings people together, empowering in his approach, who is fair, a good role model, and inspires others."

## Intent to Leave

In an effort to understand what will make Millennials leave one organization for another one, we asked the question, "What will make you leave the company?" Responses to this question have been content analyzed and findings presented below. Five key themes (see Table 4.7 and Figure 4.4) emerged as push factors to search for another job opening: negative work environment and culture (54.26 percent), toxic boss (50 percent), unfair treatment and performance–reward inequity (42.55 percent), uninteresting work (32.98 percent), and work pressure (32.98 percent).

### Negative work environment and culture

More than half of the sample—54.26 percent—considers negative work environment and culture to be the most compelling reason to leave the

Table 4.7  Intent to leave

| Intent to leave | Frequency | % |
| --- | --- | --- |
| Negative work environment | 51 | 54.26 |
| Toxic boss | 47 | 50.00 |
| Unfair treatment and performance inequity | 40 | 42.55 |
| Work pressure | 31 | 32.98 |
| Monotonous and uninteresting work | 31 | 32.98 |

Note: N = 100.

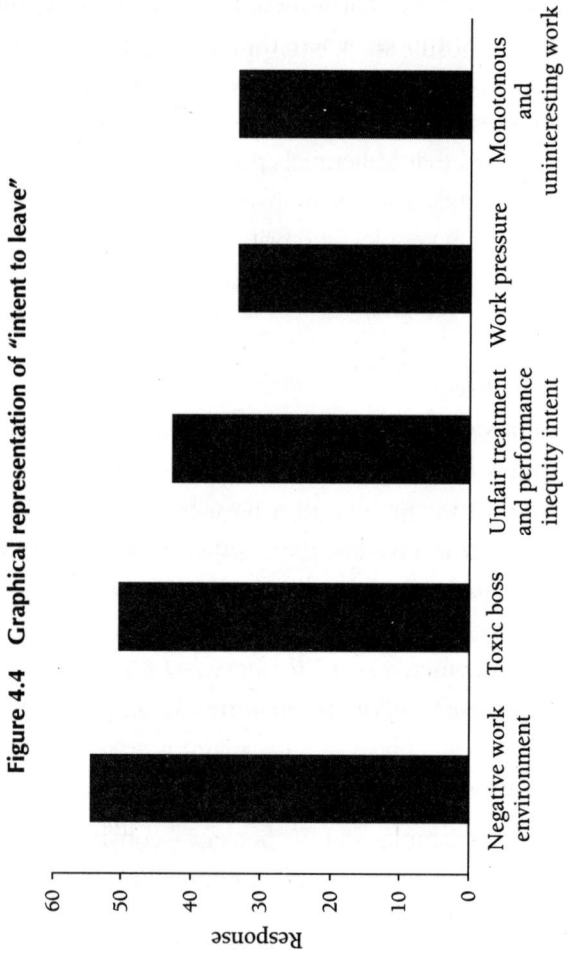

**Figure 4.4** Graphical representation of "intent to leave"

organization. Interviewees have clearly stated that if there is office politics, negativity in the work culture and lack of respect they would prefer to look for another job.

Further descriptions also brought out that they would not like an inflexible work culture; closed minded people, lack of openness, an environment of too much control and nitpicking. They are also concerned about unfriendly colleagues, hostile work environment which together create an unpleasant, insecure, and negative work environment unsuitable for good performance.

## Toxic boss

A little more than half the interviewees—51 percent—consider a toxic boss as the push factor to leave the organization. This has been expressed as follows below:

"When the leader becomes negative and critical it is time to leave;" "A leader who does not value good ideas will make me leave;" "A leader who is always nitpicking will make me leave;" "A leader who is a micromanager will make me leave;" "A leader who breathes down my neck will tempt me to find another job;" "If my head is not proper and he is not treating me well and he is not recognizing my performance, he is de-motivating me, I will surely switch to another organization;" "If I get scolded even when I do a good job, then I would leave;" If there is no clarity on company direction, then I would leave;" " when small mistakes are heavily criticized especially in front of other colleagues, I would not be able to stay for long in that organization;" "Close-minded boss will be the worst type to work for and I would leave in such a situation;" "When the boss is apathetic, it's difficult to manage;" "I will not stay long when the boss is too controlling;" "When there is no guidance, no appreciation, no encouragement and motivation from superior there is no point in staying;" "A critical boss is difficult to work with. I would look for the opportunity to leave as soon as possible;" "Not giving me my fair share of appraisal or recognition will make me leave;" "Company must differentiate between good and bad, and performance should be rewarded and recognized for healthy competition;" "There should be some sort of appreciation for those who work well." "If I am a high performer, and there is no special treatment for me, then why would a high performer stay with the organization;" "Unfair treatment;" "Lack of feeling appreciated/recognized;" "No recognition for high performance;" "Unfair appraisal;" "Biased appraisals;" "Unfair rewards."

## Unfair treatment and performance–reward inequity

A total of 42.55 percent indicated that they would look for other options if they see unfairness in treatment. They highlighted the importance of being recognized and rewarded for work done.

"I will leave if the company is more bothered about your relationship with your boss rather than nature of the work done. Appraisal should be based on performance not on relationship;" "Fairness in treatment of employees and appraisal. Individual-centric treatment where each individual is paid attention to and valued otherwise there is no point in staying in the company;" "If you feel that some partiality going on, or some sort of internal politics, if that happens and if you can't tolerate beyond a certain level, definitely the person would leave. Say if all recognition is going to this other person, where as you are also slogging, working, but the other person is getting all the credit and is hogging away your limelight, then you simply can't stand it."

## Work pressure

This has been highlighted by 32.98 percent of the interviewees. Undue work pressure, long working hours, and lack of opportunity to work from home bother them and tempt them to look for more convenient and comfortable options. This group also mentioned that they would like to have better work-life balance and if this is affected adversely in their workplace, then they would look for other job options; "It should not be all work and no play, we should enjoy life where we are working, the boss shouldn't keep you engaged over weekends, work–life balance should be there;" "For me the working style, nature of work, number of hours taken out of me, whether the work finishes in stipulated time, the work timing is more important;" "The mental stress should be low, means working hours should be flexible. Like many software companies, like Wipro, have flexible timings, and Wipro started this thing that you can work from your home also;" "Lot of vacations so that we can relax our mind, you know how engineering jobs are—too much mental work, and so there should be vacations. The company should not affect our personal lives."

## Monotonous work

Approximately one-third of the interviewed students (32.98 percent) brought out that boring work, dull work, repetitive and monotonous work, mechanical work, work which does not provide learning opportunity.

## Part III: Millennials through the Lens of HR Professionals

After perusing the Millennials' MOWP, we thought it would be appropriate to sketch the profile of Millennials through the lens of HR Professionals. It is in this perspective that unstructured interviews were conducted with 50 HR professionals belonging to middle management. They were requested to use at least five adjectives to describe the Millennials' attitudes, dispositions, and behavior. Based on the content analysis the following table has been constructed:

From Table 4.8 and Figure 4.5, it is evident that on the positive side Millennials are viewed to be energetic (rank 1), tech savvy (rank 6), curious

Table 4.8  Millennials through the lens of HR professionals

| S. No. | Adjectives for millennials | Frequency | % | Rank |
|---|---|---|---|---|
| 1. | Energetic and enthusiastic | 50 | 100.00 | 1 |
| 2. | Highly ambitious | 48 | 96.00 | 2 |
| 3. | Overconfident | 46 | 92.00 | 3 |
| 4. | Low respect for authority | 46 | 92.00 | 4 |
| 5. | Materialistic | 41 | 82.00 | 5 |
| 6. | Techno-savvy | 38 | 76.00 | 6 |
| 7. | Low commitment to organization | 36 | 72.00 | 7 |
| 8. | Me generation | 35 | 70.00 | 8 |
| 9. | Entitlement centric | 30 | 60.00 | 9 |
| 10. | Curious and learning | 30 | 60.00 | 10 |
| 11. | Creative | 28 | 56.00 | 11 |

*Note:* N = 50; the HR professionals were asked to give at least five adjectives to describe Millennials. Their responses were content analyzed and quantified, and are presented in this table.

**Figure 4.5** Graphical representation of "Millennials through the lens of HR professionals"

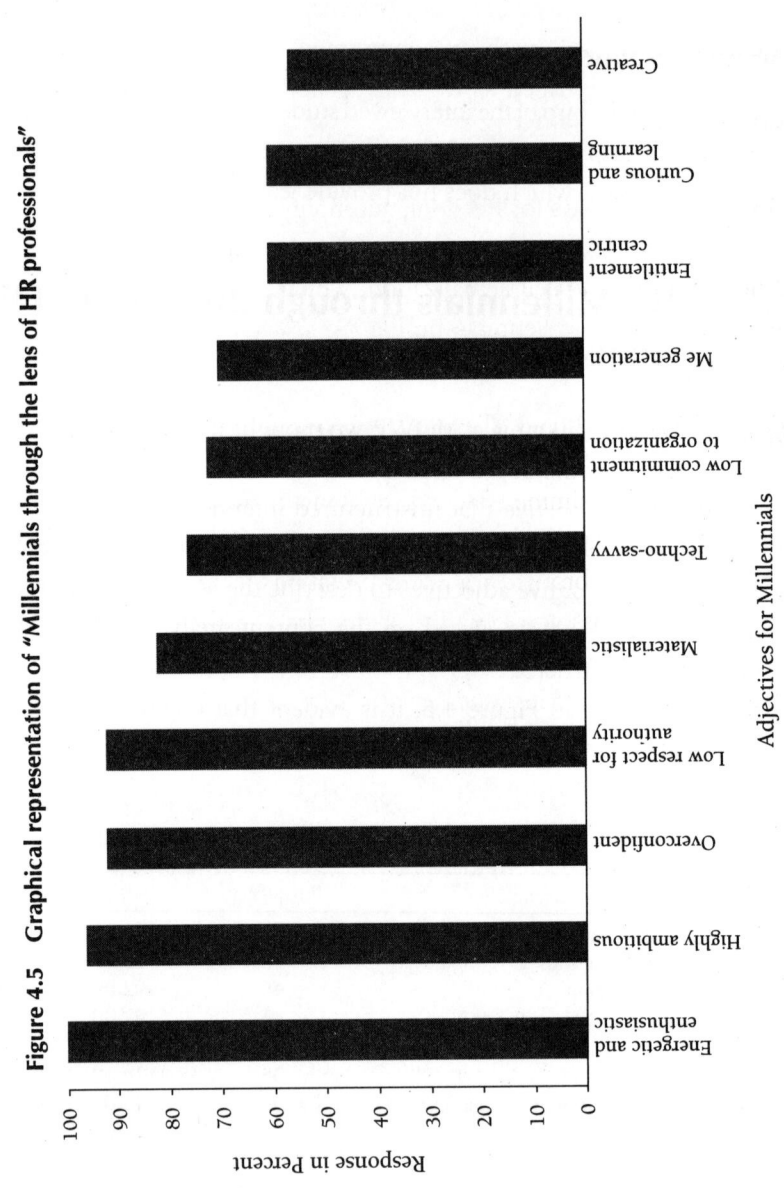

and learning (rank 10) and creative (rank 11). Apart from these four, however, they are primarily viewed as highly ambitious (rank 2), overconfident (rank 3), with low respect for authority (rank 4). They are also perceived to be materialistic (rank 4), with low commitment to the organization (rank 7). They have been described as the "Me" generation (rank 8) followed by entitlement centric (rank 9).

Surprisingly HR professionals don't see Millennials as entrepreneurial innovators, with desire for freedom, autonomy and personal space, being concerned about fairness, equity and justice, having tremendous need for self development and self actualization, which is a highly promising and potent aspect of the Millennials' profile.

# Summary and Conclusions

This chapter has examined the expectations of the Millennials from the workplace, their experience of workplace realities, and the gap between the two. It has also brought out the expectations which people have from their immediate boss, the key push factors behind the intention to leave the organization, and HR professionals' perceptions about Millennials.

We now reiterate the key findings of Chapter 4 in the following sections.

## Millennials' Expectations from the Workplace

Millennials expectations from the workplace can be summarized as follows:

- Millennials crave for a workplace which provides freedom for experimentation,
- Millennials desire to work in an organization that offers opportunities to take initiative and encourages idea generation and innovation;
- Millennials desire to work in a place where their performance contribution are amply appreciated, recognized, and rewarded; and
- Fairness and transparency are important attractors for Millennials to join an organization; and
- Millennials would like to embrace a workplace where there is plenty of opportunity for learning, growth, and self-development.

In-depth interview data broadly echoed the above cited findings from the questionnaire data. Thus according to Millennials work is a very important domain of their lives. This somewhat echoes the findings of Western literature which posits that work is central to people in industrialized countries (see Harpaz et al., 02). It has also provided rich insights into what they want from the workplace and why. It further shows that the workplace is the arena for the fulfillment of multiple needs.

## Millennials' Experience of Workplace Realities

Millennials with work experience have experienced the following workplace characteristics (in order of importance) at the workplace. Companies which they worked in had

- strong brand value;
- good physical ambience;
- freedom for coffee breaks;
- high prestige;
- ethical dealings;
- rules orientation;
- contributed to the economy; and
- good team work.

Interview data findings also echo many of the findings from the questionnaire data cited above. The workplace has been experienced as:

- Hierarchical and top-down;
- Conformity centric;
- Paying inadequate attention to unleash human creative potential; and
- Less sensitive to people development.

## A Comparative Picture of Workplace Factors: Expected vs Available

The desired workplace factors listed in section A (top 15) have been found to a much lower extent (ranking 17–45) at the workplace. Those attributes which they rated as much lesser in importance compared to the desired factors—typically physical and environment-related factors—have emerged among the top 15 at the workplace. Only two of the top fifteen attributes in the Expectations list feature in the top 15 Available list that is—encourages team work (rank 9) and learning (rank 12).

Thus while Millennials look for better opportunity for self development, greater autonomy, openness, and freedom, as well as opportunity to take initiative, unfortunately what the workplace gives them is far below the desired level. What they get is a workplace which is dominantly hierarchical and top down, customer centric, pays inadequate attention to unleash human creative potential, and less sensitive to people development. There is thus a clear contrast and a huge gap between Millennials' meaning of workplace and the workplace realities which they are confronted with.

It may be worthwhile to mention here that incongruence between expectations and reality can lead to stress disorders, low job satisfaction and negatively affect mental health. It is therefore not surprising if there is disenchantment, disconnect with the workplace, and propensity to leave organizations among Millennials.

## Expectations Regarding Immediate Supervisor

The interview data from Millennials throw up the following qualities they wish to see in their immediate supervisor's attitude and behaviour. They look for an immediate supervisor who is

- humble and listening;
- a good mentor;
- accessible and available;
- empowering in his approach;
- fair;
- a good role model and inspiring for others; and
- able to bring people together.

It may be mentioned here that according to interview data immediate superiors have been found to be

- critical;
- imposing;

- ordering rather than guiding;
- close minded and rigid.

These findings highlight the glaring mismatch between valence of expectations and reality. No wonder therefore Millennials are cynical about authority figures and express their resentment at any opportunity.

## Intent to Leave

Millennials have also indicated what makes them think of leaving an organization within a short span of time. The prominent pushers according to them are the following:

- A negative work environment filled with politics, conflict, poor interpersonal relationships.
- A toxic boss who is critical, non appreciative, distancing, unsympathetic, and above all, who tries to show his superiority.
- Unfair behavior.
- Inadequate reward for good performance.

Desire to leave is further aggravated by high work pressure and repetitive work.

## Millennials as Perceived by HR Professionals

On the positive side, Millennials have been viewed by HR professionals as

- energetic and enthusiastic;
- techno-savvy;
- curious and learning;
- creative.

On the negative side they have been viewed as

- ambitious;
- over confident;
- low respect for authority;
- materialistic;
- 'Me' generation; and
- entitlement centric.

# References

Agarwal, S. (1993). Influence of formalization on role stress, organizational commitment and work alienation of sales persons: A cross-national comparative study. *Journal of International Business Studies, 24* (4), 715–739.

Berelson, B. (1952). *Content analysis in communication research.* New York: Free Press.

Bernstein, P. (1997). *American work values: Their origin and development.* New York: State University of New York Press.

Borg, I. (1990). Multiple facetisations of work values. *Applied Psychology: An International Review, 39* (4), 401–412.

Brief, A. P., & Nord, W. R. (Eds.) (1990). *Meanings of occupational work: A collection of essays.* Lexington, Massachusetts: Lexington Books.

Buckingham, M., & Coffman, C. (1999). *First, break all the rules, what the world's greatest managers do differently.* New York: Simon and Schuster.

Burke, R. J., & Eddy, Ng (2006). The changing nature of work organizations: Implications for human resource management. *Human Resource Management Review, 16* (2), 86–94.

Cummings, T. G., & Cooper, C. L. (1979). *Cybernetic framework for studying occupational stress.* Minneapolis, Minnesota: Minnesota Press.

Dansereau, F., Jr., Graen, G., & Haga, W. J. (1975). A vertical dyad linkage approach to leadership within formal organizations: A longitudinal investigation of the role making process. *Organizational Behavior and Human Performance, 13,* 46–78. doi:10.1016/0030-5073(75)90005-7

De Vos, A., & Meganck, A. (2007). What HR managers do versus what employees value: Exploring both parties views on retention management from a psychological contract perspective. *Personnel Review, 38* (1): 45–60.

Dienesch, R. M., & Liden, R. C. (1986). Leader-member exchange model of leadership: A critique and further development. *Academy of Management Review, 11* (3), 618–634. doi: 10.2307/258314

England, G. W., & Misumi, J. (1986). Work centrality in Japan and the United States. *Journal of Cross Cultural Psychology, 17* (4), 399–416.

Erez, M., & Earley, P. C. (1993). *Culture, self-identity and work.* Oxford University Press: New York.

Ferris, G. R. (1985). Role of leadership in the employee withdrawal process: A constructive replication. *Journal of Applied Psychology, 70* (4), 777–781.

Fiedler, F. E. (1967). *A theory of leadership effectiveness.* New York: McGraw-Hill.

French, J. R. P., Jr., Caplan, R. D., & Harrison, R. V. (1982). *The mechanisms of job stress and strain.* Wiley: London.

Furnham, A. & Schaeffer, R. (1984). Person-environment fit, job satisfaction and mental health. *Journal of Occupational Psychology, 57* (4), 295–307.

Furnham, A. & Walsh, J. (1990). Consequences of person-environment incongruence: Absenteeism, frustration and stress. *The Journal of Social Psychology, 131* (2), 187–204.

Johnson Controls. (2010). *Generation Y and the workplace, Annual report 2010.* London: Johnson Controls Global Workplace Solutions..

Gerstner, C. R., & Day, D. V. (1997). Meta-analytic review of leader-member exchange theory: Correlates and construct ideas. *Journal of Applied Psychology, 82* (6), 827–844.

Glenberg, A. M., & Andrzejewski, M. E. (2008). *Learning from data: An introduction to statistical reasoning* (3rd ed.). New York and London: Lawrence Erlbaum Associates.

Graen, G. (1976). Role-making processes within complex organizations. In M. D. Dunnette (Ed.), *Handbook of industrial and organizational psychology* (pp. 1201–1245). Chicago: Rand McNally.

Graen, G., & Scandura, T. A. (1987). Toward a psychology of dyadic organization. In B. Staw & L. L. Cummings (Eds.) (pp. 175–208). Greenwich, Connecticut: JAI Press.

Graen, G., Liden, R. C., & Hoel, W. (1982). Role of leadership in the employee withdrawal process. *Journal of Applied Psychology*, 67 (6), 868–872, doi:10.1037/0021-9010.67.6.868

Graen, G. B., & Cashman, J. (1975). A role-making model of leadership in formal organizations: A developmental approach. In J. G. Hunt & L. L. Larson (Eds.). *Leadership Frontiers* (pp. 143–165). Kent, Ohio: Kent State University Press.

Graen, G. B., & Schiemann, W. (1978), Leader member agreement: A vertical dyad linkage approach, *Journal of Applied Psychology*, 63 (2), 206–212.

Harding, S. D., & Hikspoors, F. J. (1995). New work values: In theory and in practice. *International Social Science Journal*, 145 (3), 441–456.

Harpaz, I. (1990). The importance of work goals: An international perspective. *Journal of International Business Studies*, 21 (1), 75–93.

———. (1999). The transformation of work values in Israel: Stability and change over time. *Monthly Labor Review*, 122 (5), 46–50.

Harpaz, I., Honig, B., & Coetsier, P. (2002). A cross-cultural longitudinal analysis of the meaning of work and the socialization process of career starters. *Journal of World Business*, 37 (4), 230–244.

Hecht, T. D., & Allen, N. J. (2005). Exploring links between polychronicity and well-being from the perspective of person-job fit: Does it matter if you prefer to do only one thing at a time? *Organizational Behavior and Human Decision Process*, 98 (2), 155–178.

Holland. J. (1973). *Making vocational choices: A theory of careers*. Englewood Cliffs. New Jersey: Prentice Hall.

———. (1985). *The self-directed search—professional manual*. Odessa, Florida: Psychological Assessment Resources.

Horwitz, F. M., Heng, C. T., & Quazi, H. A. (2003). Finders, keepers? Attracting, motivating and retaining knowledge workers. *Human Resource Management Journal*, 13 (4), 23–44.

Jablin, F. M., & Sussman, L. (1983). Organizational group communication: A review of the literature and model of the process. In H. H. Greenbaum, R. L. Falcione, & S. A. Hellweg (Eds.), *Organizational Communication: Abstracts, analysis and overview*. Newbury Park, California: Sage.

Kanungo, R. N. (1983). Work alienation: A pan-cultural perspective. *International Studies of Management and Organization*, 13 (1/2), Cross-Cultural Management: II. Empirical Studies (Spring-Summer, 1983), 119–138.

Kaplan, H. R., & Tausky, C. (1974). The meaning of work among the hard-core unemployed. *Pacific Sociological Review*, 17 (2), 185–198.

Katz, D., & Kahn, R. (1966). *The social psychology of organizations*. New York: Wiley.

———. (1978). *The social psychology of organizations* (2nd ed.). New York: Wiley.

Leonard, N. H., Beauvais, L. L., & Scholl, R. W. (1999). Work motivation: The incorporation of self concept based processes. *Human Relations*, 72 (8), 969–998.

Liden, R. C. and Graen, G. (1980). Eneralizability of the vertical dyad linkage model of leadership. *Academy of Management Journal*, 23 (3), 451–465.

Lipkin, N. A. and Perrymore, A. J. (2009). *Y in the workplace: Managing the "Me First" Generation*. New Jersey: The Career Press Inc.

Lyons, S. (2004). An exploration of generational values in life and at work, *Dissertation Abstracts International*, 3462A (UMI No. AATNQ94206).

Mannheim, B. (1993). Gender and the effects of demographics status and work values on work centrality. *Work and Occupation, 20* (1), 3–22.

Morin, E. M. (2004). The meaning of work in modern times, *10th World Congress on Human Resources Management*, Rio de Janeiro, Brazil, August, speech.

Morse, N. L., & Weiss, R. S. (1955). The function and meaning of work and job. *American Sociological Review, 20* (2), 191–198.

MOW International Research Team. (1987). *The meaning of working*. London: Academic Press.

Ng, Thomas W. H., & Feldman, D. C. (2009). Age, work experience and the psychological contract. *Journal of organizational behaviour, 30* (8), 1053–1075.

Parker, R. S. (1971). *The future of work and leisure*. London: MacGibbon & Kee.

Roehling, M. V., Cavanaugh, M. A., Moynihan, L. M., & Boswell, W. (2000). The nature of the new employment relationship: A content analysis of the practitioner and academic literatures. *Human Resource Management, 39* (4), 305–320.

Ros, M., Schwartz, S. H., & Surkiss, S. (1999). Basic individual values, work values and the meaning of work. *Applied Psychology: An International Review, 48* (1), 49–71.

Ruiz-Quintanilla, S. A. and Wilpert, B. (1991). Are work meanings changing? *European Journal of Work and Organizational Psychology, 1* (2/3), 91–109.

Shamir, B. (1991). Meaning, self and motivation in organizations. *Organizational Studies, 12* (3), 405–424.

Smola, K. W., & Sutton, C. D. (2002). Generational differences: Revisiting generational work values for the new millennium. *Journal of Organizational Behavior, 23* (4), 363–382.

Stanton, S. W. (2008). *Decoding Generational Differences: Fact, fiction...or should we just get back to work?* Deloitte LLP.

Tajfel, H., & Turner, J. C. (1986). The social identity theory of inter-group behavior. In S. Worchel and L. W. Austin (Eds.), *Psychology of Intergroup Relations*. Chicago: Nelson-Hall.

Turnley, W. H., & Feldman, D. C. (2000). Re-examining the effects of psychological contract violations: Unmet expectations and job dissatisfaction as mediators. *Journal of Organizational Behavior, 21* (1), 25–42.

Twenge, J., & Campbell, W. (2009). *The narcissism epidemic: Living in the age of entitlement*. New York: Simon & Schuster.

Twenge, J., & Foster, J. (2008). Mapping the scale of the narcissism epidemic: Increases in narcissism 2002–2007 within ethnic groups. *Journal of Research in Personality, 42* (6), 1619–1622.

———. (2010). Birth cohort increases in narcissistic personality traits among American college students, 1982–2009. *Social Psychological and Personality Science, 1* (1), 99–106.

Twenge, J. (2006). *Generation Me*. New York City: Free Press.

Twenge, J. M., Campbell, S. M., Hoffman, B. J., & Lance, C. E. (2010). Generational differences in work values: Leisure and extrinsic values increasing, social and intrinsic values decreasing. *Journal of Management, 36* (5).

Twenge, J. M., Konrath, S., Foster, J. D., Campbell, W. K., & Bushman, B. J. (2008). Egos inflating over time: A cross-temporal meta-analysis of the narcissistic personality inventory. *Journal of Personality, 76* (4), 875–901.

Visweswaran, C., & Deshpande, S. P. (1996). Ethics success and job satisfaction: A test of dissonance theory in India, *Journal of Business Ethics, 15* (10), 1065–1069.

Warr, P. (1982). A national study of non-financial employment commitment. *Journal of Occupational Psychology, 55* (4), 297–312.

Yang, Liu-Quin, Che, H., & Spector, P. E. (2008). Job stress and well-being: An examination from the view of person–environment fit. *Journal of Occupational and Organizational Psychology, 81* (3), 567–587.

Yiu, L., & Saner, R. (2011). Talent recruitment, attrition and retention: Strategic challenges for Indian industries in the next decade. Geneva: Centre for Socio-Economic Development.

Zemke, R., Raines, C., & Filipczak, B. (2000). *Generations at work: Managing the clash of veterans, boomers, xers and nexters in your workplace* (2nd ed.). New York: Amacom.

# Architecting the Organization of Tomorrow

**5**

We begin this chapter by narrating an exciting and meaningful story. There was once a school teacher who used to tear a world map and give the bits and pieces of paper to the students asking them to reconstruct the map. Invariably students failed at this exercise. However, once there came student who successfully reconstructed the map. The teacher was aghast because in five years of conducting the exercise, not a single student had succeeded. This made him very curious and he rushed to the student, patted him on the back and exclaimed, "Young boy you must be a genius, how did you do it?" The reply of the boy is profound and meaningful and conveys the basic tenets underlying this chapter. He said, "Teacher, I didn't try to piece together the world map. I tried to put together the picture of the boy which I found on the scraps of paper and to my surprise, I found that I had succeeded in constructing the world map."

Reflection on the above story brings out the key philosophy underlying this concluding chapter—"Architecting the Organization of Tomorrow." It reflects the following essential wisdom:

- Build the Millennials and the youth and in turn the world will be built.
- Build the Millennials and the young generation and they will build flourishing, competing, and excelling organizations.

Millennials and the young generation generally operate at the frontline of the organization, playing a critical role for execution of action plans, as well as directly dealing with stakeholders like customers, employees, and others. Youth are the forerunners in experimentation, innovation, and new idea generation and therefore symbolize the essence of transformation, change, and creativity. If they are frustrated, disengaged, and disenchanted, neither will grand organizational plans fructify nor will creative ideas bring new life to organizations. Vineet Nayar in his book *Employees First, Customers Second* (2010) passionately advocated this point, exhorting organizations to be sensitive to the needs, aspirations, and ambitions of their people, and more so of the youth. Further he seems to propagate that those organizations which evolve their human processes and align them with the needs, expectations, and aspirations of their people are bound to excel and do better than others.

It must be highlighted that the importance of enthusiasm, passion, excitement, and commitment of those at the frontline are critical for an organization in pursuing its larger goal. This is an ageless and timeless truism equally applicable in the management of Millennials. Unless Millennials are fired up with the passion to innovate, create, and experiment, it would be difficult to build excelling, competing, and winning organizations of tomorrow. Organizations must therefore make conscious efforts to create a workplace which can be exciting, inspiring, and challenging and enabling expression of innovation, creativity, and experimentation.

It is in this spirit that the present chapter has been sketched.

The chapter weaves together the findings regarding:

- Millennials' meaning of workplace and experienced reality;
- Preferred boss[1] through Millennials' lens; and
- Millennials' profile from the lens of HR professionals.

This interweaving has been done with a view to create the backdrop for building the organizations of tomorrow in order to enable the reader to see the disconnect and the gap between:

---

[1] Boss and superior have been used interchangeably. The terms refer to one's immediate superior to whom one directly reports.

- what they want and what they get; and
- who they are and how they are perceived.

This chapter also examines the valley of the corporate world focusing on the various facets of the organization—strategy, structure, systems, processes, styles, and culture to apprise the readers about the existing corporate reality. Finally the chapter dwells on the needed shifts in the organizational architecture for creating a fit between Millennials' expectations and the workplace realities.

The quest of humanity has been the history of struggle to build nations, institutions, and organizations responsive enough to meet citizens and individuals' needs, demands, and aspirations. Those nations which succeeded in bringing a convergence between the two took big strides towards progress without suffering much turmoil, revolt, and revolution. However nations which failed to create convergence between citizen's demands and aspirations with strategic plans and policy, experienced public outcry, revolt, and even revolution. The French Revolution of the 19th century, Russian, and other East European revolutions of the 20th century, amply prove this basic thesis. In the 21st century the recent revolutions in Egypt, Libya, Tunisia, Bahrain, and other parts of the Middle East, further reinforce the above paradigm—inadequate convergence between human aspirations and responsiveness of various institutions of a nation.

India is witnessing a similar churn in public life as indicated by the recent movements by civil society. For example, Anna Hazare's movement against the poor responsiveness of the government on various issues affecting the common man clearly illustrates the result of non-convergence between citizens' aspirations and the response of governmental institutions. There has been an outpouring of public support for Anna Hazare because the issue of corruption raised by him is something which Indians resonate with. Millions of people throughout the country—especially Millennials—have come forward to express solidarity for the cause in a manner not seen since Gandhi's call for freedom from the British. This is a sign of the times; it shows that youth are getting restless and vociferous and seek greater transparency, involvement, engagement, and fulfillment of their aspirations and needs.

At the organizational level, it is invariably observed that when managements craft organizations responsive enough to match human needs and aspirations, both individuals and organizations flourish. There is a sense of excitement, satisfaction, and commitment which in turn results in performance excellence as well as worthwhile and sustainable contributions. If the organization however fails to synchronize the two there is helplessness and powerlessness and suboptimal performance both at the individual level and the organizational levels. Millennials would not find enough meaning to stay committed to the organization and they would feel tempted to look for other alternatives, a behavior which in our observation is, unfortunately, branded as disloyalty by the organization. In case they do not succeed in moving out of the organization, they continue to stay but experience tremendous alienation and estrangement expressed in the form of disengagement and withdrawal.

It is relevant to highlight that human beings and human needs are not static (Maslow, 1987). They dynamically change, grow, and transform with the passage of time and stages of economic prosperity as well as stages in their lifestyles and degree of enlightenment and knowledge. In fact human needs are constantly shaped by social, political, economic, informational, and technological shifts taking place in society. Viewing human societies in a historical perspective over the last few centuries brings out that human needs have drastically shifted from the Agrarian Age to the Industrial Age, from the Industrial Age to the Information and Knowledge Age. In other words, the need profile of the emerging era is very different from the needs profile in the preceding eras. The prerequisite for this is the shift from the mindset of yesterday to the mindset of tomorrow.

In this context of changing human needs today therefore the way in which nations and organizations have dealt with human beings in an erstwhile era, maybe completely obsolete and irrelevant for architecting organizations and societies of tomorrow. Future nations and organizations will therefore have to be shaped and built differently in order to stay aligned with the needs and aspirations of the emergent generation.

To build organizations for the future, there is a dire need to have an in-depth understanding of the needs, dreams, aspirations, personality, and value dispositions of the Millennials, which would no doubt tend to be different from those of the previous generation. Such understanding will, needless to say, result in creating the right set of assumptions about Millennials' nature and their dispositions for building the organization of tomorrow. Unfortunately organizations of tomorrow are in danger of being poorly managed and led because they are using the processes of today and the assumptions and mindsets of yesterday while managing Millennials. In fact this has been a perennial issue in societies transitioning from one age to the other. Invariably there has been a lag, and therefore there is a struggle to move from past mindsets to the present and future realities. Those organizations which proactively respond to the emerging realities at social–psychological and cognitive levels of the individuals are in a better position to handle the generational transition and excellently meet organizational goals—sustainable performance and growth.

From the above exposition it is clear that organizations and leaders must develop sensitivity and capability to understand and appreciate the emerging needs of the new generation and proactively shape organizational structure and architecture responsive enough to meet the needs, dreams, and aspirations of the next generation. In other words in the context of our study, organizations and leaders must map out the Millennials' dreams, needs, and aspirations and appropriately architect organizations, the culture, and leadership styles. Organizations and leaders need to shift their mindsets—attitudes, behavior, and styles—from the shackles of the past and present to proactively respond to the emerging realities of the future. If this fundamental shift in perspective takes place then organizations would be in a position to design and evolve organizational strategies, structure, systems, processes, leadership skills, and styles enabling them to cope with the challenges of the future. The biggest block to align the present with the future however lies in the collective mindset of the older generation. Once the collective mindset is changed, appropriate convergence and alignments at the organizational level will smoothly follow.

Perusal of management literature of the 20th century powerfully brings out that organizations are architected around the beliefs held by owners of organizations and their managements. The strong focus of organizations of the Industrial Era was to ensure predictability, stability, and compliance. Even today in the Information and Knowledge Era organizations continue to exhibit this orientation and mindset.

Most organizational processes, systems, and strategies are evolved for the purpose of attaining these goals, the assumption being—rightly or wrongly—that the achievement of these goals will automatically lead to organizational excellence. Whether we talk of control systems or process-centric frameworks and organizational planning process, the whole endeavor has been to bring predictability, stability, and compliance in organizational functioning. The overarching emphasis on predictability, stability, and compliance relegates the forces driving creativity, innovation, experimentation, freedom, and empowerment into the background.

## ⓜ Valley of the Corporate World

Our experience of the past few decades in the corporate sector has provided us many deep insights into organizational functioning. Dealing with training of more than 100,000 managers, consulting with CEOs and top teams of more than a 100 organizations, has provided many valuable and enriching experiences and insights. The valley of the corporate world presented below draws heavily from these experiences.

The value which organizations attach to human beings at the workplace can be surmised from the fact that they are viewed as a resource, like materials and other factors of production. Few organizations view them as assets and treat them accordingly. Another indicator is the tendency to slash company spending on employee training and also cut jobs, as soon as there are problems of any kind facing the company. This shows that the organization sees the person as highly expendable and replaceable.

Many MNCs in India, China, Egypt, Mauritius, Mexico, South Africa, and Brazil tend to expect their subsidiaries to adopt practices, processes, and culture and training used by the corporate office, even though unsuitable to the local realities of the units and subsidiaries. Even domestic multi-location and multi-business companies tend to follow a similar pattern of compelling people to adapt to the existing organizational practices and culture regardless of their region specific requirements. This continues in many ways even today, despite the lessons brought out by Percy Barnevik, Ex-CEO ABB, that successful global organizations are glocal and must primarily respond to local requirements rather than being purely head-office centric in their approaches. However, the approach taken by organizations in general reflects that most organizations are too preoccupied with ensuring predictability and stability, many times at the cost of creating institutions of excellence innovative enough to compete and excel. This betrays a total lack of sensitivity to nuances of different businesses and human needs and aspirations especially of the younger generation. This clearly brings out the prevalence of unilateral and top-down approach adopted by most organizations while dealing with both their people as well as the business, in their quest for uniformity, control, and compliance centricity.

Another common feature across organizations is the obsession with designing training programs to socialize new incumbents into the existing realities of the workplace. Strong efforts are made to evolve strategies and processes enabling organizations to powerfully condition new entrants to existing realities. Very few organizations make efforts to understand the following:

- Who are the new entrants?
- What are their dreams?
- What are their ambitions?
- What are their needs?
- What is their social–psychological disposition?
- What is the kind of life they would like to lead which can make them happy, excited, innovative, creative, and productive?

The outcome of this one-way socialization is a form of cloning which takes place with the intention of creating a strong culture. When the work culture is strong, it results in robotization of the thought processes, attitudes, and behavior of individuals. In turn these people tend to adopt a similar approach while inducting new entrants down the line thereby ensuring the perpetuation of this vicious cycle. The pressures for conformity in behavior are so strong at the workplace that anyone who diverges from the existing culture is promptly pulled back. In fact in strong culture organizations such individuals face social censure till they fall in line.

The well-known experiment performed on chimpanzees (Stephenson, 1967) has by now become a classic one to explain the conformity-centric forces which lead to the building of the organizational culture. The experiment consisted of five chimpanzees in an enclosure with a bunch of bananas hung on the top. A stepladder was placed below the banana bunch making it easy to reach the bananas. Every time the chimpanzees reached out to pluck the bananas, a strong jet of cold water was sprayed on them and they withdrew to escape the water jet which they disliked. After all the chimpanzees experienced this, they stopped trying for the bananas. The experimenter then introduced a new chimpanzee into the enclosure and as expected, this one also tried to get the bananas. Immediately the other chimpanzees pulled him down because of their conditioning that reaching out for the bananas lead to a spray of cold water.

The above example clearly indicates that strong culture organizations normally do not permit deviance of any kind, thereby promoting compliance and killing creativity and innovation. This constrains an organization's ability to anticipate and prepare for the future. It is human nature to transmit what they have received and this is how cultures get perpetuated making it difficult for new cultures to emerge.

Management gurus of the industrial era—Taylor, Fayol, and others—advocated the theory of evolving systems and processes primarily geared to control employees, bring compliance centricity, and force them to execute the plans evolved by the "specialists" in the organization. In fact, Henry Ford went to the extent of saying (about workers), "All I want is a good pair of hands. Unfortunately, they come attached to a person" (Ford and Crowther, 1922).

Deeper scrutiny of the above exposition powerfully reveals the underlying assumption about human beings which dominated the thinking in the Industrial Age.

In his pioneering work, *The human side of enterprise,* McGregor (1960) captured the assumptions of man in the Industrial Age as Theory X comprising of the following:

- The average human being has an inherent dislike of work and will avoid it if he can.
- Because of this human characteristic of dislike of work, people must be coerced, controlled, directed, and threatened with punishment towards the achievement of the organization's objectives.

- The average human being prefers to be directed and wishes to avoid responsibility, has relatively little ambition and wants security above all.

Many thinkers such as Gulick, Taylor, Fayol, Mooney, Urwick (cited in Gibson 1966) have highlighted that in the Industrial Era, human beings were viewed to be similar to machines—predictable, repairable, and replaceable. According to Downs (1965), they were also seen to be distrustful, suspicious, jealous, and deceitful.

These have been the salient assumptions about human beings and therefore organizational processes and practices were designed around these basic assumptions. The exploitative, manipulative, and insensitive actions of managements can be traced to such negative assumptions about human nature and hence the quest for ensuring predictability, reliability, and role clarity to keep the wheels of the organization in motion. Unfortunately such assumptions about human nature persist in many organizations even today.

A host of thinkers like McGregor (1960), Heilbroner (1980, 1970), Fromm (2003, 1973), Argyris (1962), Bennis (1994, 1966), Rogers (1961), Gibson (1966), Aktouf (1992), Drucker (1988), and Herzberg (1980, 1966, 1976) have been vehement critics of these postulates about human nature and have rejected them outright. In their view human beings are self conscious, take self responsibility, have right judgment and free will, enjoy work, and seek a sense of challenge; they have natural creative and innovative urges; they aspire to grow and self evolve.

Eric Fromm went to the extent of saying,

> Man is not a means to reach this or that end ... but that he is himself the bearer of his own end ... not only on his capacity for individual action but also on his capacity for participation in history and on the fact that each man bears within himself humanity as a whole. (Cited in Aktouf, 1992)

McGregor (1960) derided the negative assumptions about human beings in the Industrial Era and propagated Theory Y. According to him, a human being does not inherently dislike work; work for him is a source of satisfaction and is as natural as play or rest. Human beings are self directed, self controlled, and dislike being coerced, manipulated, and controlled. Human beings have learning orientation and continuously seek responsibility. They have high degree of imagination, ingenuity, and creativity in solving organizational problems. In fact McGregor concluded that in the modern industrial life, human intellectual potential is only partially utilized because of wrong assumptions about human nature. Despite the concerns raised by various thinkers regarding the inaccurate views about human nature, practitioners have unfortunately, continued to hold many of these assumptions even today, thus continuing to build organizations of today and tomorrow with the mindset of yesterday.

## The Millennial Generation: Who Are They and What Do They Expect?

At this stage it may be worthwhile to highlight (even at the cost of being repetitive)

1. The profile of Millennials.
2. Their expectations from the workplace.
3. The expected versus experienced workplace realities according to the Millennials.

Such an exposition will help readers understand the Millennials' expectations and their experienced realities.

1. Understanding who they are in terms of their personality, value preferences, and demographics would also be useful in getting insights into their work place expectations and behavior.

Key findings from the study about the Millennials' profile are briefly sketched below:

- They are high achievers, ambitious, and would like to strive hard to reach their goals.

- They are highly self-driven, have an internal locus of control, and have capability to confront failures; they reflect and strive to convert failure into success.
- Personal growth and development (in a psychological sense) is the most important value for Millennials; followed by self-fulfillment value, progressive orientation, and community development, in that order.
- Prior work experience, educational background, parental background, and place of upbringing significantly influenced the personality and value preferences of the Millennials.
- In fact given their high achievement orientation and high internal locus of control, it is not surprising that Millennials have such high expectations from the workplace.

2. Culling out the top 10 workplace expectations of Millennials reveals that Millennials look for an organization which encourage innovation and idea generation; recognizes performance; believes in fairness and justice; provides opportunity for personality development; recognizes contribution; provides opportunity to take initiatives; encourages learning; gives autonomy and freedom to express views and encourages leadership development, trust, and transparency. The valence which Millennials attach to the workplace clearly indicates that they value a workplace where there is scope to exercise their creative capabilities; where there is fairness, equity, and justice; where there is opportunity to exercise freewill—freedom, autonomy, and initiative and where there is scope for self-development and self actualization. In contrast, workplace attributes connected with materialistic needs and hygiene factors do not prominently feature in the Millennials' wish list.

3. Workplace realities experienced by Millennials are however a picture of contrast—higher level factors like freedom, autonomy, fairness, justice, empowerment, and opportunity for self-development, do not feature prominently in the top-rated workplace realities experienced by the Millennials. Workplace attributes such as strong brand value, good physical ambience, freedom for coffee breaks,

high-prestige organization, ethical dealings, rules orientation, and good team work feature high on the availability list.

It would also be worthwhile to reiterate here the perceptions of HR professionals about what Millennials value in their lives. According to them, Millennials are materialistic, careerist, overambitious, low on commitment to the organization and high on commitment to self, highly energetic; they have low respect for authority; they are the 'Me' generation, they are entitlement centric and focus more on rights rather than duties; they are tech savvy, well-informed, and creative. Of these nine perceptions about Millennials, only two—energetic and creative—have a positive connotation while the rest are pejorative.

The findings have been reiterated here with a view to highlight the gap between Millennials' priorities (self perceived) and HR professionals' perceptions and assumptions about them. We must not forget that these are the very same people who play a significant role in shaping and evolving the HR policies, systems, and plans which have a deep impact on the lives of the employees.

These workplace expectations of Indian Millennials reveal a close affinity to the positive conceptualization of human nature by thinkers like McGregor, Fromm, etc., cited in the preceding paragraphs. They are, in fact, diametrically opposite to the concept of human nature propagated by the leading thinkers of scientific management which ironically enough continue to prevail in many organizations even today.

Viewing these two sets of findings together shows a large gap between what Millennials want and what organizations offer. It is no wonder that organizations are plagued by the problems of low commitment, high turnover, and struggle to retain the right talent. The lack of fit between desired and available factors at the workplace, result in Millennials feeling conflicted and restlessly searching workplaces which provide them a better fit more in line with their aspirations. Enhancing individual-level commitment depends on factors like perceived organizational support, organizational justice, met expectations, person–organization fit, and leadership. Those organizations which pay attention to enhance such conditions at the workplace would be able to increase the commitment levels of the Millennials.

After highlighting the Millennials' valence of workplace, it is equally important to sketch the expected profile of the superior from the Millennials' lens vis-à-vis their experienced reality with bosses. As discussed earlier, Millennials would like to work with superiors who

- are humble;
- give honest feedback for performance;
- are men of ideas;
- work as mentors and guides;
- are open and approachable; and
- build teams.

Another important finding is regarding the push factors which are likely to prompt Millennials to look for jobs in other organizations. Millennials clearly indicated in the in-depth interviews that they will leave an organization with the following characteristics:

- Negative work environment.
- Toxic boss.
- Unfair treatment and performance inequity.
- Work pressure.
- Monotonous and uninteresting work.

This clearly brings out that the attitude of the boss/superior has an important role to play in their decision to leave along with work culture which is negative and politicized, which is not fair in rewarding performance and where the work is too demanding and quality of work is dull and monotonous.

# Architecting the Organizations of Tomorrow: Needed Paradigm Shifts

In this section we now propose to sketch the contours of the organization which could fulfil the Millennials' workplace aspirations. This section focuses on ways to create the future workplace around the most highly desired Millennials' expectations from the workplace (top 10 items), which have been broadly grouped into the following:

1. Entrepreneurial innovation.
2. Equity, justice, and fairness.
3. Self-development.
4. Free will.

## Entrepreneurial Innovation

The hierarchical, seniority-centric styles of organizations must shift and organizations should morph into more open and idea-driven workplaces. Such a shift would unleash the enormous creative potential of the Millennials. It is only in such a free and open culture that Millennials will be able to experiment, explore, take risks, and use the power of ideas to come up with novel and innovative solutions. Individual creativity will no doubt contribute to organizational innovation, effectiveness, and survival (Amabile et al., 1996 and Shalley, Zhou, and Oldham, 2004). In fact transformational leadership styles have been found to contribute to individual creativity (see Zhang and Bartol, 2010). Towards this end leaders and organizations need to first value Millennials both as worthy individuals, as well as for their enormous entrepreneurial urge, and nurture their ideas by creating an enabling environment. The culture of the organization must promote the curious, questioning, and dissenting mind, which is of paramount importance for promoting entrepreneurial innovation.

Organizations must respond to a very basic human need—the need to create—if they want to enhance their sense of ownership and commitment to the organization. One's creative contribution to the organization very powerfully binds a person and creates a sense of attachment and ownership to the organization. Such a powerful sense of ownership is what makes people relentlessly persist in the face of all odds in a bid to protect their creation. According to Csikzentmihalyi (1990) those who create, experience a sense of flow, a state of concentration, or complete absorption with the activity at hand and the situation. It is a state in which people are so involved in an activity that nothing else seems to matter. According to him, "People are most happy when they are in a state of *flow*. The flow state is an optimal state of intrinsic motivation, where the person is fully immersed in what he or she is doing...."

Organizations must also allow people to express their uniqueness and individuality. This is a basic need seen across generations and is expressed through individual preferences in dress, food, and music. Youth, however, tend to hold this as their banner and anthem—to be unique and different, especially from previous generations. Should this human urge be stymied in the current generation as well when they join the workplace? Should the pressures for conformity be exerted even at these levels? How can this need be positively channeled at the workplace are the questions which organizations need to address.

In most of the organizations unfortunately, the general experience has been that people at the entry levels are stifled and their ideas not even heard properly, let alone being valued. Millennials are treated as immature, non-pragmatic, and highly idealistic. This indicates inaccurate perceptions about the mindsets and value predispositions of the Millennials which need to be corrected. The organization must take care to provide dignity to the Millennials as they enter the workplace. This is because Millennials are the torch bearers for future idea generation and innovation. Organizations must tolerate differences and create space for multiple voices.

In fact, at this level we have heard the cry for freedom, "Make us accountable, but don't shackle us down by bureaucratic procedures;" "Evolve enabling practices;" "Don't treat us like a cog in the wheel;" "Tell us what to do, not how to do it;" "Don't breathe down our necks;" "Allow us to speak out, express our thoughts and raise questions about the organization," etc. These are the typical expressions used by the Millennials.

At the leadership level this implies that Millennials' superiors must be empowering, must believe in delegation and decentralization; they should work more as mentors and coaches, philosophers and guides, since Millennials dislike the direct and visible exercise of authority and power. In fact, empowering leadership is fundamental to experience of psychological empowerment which in turn leads to intrinsic motivation and creative-process engagement (Zhang and Bartol, 2010). Superiors should be excellent listeners, be appreciative with attitude to tolerate differences, mistakes and promote experimentation. They must be supportive of Millennials' zest for experimentation and exploration. They must create psychological space and provide autonomy, which is one of the most cherished and valued desire of the Millennials.

Above all, organizations must create conditions by which Millennials experience a sense of ownership in the organization. This is possible when they are given the freedom to create and innovate. It is this opportunity to create which brings in the involvement, commitment, and sense of ownership. Once they create something which adds value in the organization and get appreciated for the same, this becomes the biggest aphrodisiac for them to stay on and work with the organization. This is not at all surprising because their core creative need gets a channel and every human being has a fundamental need to be creative.

## Equity, Justice, and Fairness

The concept of equity, justice, and fairness is something which is weighed against a referent group in the minds of individuals and therefore what one gets is not as important as what other peers get in return for similar contribution. This implies that Millennials crave recognition, appreciation, and rewards which are based on contributions in a just way. Today Millennials have a clear credo of rights and entitlement. This was amply demonstrated in the recent civil society movement led by Anna Hazare, in which youth were found to be the most vociferous supporters of the movement. Youth were agitated and reacted to the perceived unfairness, favoritism, nepotism, and corruption indulged by politicians, bureaucrats, and some corporate icons.

In the organizational context, Millennials desire that rewards should be commensurate with the efforts and contributions as well as competencies, and passion to innovate. This challenges the manner in which appraisals, promotions, and reward systems are administered in most of the organizations. The challenge lies not in terms of changing the content of the appraisal system but in administration of the existing appraisal systems. In fact the challenge lies in fair and just administration of the existing appraisal system. Unfortunately when people are dissatisfied with the appraisal system, it is the content which is first attacked rather than improving the process and changing the mindset of those who administer it and those who use it.

Millennials' desire to work with leaders who are bold enough to differentiate high performers and low performers; who value high performers and reward them; who are not biased, do not have favorites, discourage *chamchas* (sycophants), and are always prepared to explain discrepancies between expected rewards and actual rewards.

Millennials tend to get more bothered when undeserving peers get high rewards as compared to those who have done a better job. Thus the cry is not for rewards per se, but for justice in reward and recognition. This is possible when the leaders demonstrate impartiality, courage of convictions, unbiased attitude, and use their senses to understand the facts rather than merely perceiving facts through others eyes. In other words leaders must do their home work, be aware of each one's contributions, have a finger on the pulse of those working with them and be patient enough to constantly counsel and coach to raise lower performers into the higher performance zone.

## Self-development and Self-actualization

Millennials intensely desire to join an organization where there is a stimulating, exciting, challenging, and learning environment. This is because they deeply desire to learn, develop, evolve, and actualize their potential; this is the desire to become the best that they can be. This is possible only when organizations are both teaching and learning entities. Learning can be promoted by a culture of sharing, discussing, dialoging, questioning, exchange of ideas, brainstorming, and constant exploration of possibilities. The organization must continuously scan the environment and the horizon and share and disseminate the information and get ideas, views, and reactions from the Millennials. There is a need to develop strategy making not only top-down but also bottom-up. With the dynamic changes in the environment and knowledge explosion, Millennials know that they will rapidly become obsolete and therefore they aspire to constantly upgrade their skills, refresh their horizons, and heighten their competencies by going for higher education, courses in niche areas and attending various training programs. The organization will thus have to become a university for lifelong learning and promote the quest for new knowledge and new skills.

Superiors must have a ceaselessly learning, developing, and evolving mindset. It is only such leaders who can promote and support learning among the Millennials. They must accept that Millennials would be more up to date and have the latest information rather than feel threatened by them and competing with them. Only then will superiors be in a position to facilitate the credo for learning and development among the Millennials. Superiors will have to modify their roles from controllers to shapers, developers, and enablers. Their styles need to become more involving, engaging, and participative. To be able to successfully adopt this style, they will need to become mentors and coaches, guiding, shaping, and developing Millennials. Most importantly, the leader should be sensitive enough to give appropriate feedback for developmental purpose rather than for the purpose of control.

## Free Will

The core finding which emerged from the factor analysis of Millennials' expectations is entrepreneurial innovation, which is closely linked to "free will," i.e., opportunity to exercise autonomy, freedom, and initiative at the workplace. This indicates that bureaucratic, mechanistic, and too much process centricity is anathema for Millennials. They dislike authoritarian culture, pyramidal structure, and overly rule-bound organizations that restrict and hamper expression of free will at the workplace.

In other words the entire structure of the organization will have to be changed from tall, pyramidal, head office driven to flat, web-centric and networking oriented. They will have to move from thick-boundary to thin-boundary organizations which are borderless and seamless in operation, where change is a way of life. Millennials would like to work with those leaders who are not authority centric, status conscious, stiff, who maintain the status quo, who are both change and risk averse. They would like a boss who is open, accessible, amiable, and affable, who does not throw his weight around, who does not pull rank on subordinates, and who does not use symbols of power around him.

In the foregoing narrative we have highlighted the relevant contours of the organization which can galvanize, inspire, motivate, and develop a sense of esteem and engagement among the Millennials. We have also discussed the leader's role and style in inspiring and motivating Millennials. It would be appropriate to mention here an age-old debate between the superiority of process centricity over leader centricity in the organization. Today, there is a dominant assumption in the corporate world that process centricity can take care of all organizational problems including human aspirations and needs at the workplace. In the last decade process has in fact become the buzzword for creating great organizations. In fact our experience of consulting in the corporate sector showed us that organizations view process centricity as a more powerful tool for motivating people as compared to the role which leaders with human sensitivity can play in creating excitement and sense of enthusiasm among people.

Process centricity leads to standardization thereby dealing with people uniformly without differentiating among them and without acknowledging their unique qualities. This approach ignores the uniqueness of individuals and their capabilities thereby making them feel undervalued and somewhat ignored and even feeling they are not understood. In this context it is possible to say that an extremely process-centric approach devoid of leaders with human sensitivity fails to unleash the full potential of Millennials. In fact the process-centric approach boomerangs because Millennials dislike rules, regulations, and frameworks.

While both process and leadership are undoubtedly important in building and motivating people, however in our experience the role of leadership in galvanizing people is far more potent. In fact all the processes and systems are executed and implemented by leaders. Unless the leader has the appropriate competencies, attitudes, and mindsets, systems and processes can collapse thus failing to achieve the desired objectives for galvanizing and motivating Millennials. The fact that people do not leave organizations rather they leave their bosses, further reinforces the importance of leaders in retaining, motivating, exciting, and galvanizing Millennials. Millennials belong to the future generation and certainly ought not to be managed with mindsets of the past.

Organizations on their part must evolve suitable mechanisms to prepare their existing leaders for handling the generations of tomorrow. If it does not happen then helplessness, powerlessness, alienation, job hopping, and restless search for a better organization will keep happening among the youth and Millennials. In a nutshell it can be summarized that for dealing with the generations of tomorrow—the Millennials—we need leaders who are non-hierarchical, non-status-quoist, less arrogant, less rule and process bound, less focused on compliance enforcement, less rigid, and less distancing. Needless to say, such toxic behavior must be replaced by empowering, enabling, supporting, listening, experimenting, taking risks, and tolerance for mistakes. They must also demonstrate idea and innovation focus, be courageous, open, fair and just, be a coach and mentor, philosopher and guide, and above all, be entrepreneurial in approach. Such a leader will be able to meet the Millennials' need for free will, self-development and learning, creativity and fairness and justice, not only directly through his style but also by effectively implementing needed enabling processes and practices.

## Future Directions

In this section an effort is made to create checklists which will enable organizations and organizational members to build organizations of tomorrow responsive enough to meet Millennials' expectations, desires, and aspirations.

Based on the findings of the research we have developed two kinds of checklists (a) for the organization and (b) for the senior management and leaders. Once organizations and leaders respond to the questions in the checklist they will be able to assess where their organizations and leaders stand vis-à-vis Millennials' valence of workplace. This will enable them to identify the direction in which both organizations and leaders need to move and what action plans need to be initiated in order to develop a fit between Millennials' expectations and workplace realities. These have been presented in two categories below:

1. Organizational DNA for meeting Millennials' expectations.
2. Leadership code for meeting Millennials' expectations.

# Organizational DNA for Meeting Millennials' Expectations

Organizations need to demonstrate practices and processes which can create a culture facilitating openness, initiative, willingness to try, sense of empowerment, and ownership, so that the passion of youngsters to be entrepreneurial and innovative is given free rein in the organization. Questions have been designed to highlight the needed work culture in an organization in order to align with Millennials' aspirations. These are now presented in the following sections.

## Questionnaire on organizational DNA

### *Instructions*

Given below is a set of statements each on a five-point scale—1 being very low agreement and 5 indicating very high agreement. Kindly indicate for each statement the number on the scale (1 to 5) which reflects the extent to which you agree with that statement:

I agree to a

| Very low extent | Low | Moderate | High | Very high extent |
|---|---|---|---|---|
| 1 | 2 | 3 | 4 | 5 |

| S. No. | Statement | Rating 1 to 5 (mention the number for each statement) |
|---|---|---|
| 1. | There a contribution-centric reward system in this organization | |
| 2. | This organization encourages participative decision making | |
| 3. | There is open and free flow of information in this organization | |
| 4. | There is a flat organizational structure here | |
| 5. | This organization encourage high involvement and engagement | |
| 6. | The organizational practices and culture help people feel a sense of ownership and empowerment | |
| 7. | The organization tolerates unintended mistakes and failures | |

*Table continued*

*Table continued*

| S. No. | Statement | Rating 1 to 5 (mention the number for each statement) |
|---|---|---|
| 8. | People feel valued and respected in this organization | |
| 9. | People freely express ideas in this organization | |
| 10. | People have the opportunity to learn and develop themselves | |
| 11. | Curiosity is valued in this organization | |
| 12. | The organization is sensitive about Millennials' aspirations | |
| 13. | Efforts are made in this organization to build processes to meet Millennials' aspirations | |
| 14. | The recognition and reward practices and policies in this organization are fair and just | |
| 15. | Celebration and coming together of the community are encouraged in this organization | |

## Leadership Code for Meeting Millennials' Expectations

Millennials would like to work with superiors who understand their expectations, aspirations, and value dispositions. Questions have been designed to highlight the needed profile of the leader, in order to align with Millennials' aspirations. These are now presented as follows.

### Questionnaire on leadership code

### Instructions

Given here is a set of statements, each on a five-point scale—1 being very low agreement and 5 indicating very high agreement. Kindly indicate for each statement the number on the scale (1 to 5) which reflects the extent to which you agree with that statement:

I agree to a

Very low extent    Low    Moderate      High      Very high extent

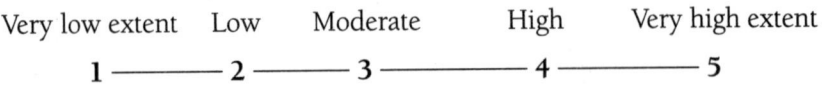

| S. No. | Statement | Rating 1 to 5 (mention the number for each statement) |
|---|---|---|
| 1. | I spend time trying to listen to and understand the needs and aspirations of the youngsters working with me | |
| 2. | I am concerned about the effect my behavior has on young members of the team | |
| 3. | I display a supportive style | |
| 4. | Younger team members freely approach me when they face problems | |
| 5. | I share information about the work and organization with younger team members | |
| 6. | I openly say that each of my young colleagues is important to me and that I value their contribution | |
| 7. | When someone gives me a new idea or shares a thought, I give it due consideration | |
| 8. | I ensure greater participation and involvement of the team in many activities | |
| 9. | I provide the freedom and autonomy for people to take initiative | |
| 10. | I strive to be fair and just in my decisions and actions | |
| 11. | I make the effort to mentor and coach Millennials in my team | |
| 12. | I give them a sense of challenge which keeps them excited and involved | |
| 13. | I appreciate the work youngsters are doing and express how important it is to the organization | |
| 14. | I allow Millennials to experiment and take risks | |
| 15. | When Millennials do work with good intention and make mistakes, I tolerate the same | |

# References

Aktouf, O. (1992). Management and theories of organizations in the 1990s: Toward a critical radical humanism? *The Academy of Management Review, 17* (3), 407–431.

Amabile, T. M. (1996). *Creativity in context: Update to the social psychology of creativity.* Boulder, Costa Rica: Westview Press.

Argyris, C. (1962). *Interpersonal competence and organizational effectiveness.* Homewood, III: Irwin Press.

Bennis, W. G. (1966). *Changing organizations.* New York: McGraw-Hill Book Company.

———. (1994). *On becoming a leader.* New York: Perseus Books.

Csikzentmihalyi, M. (1990). *Flow: The psychology of optimal experience*. New York: Harper & Row.

Downs, A. (1965). Non-market decision making: A theory of bureaucracy. *American Economic Review*, 55 (1/2), 439–446.

Drucker, P. (1988). The coming of the new organization. *Harvard Business Review*, 66 (1), 45–53.

Ford, H., & Crowther, S. (1922). *My life and work*. Garden City, New York: Garden City Publishing Company Inc.

Fromm, E. (1973). *The anatomy of human destructiveness*. New York: Holt: Rinehart and Winston.

———. (2003). *On being human*. New York: The Continuum International Publishing Group Ltd.

Gibson, J. L. (1966). Organization theory and the nature of man. *The Academy of Management Journal*, 9 (3), 233–245.

Heilbroner, R. (1970). *The wordly philosophers*. New York: Washington Square Press.

———. (1980). *Marxism: For and against*. New York: Norton.

Herzberg, F. (1966). *Work and the nature of man*. Cleveland, Ohio. Holland.

———. (1976). *The managerial choice: To be efficient and to be human*. Homewood: Illinois: Dow-Jones-Irwin.

———. (1980). Humanities: Practical management education. *Industry Week*, 206 (7), 69–72.

Maslow, A. H. (1987). *Motivation and personality* (3rd Ed.). New York: Harper & Row.

McGregor, D. (1960). *The human side of enterprise*. New York: McGraw-Hill.

Nayar, V. (2010). *Employees first, customers second: Turning conventional management upside down*. Boston: Massachusetts: Harvard Business Press.

Rogers, C. (1961). *On becoming a person: A therapist's view of psychotherapy*. London: Constable.

Shalley, C. E., Zhou, J., & Oldham, G. R. (2004). The effects of personal and contextual characteristics on creativity: Where should we go from here? *Journal of Management*, 30 (6): 933–958.

Stephenson, G. R. (1967). Cultural acquisition of a specific learned response among rhesus monkeys. In D. Starck, R. Schneider & H. J. Kuhn (Eds.), *Progress in primatology* (pp. 279–288). Stuttgart: Fischer.

Zhang, X. M., & Bartol, K. M. (2010). Linking empowering leadership and employee creativity: The influence of psychological empowerment, intrinsic motivation, and creative process engagement. *Academy of Management Journal*, 53 (1), 107–128.

# Index

ABG, 2
achievement motivation, 29, 116
   behavior motivation, 51
   definition of, 50
   individual level, 51
   people with high, 50–51
      features of, 51–52
   study of, 51
   Ying-Feng Kuo questionnaire to study, 74
achievement orientation, 61–63, 72
   by background variables
      $F$ test, 76
      $t$ test, 75
      Tukey table, 77
Action Regulation theory, 20
agrarian age, 204
agricultural family background, MOWP expectations of, 114–15
Airtel, 2
Antoinette, Marie, xxiii
appraisal, 176
attitude, work, 28
autonomy, 15

behavior, work, 28
behavior, workplace
   personality factors role, 21
Bhagavad-Gita, 9
Biocon, 2
Buddha
   essence of philosophy, 11
   statement by, xxiii
   work role, in human life, 10–11

Burroughs, John, 6
business world, present day, xxiv

capitalism, modern
   PWE contribution to, 8
career expectations, 24
career success, 8
centrality of job, in workplace, 22
CEO, role of, 11–12
*chamchas*, 173
civil society, movements by Indian, 203
communism, 1
community development value, 68–70, 116
   by background variables
      $F$ test, 87
      $t$ test, 86
      Tukey table, 88
Company's brand image, 105
   factor by selected demographic variables, 140–42
   meaning of, 111
conducive physical ambience, 104, 113
   factor by selected demographic variables, 134–36
   meaning of, 110–11
Confucius, 10
corporate executives, survey on, 20
corporate responsibility, 24
corporations, factors for collapse of, 2
customer delight, 177

DDI study, 3
democracy, 1
democratic institutions, statement by Lincoln, 1

demographic variables, influence on MOWP, 28
  company's brand image (*see* Company's brand image)
  conducive physical ambience (*see* Conducive physical ambience)
  entrepreneurial innovation (*see* Entrepreneurial innovation)
  fair and ethical (F&E) workplace (*see* Fair and ethical [F&E] workplace)
  process centricity with shared vision, 108
  sense of community (*see* Sense of community)
  sense of security (*see* Sense of security)
  sharing and celebrating culture (*see* Sharing and celebrating culture)
  techno-savvy (TS) workplace (*see* Techno-savvy [TS] workplace)
  total score, 107
dharma, 9. *See also* Work, in human life
distributive justice, 20

employee creativity, importance of, 98
*Employees First, Customers Second*, 202
entrepreneurial innovation, 103, 113, 117
  factor by selected demographic variables, 126–28
  meaning of, 107
  work experience impact on, 108
equity, 20, 101
equity theory, 20
ethical, 105
expectations of millennials, from workplace, 98, 152–54, 193
  comparison of questionnaire and findings of interview data, 169–70
  availability, 179–80
  contribution toward society, 169
  identity and social status, 164–65
  meaningful engagement (*see* Meaningful engagement)
  money and material comforts, 166–67
  opportunity to experiment and express creativity, 165–66
  platform to grow and actualize myself, 163–64
  results from interview data, 160–63
  sense of community, 168–69
  sense of security and safety, 169
experienced organizational reality, 171–73
  ambitious to grow, 177–78
  conformity centric, 173–74
  experienced organizational reality, 171–73
  good place to work, 178
  hierarchical/top-down character, of organization, 173
  learning and innovating organization, 178–79
  obsessed with ROI, 176–77
  pay less attention, to loose human creative potential, 174
external locus of control individuals, 49

fair and ethical (F&E) workplace, 112–13
  factor by selected demographic variables, 142–44
fairness, 20, 101, 154
Ford, Henry, 208
free will, 218–20
French Revolution, xxiii, 203

Gen Y, 23
goal setting model, 20
good leader, expectations from, 181–82
group-based work, 24–25

hard work, in post-religious reformation in Europe, 8
Hazare, Anna, 203, 216
hierarchical character of organizations, 173
higher order needs, 20
horizontal job loading, 22
HR professionals, Millennials through lens of, 191–93, 196
human aspirations and nature, mismatch between, impact of, 11
human behavior
  locus of control (*see* Locus of control)
human beings, 204, 209–10
  attributes as per ancient Indian scriptures, 14
  basic needs of, 15
  in industrial age, 209

institutional arrangements for liberation of, 17
   religions, 18
human capability, 17
human nature
   features of, 16
   patterns of
      assumptions about, 13
      beastly and godly attributes of, 14
      impact of mismatch between aspiration and, 11
human needs, 204
human passion, 17
human personality, Freudian sense of, 15
human potential, 17
human societies and institutions
   challenge for, 15
   in historical perspective, 204
human soul, Hindu philosophy on, 12

ICICI, 2
identity, 164–65
immediate supervisor, expectations from, 195–96
individual creativity, 214
individual expectations and experience, lower harmony and mismatch between, xxviii
individualism, xxiv
industrial age, 204–5, 208
   assumptions of man in, 208–9
   human beings as machines, 209
information age, 204
innovating organization, 178–79
intent to leave, 187–91, 196
internal locus of control individuals, 48–50
intrinsic motivation, 21
Islamic work ethics, 10

job enlargement, 22
job enrichment, 22
job loading, 22
Johari Window model, 15
JSW, 2

karma, in human life, 10
knowledge age, 204

leader–follower relationship, 180
learning organization, 178–79
Lincoln, 1
locus of control, 29–30
   by background variables
   influence of demographic variables, 72
   internal, 48–50
   people with high and external, 48
   work locus of control (WLOC) (see Work locus of control [WLOC])
lower order needs, 20
L&T, 2

Mahabharata, 9–10
man
   Confucianism on nature of, 12
   mechanistic model of organization assumption, 14
   positive with potential for self-realization, 13
   Shakespeare views on, 12
manager quality, 24
Mandela, Nelson, 48
Maslovian concept, of workplace, 20
mass aspirations, stress on, 1
material comforts, 166–67
*McKinsey Quarterly* survey, 23
meaningful engagement
   meaning of, 167
meaning of workplace (MOWP)
   creation of higher, factors for, 21
   definition of, 18, 26
   demographic and personality attributes, 26–30
   demographic variables impact on, 119–21
   differences by background factors, 125–44
   factors of, 102–6
   job characteristics, importance of, 22
   levels of, 20
   mean values, 99–100
      outcomes of, 101–2
   outcome of alignment between individuals, 18
   personality and values on, impact of, 115–17, 121

research design and framework for
instrument design, 31–35
objectives of, 30–31
Millennial(s)
background profile of
demographic background variables, 54–56
expectation from workplace, graphical representation of, 162
factors of MOWP, 102–6
fit between expectations and workplace realities, 97
generation
expectations and experienced realities of, 210–12
profile of, 210–11
MOWP preference of, 118
personality of (*see* Personality, of Millennials)
psychosocial profile of, 56–59
role in organization, 202
through lens of HR professionals (*see* HR professionals, millennials through lens of)
values of (*see* Values, of Millennials)
variables influencing personality and personal values priorities of
achievement motivation, 61–63
community development value (CD value) (*see* Community development value [CD value])
locus of control, 63–65
personal growth value, 65–67
progressive orientation value (*see* Progressive orientation value)
self-fulfillment (SF) value (*see* Self-fulfillment [SF] value)
workplace characteristics, as experienced by
means and standard deviations of MOWP items, 155–59
modern organizations, 45
money and material comforts, 166–67
motivation, work, 19
definition of, 29
levels of, 20
personality factors role, 21

motivators, 24
multiple regression analysis (MRA), stepwise
with dimensions of personality and values, to predict MOWP, 145–49

n-Ach analysis, 51
nation
asset of, 7
goal of, 16
needs
hierarchy of, 20
SDT definition of, 21

older Millennials, 66
organization man, in contemporary world, 13–14
organizations
architecture for tomorrow
entrepreneurial innovation, 214–16
equity, justice, and fairness, 216–17
free will, 218–20
self-development and self-actualization, 217–18
attachment to human beings, at workplace, 206
challenges before, 3
DNA for meeting millennials' expectations, 221–22
features of, 207
Indian, 46
study on, 153
of industrial era, focus of, 205
meeting Millennials' expectations
DNA for, 221–22
leadership code for, 222–23
modern (*see* Modern organizations)
response to emerging realities, 205

Path Goal theory, 19
performance-based recognition, 101
personal growth value, 65–67, 116
by background variables
personality
assessment by using framework and instruments
achievement motivation, 50–52
locus of control, 47–50
personal values, 52–53

definition of, 28, 47
differences by background factors, 75–91
factors, role of, 21
impact on MOWP, 28
of Millennials, 59–60
personality development theory, 114
personal values
  components of, 52
  definition of, 28
  impact on MOWP, 115–17
  influence work-related outcomes, 53
  Rokeach value survey (RVS) (see Rokeach value survey [RVS])
pre-modern societies, individual identity growth in, xxiii–xiv
Price Waterhouse Coopers study, 24
process centricity, with shared vision, 103, 113
  factor by selected demographic variables, 129–30
  meaning of, 108
progressive orientation value (PO value), 70–72, 116
  by background variables
Protestant Work Ethic (PWE), 8

Ramayana, 10
reality and expectations, gap between, 153
rewards
  extrinsic, 22
  intrinsic, 22
Rokeach value survey (RVS)
  measurement of personal and societal values, through 25-item scale, 73–74
rotated component matrix, MOWP, 122–23

scales, psychometric properties of, 124
SDT theory, 21
self-actualization, 217–18
self-development, 217–18
self-efficacy, poor and high, 21
self-fulfillment (SF) value, 67–68, 116
  by background variables
sense of community (SOC), 104, 168–69
  desire of MBA students, 109
  factor by selected demographic variables, 130–32
  meaning of, 108
sense of security, 104, 113
  factor by selected demographic variables, 132–34
  meaning of, 109
  people with agricultural background, preference of, 110
Shakespeare, 12
sharing and celebrating culture, 104, 113
  factor by selected demographic variables, 136–38
  meaning of, 110–11
silo functioning, 175
social status, 164–65
society, goal of, 16
Sri Ramakrishna, 9

talents, scarcity of, 4
Taylorian view, of man, 12
techno-savvy (TS) workplace, 104, 113
  factor by selected demographic variables, 138–40
  meaning of, 111
*The human side of enterprise*, 208
top-down character of organizations, 173
toxic boss, 181
transparency, 154
turnover, increase in Indian organizations, 153

UTI, 2

values
  definition of, 52
  of Millennials, 59–60
vertical job loading, 22
Vitamin Model, Warr's, 22

wealth, accumulation of, 8
work content, 22
work environment, features of, 22
working, 8
  dimensions of, 18
  meaning of, 7
working population, in India till 2050, 98
work, in human life

domains of, 21
emphasis on intrinsic aspect of, 25
importance of, 7
in Indian context, 9
meaning of, 5, 7–8
role of, 8–9
work institution, goal of, 16
work–life balance, 102
work locus of control (WLOC), 74
workplace, xxvii
PWE role in, 8
workplace(s)
challenges in, 3
techno-savvy (see Techno-savvy [TS] workplace)
work-related attitudes
expectation from immediate boss
humble and listening, 183
importance of valid and honest feedback, 185
inspiring and empowering, 183–84
just and fair, 184
nurturing mentor and guide, 185–86
open and approachable, 186
smart and clear thinker, 185
team builder, 186–87
intent to leave
monotonous work, 191
negative work environment and culture, 187–89
toxic boss, 189–90
unfair treatment and performance, 190
work pressure, 190–91
"Yes Sir" kind of organization, 166
youth
adaptation to new technologies, 30
entering organizations, characteristics of, 23

# About the Authors

**Pritam Singh** is the Director General of International Management Institute, India. Previously, he has been the Director of Management Development Institute (MDI), Gurgaon, India (1994–1998 and 2003–2006), and Indian Institute of Management, Lucknow (IIML), India (1998–2003).

An inspiring role model, Dr Pritam Singh has spent his entire life tirelessly doing what he does best: awakening students, academia, corporate heads, and policymakers to raise their excellence to the next level. As the chairman and member of several policymaking committees and bodies of Government of India, he has stamped his perspective on policy issues that surround both management education and corporate management in India. He sits on the boards of more than 20 reputed private- and public-sector organizations, helping them initiate change processes and charter winning corporate strategies. As a consultant, Dr Singh has worked with more than 200 CEOs in India and abroad and conducted more than 100 retreats for the top management of both private- and public-sector organizations as well as multinational corporations.

As an academic administrator, Dr Singh's record is unparalleled. With his entrepreneurial vision and path-breaking innovative methods, Dr Singh turned around the fortunes of both MDI (where he was director in the periods 1994–1998 and 2003–2006) and IIML (1998–2003), and, quite fittingly, earned the repute of being the "Midas Touch" director.

A thought leader with extraordinary insight, Dr Singh is the author of seven academically reputed books, three of which are award winning. He has also published over 60 research papers in various national and international journals. He is a globally sought-after speaker and has addressed various Indian and global audiences including chambers of commerce in various countries, notably, the Netherlands, France, Germany, Greece, Russia, UK, USA, Thailand, Mauritius, Egypt, and so on.

Dr Singh is and has been a member and the chairman of several important government committees:

1. Chairman, Sub-committee on Institutional Management and Leadership Development in Higher Education, Planning Commission of India (for Twelfth Five Year Plan, 2012–2017).
2. Member, Banking Selection Board (for selecting chairperson, managing directors, and executive directors).
3. Member, Department of Personnel and Training, Government of India committee on leadership building for the Indian Administrative Services officers.
4. Member, Ministry of Home Affairs, Government of India committee for the capacity building of Indian Police Service officers.
5. Member, Tenth Five Year Plan for Higher Education.

His distinguished services were acknowledged by the country when the President of India conferred on him the prestigious Padma Shri in 2003 for excellence in education. It was for the first time that any professor and a serving director of a management institute in India received this coveted award in the field of management education.

Dr Singh is an MCom (Gold Medalist), Banaras Hindu University (BHU); PhD in Management, BHU; DLit, UP Technical University; and Fulbright Fellow, Kelley School of Management, Bloomington, Indiana, USA.

**Asha Bhandarker** is the Raman Munjal Chair Professor of Leadership Studies and the Dean of Research and Consulting at MDI, Gurgaon. She is a distinguished psychologist and a management thinker. She has been awarded the best teacher award at MDI and has received the best book award for her book *Winning the Corporate Olympiad: Renaissance Paradigm*. Her recent publications are *In Search of Change Maestros* and *Shaping Business Leaders: What B Schools Don't Do*. She has five published books and many research papers and cases in various national and international journals to her credit. Dr Bhandarker has been a Senior Fulbright Scholar and a visiting professor at Darden School of Business, University of Virginia, and at George Mason University, Virginia, USA. She has also been a visiting fellow at the London Business School.

**Sumita Rai** is Associate Professor of Organizational Behavior at MDI, Gurgaon. She is a PhD from Indian Institute of Technology (IIT), Kanpur, India. Dr Rai, with around 10 years of experience in management teaching before joining MDI, had been at IIM Lucknow and IIM Indore. She has presented and published more than 25 papers in national and international journals. Dr Rai's areas of interest are leadership, employee motivation, values, and organizational culture.

## The Research Team

**Ajay K. Jain** is Associate Professor of Organizational Behavior at MDI, Gurgaon. He has done his PhD from IIT Kanpur and a post-doctoral fellowship from Indian School of Business, Hyderabad, India. He has more than 10 years of work experience. Dr Jain's research interests are emotional intelligence, organizational citizenship behavior, and leadership.